A Village Transformed

Keyworth 1750–1850

A Village Transformed
Keyworth 1750–1850

John Atkins

Bob Hammond

Peter Roper

Keyworth and District Local History Society

1999

First published in 1999 by Keyworth & District Local History Society, c/o
Keyworth Library, Church Drive, Keyworth, Notts NG12 5FF.

Made and printed in Great Britain by The Local History Press Ltd, 3 Devonshire
Promenade, Lenton, Nottingham NG7 2DS.

ISBN 0 9524602 1 1

British Library Cataloguing-in-Publication Data
A catalogue record for this book is available from the British Library

Contents

List of Figures

List of Plates

Foreword

Every city, every town, every village, every farm, every field has a history, but it takes committed local historians to research and then write each of the many thousands of local studies which go towards building up the overall picture of how our country evolved across time. The Keyworth and District Local History Society deserves every congratulation for masterminding this impressive study of a village which is known today chiefly as a residential satellite of Nottingham. Keyworth at the end of the twentieth century has a population of nearly 9,000, the great majority of whom live in the new homes built since the 1960s, but for a thousand years it was a small agricultural settlement clustered around its medieval church. Mentioned in Domesday, when it had a population of perhaps 80, Keyworth still had only 325 residents at the time of the first census in 1801. Our authors note that in the 1670s it was a 'very ordinary village'. It had no resident landlord or vicar, and perhaps because it lay some distance from the main local roads turnpiked in the eighteenth century (what are now the A60, in 1737–8, and the A606, in 1753–4), Keyworth was too far distant from Nottingham to be influenced by urban life, although young people departed in search of fame and fortune elsewhere.

Keyworth was never destined to make headlines but, like many villages of its type, by the mid-eighteenth century the mixed farming system relying on open field arable was under pressure. Responding to the conditions all around them the landowners and farmers set out to reorganise the land. This seems to have been achieved in the 1750s without rancour or dispute, presumably because those who were in a position to take a lead recognised the need for change. By the 1790s a further phase of change, perhaps driven by agricultural conditions during the Anglo-French wars, brought Parliamentary enclosure of the common fields in Keyworth just as it did in many surrounding villages. Even this seems to have been a rational response by a group of landowners and farmers who saw the way the wind was blowing, and agreed to fund the necessary changes in tenure and organisation. Keyworth was clearly not one of those villages where enclosure represented class war with the weakest going to the wall. Property boundaries were necessarily altered, and common grazing disappeared, but beyond these alterations the impact of enclosure was circumscribed. Some of the new landscape created by the commissioners can still be seen on the ground today, including property boundaries and hedges. Despite nineteenth century development which turned Keyworth into an industrial village, destruction of the older landscape really began only in the 1960s when Messrs. Wimpey and Goulding developed a commuter village on some of Keyworth's historic fields.

Keyworth demonstrates just how the enclosure war beloved of some politically-inclined historians has to be tempered against the relative ease with which change took place in many parishes. John Atkins, Bob Hammond and Peter Roper, have undertaken a remarkable reconstruction, made the more difficult by the fact that there were relatively few records from which they could work. Often using inferences from East Leake, Cotgrave and elsewhere, they have managed to reconstruct the history of Keyworth more or less from the seventeenth to the nineteenth centuries, building out from their starting point of the 200th anniversary of the enclosure award. Their account is scholarly but highly readable, and it shows how even in the case of a village for which few documentary sources survive, committed historians can still find out a great deal about the past. By studying field boundaries, road patterns and house styles, and by carefully reconstructing life in Keyworth based on what was happening in similar villages elsewhere, they have produced a clear and coherent account of the transformation of Keyworth through the process of Parliamentary enclosure two centuries ago. They deserve our congratulations for this excellent study, which shows just why local history can and should be both interesting and rewarding.

John Beckett
August 1999

Preface

The writing of this book was occasioned by the bi-centenary of the parliamentary inclosure of Keyworth: the passing of the Act in 1798 and the Award made public on Christmas Eve, 1799. This was undoubtedly one of the most significant events in the history of this village, as were thousands of similar parliamentary inclosures of other villages during the late eighteenth and early nineteenth centuries, when the landscape, patterns of landownership and land use, as well as social relations, were transformed, almost overnight, through large tracts of the English countryside. The title of the book is no exaggeration.

Although inclosure was primarily concerned with land and farming, it had a direct impact on other aspects of village life: on roads, their course, width and maintenance; and, through measures taken to deal with tithes, on the relationship between the clergy and their flock. But its direct effects upon the communal regulation of farming and many other areas of village life were at least as radical. A study of inclosure, therefore, while giving priority to the land, cannot ignore those other areas, ranging from religion to industry. Equally, to assess the effects of inclosure, it is necessary to examine the pre-inclosure picture, with a general survey of Keyworth in the eighteenth century, as well as the process of inclosure itself and its outcomes. The book therefore divides into three parts: the pre-inclosure scene; the procedures and people involved in inclosure itself; and, finally, the aftermath to the upheaval and its modern legacy.

While the focus is on Keyworth, it also considers the wider context in which village life in general, and farming in particular, developed during the period of parliamentary inclosure. For while each village is unique, many of its features and experiences are repeated with minor variations over a wide area, especially in the Midlands. This book is therefore offered as a case-study, representing many aspects of the history of rural England during the late eighteenth and early nineteenth centuries, but exemplified in the specific detail of one locality.

Readers may query the spelling of *inclosure* here adopted. It was the normal way of writing the word two hundred years ago, and as that is the period we are mainly concerned with, we have kept to it rather than use the more common spelling — *enclosure* — in use today.

We wish to acknowledge support received from many quarters. The late Dr Alan Harris of the University of Hull got us started with initial advice on background reading, and we are particularly grateful to Professor John Beckett of the University of Nottingham for agreeing to write a foreword — which, we hope, will commend the book to academic and amateur historian alike. Closer to home, a group of fellow-members of the Keyworth and District Local History Society investigated the inclosure of neighbouring villages to identify some of the similarities and differences between them and Keyworth. They also scanned newspapers of two hundred years ago for references to Keyworth and to inclosure. We thank them all: Ann Ashley, Lesley Coote, Tom Heald, John Howarth, Jean Smith, John Thelwell and Alice Yardley. Three other members of the Society deserve special mention: Carol Allison, who made her research finds on probate inventories available to us; Keith Barton, who has drawn figures 2 and 3; and Alan Spooner who has performed an invaluable task as literary editor.

The publication of this book, then, would not have been possible without the interest and cooperative involvement of the Keyworth and District Local History Society as a whole. The writing of the text, too, was a collaborative effort, with the three authors consulting each other over their respective contributions. (While they take collective responsibility for any shortcomings, there has been some division of labour, with Bob Hammond being primarily involved in Part I, Peter Roper in Part II, and John Atkins in Part III.) The Society has found the production of this book to be an enjoyable learning experience — which we hope will continue as we receive feedback from what we have produced.

Acknowledgements

The authors are extremely grateful for a grant towards production costs from the Awards for All scheme.

They also thank Susan Griffiths of the Local History Press, Lenton, Nottingham, for her expert advice on typographical and production matters; and Linda M. Dawes of Cartographic Designs, Bottesford, Leics., for her drawing of figures 4, 5, 6, 8, 11, 18, 19, 25, and 26.

Thanks for permission to reproduce material are due to Bedfordshire and Luton Archives and Records Service (Plate 2); Bodleian Library (figure 14); British Library (figure 17); Museum of the History of Science, Oxford (Plate 1a); Oxford University Press (figure 7); Public Record Office (cover); Science and Society Picture Library, Science Museum, London (Plates 1b & 1c); and the Department of Manuscripts and Special Collections, The University of Nottingham Library, for material cited from their papers, in particular the Manvers and Newcastle papers.

Abbreviations

BL	British Library
DNB	Dictionary of National Biography
K&DLHS	Keyworth and District Local History Society
NA	Nottinghamshire Archives
NUDM	Nottingham University Library Manuscripts Department
PRO	Public Record Office

PART I: THE OLD VILLAGE

Chapter 1

A changing world

Agriculture is the mainspring and — looking at it another way — the end result of a flourishing, well populated state. These two complementary propositions demonstrate both that England is well cultivated and why.[1]

This chapter sets out the context in which communal open field farming came to be recognised as outmoded and was gradually replaced by independent farmers cultivating compact holdings. So universal was this change — and inevitable in hindsight — that there is only one substantial case of pre-inclosure field organisation left in England today, in our own county at Laxton, which has become a living museum of the past, visited from all parts of the world.

It is during the eighteenth century that the formation of modern Britain is most clearly seen. The earlier centuries had witnessed the clearing of the ground and the laying out of the foundations, but it was in the eighteenth that building work proceeded apace. During the first decade Scotland was united with England. Forty years later the residual embers of the Stuart cause were extinguished at Culloden. Abroad, the country spent no less than 35 years in wars with France, including the revolutionary and Napoleonic wars at the end of the century which had a bearing on the progress of parliamentary inclosure. It strengthened its hold on India, gained Canada, but lost its other American colonies. It experienced the beginnings of the Industrial Revolution which both forced and facilitated agricultural change.

In 1700, except for London with a population of half a million, there were only seven towns with more than 10,000 inhabitants.[2] Of these, four (Colchester, Exeter, Norwich and York) had been regional centres since medieval times. The other three (Bristol, Newcastle and Yarmouth) were ports. Twenty three towns had populations of over 5,000. The vast majority (over 80%) of England's five million people lived in villages and small towns dependent upon local agriculture. By the end of the century, London's population had grown to 900,000, there were 50 towns with a population greater than 10,000, and the proportion living in small towns and villages had decreased to under 70%. Overall there were nearly double the number of people at the end of the eighteenth century that there were at its beginning. Within this uneven growth there were some spectacular examples. One such was Birmingham where, in 1700, the population was between five and seven thousand; this grew to over 70,000 by the end of the century.[3] By comparison, the growth of Nottingham was modest: though with a population in 1700 similar to that of Birmingham it had expanded to only 11,000 by mid-century and to 29,000 at the time of the census of 1801. Thus the eighteenth century was a time during which more mouths had to be fed, but when an increasing proportion of the population was living in towns with their diversity of manufactures and trades.

These developments were accompanied by a host of others which were simultaneously consequences and stimulants of change. Fundamental were improvements in communications, the movement of ideas, people and goods. Freedom of the press we take for granted; at the beginning of the eighteenth century, if it was not a novel concept, it was limited in practice. Prior to 1695, when the Licensing Acts lapsed, the government censored all publications, it was mandatory for published works to be registered with the Stationers' Company, and the number of master printers was limited to 20. Printing was confined to London, Oxford and Cambridge. Immediately following the change in the law, printing presses were operating in Bristol, Shrewsbury, Exeter and Norwich.[4] By the 1730s almost every substantial provincial press published a newspaper and thereby created an advertising network linking London with the provinces. Nottingham had a weekly newspaper, the *Nottingham Post*, as early as 1710. The number of master-printers in London grew to 75 in 1720 and to more than 120 in 1760. In 1785, a guide to printing and publishing listed 49 country newspapers printed in 34 towns. In Nottingham, Thomas Peat (1708–1780) founded *The Gentleman's Diary* or *Mathematical Repository* in 1744 and edited it until his death.[5]

The potential for trade from this diffusion of information was hampered by the available means of transport. People and goods could be carried by horse or by boat. Carriage by sea or along navigable rivers had been exploited from time immemorial; the importance of such towns as Yarmouth, Bristol and Newcastle referred to above testify to that. Where suitable rivers were not available, everything was moved by man or horse power; consequently the 'roads' were, at best, no more than adequate for these means. Sufficient numbers of packhorse bridges survive to demonstrate the limitations that this implied. Goods too heavy or bulky for a packhorse required a wagon and a wagon required a wholly different road from that for a horse. It needed to be wider and smoother. Throughout the century there was a search for road improvements, although where these occurred, they always fell short of the need, for the simple reason that full advantage was taken of them by increased usage by better carriages and wagons. Improvement in one place served to emphasise the deficiency elsewhere — a phenomenon very familiar to us today.

The responsibility of parishes for the upkeep of roads within their boundaries, which had existed since Elizabethan times, was not effective in maintaining an adequate network for the carrying of goods over long distances. This

Figure 1 **Growth of the network of Turnpike Roads 1740–1770**

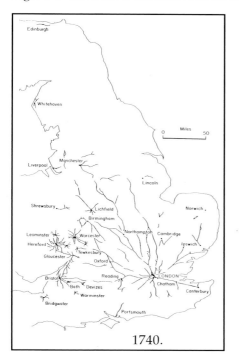

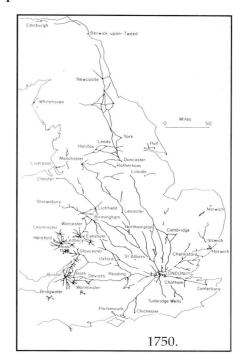

After Pawson, 1977, pp.138, 139, 151. With permission.

need began to be met by the Turnpike Trusts. These trusts, authorised by Acts of Parliament, constructed new or improved existing roads and levied traffic tolls to pay for their upkeep. The rapid growth in turnpikes during 1740–1770 is best illustrated by the maps in Figure 1. For the carriage of freight these roads could only make it possible to exploit the best of horse and wagon but became inadequate for the burgeoning trade generated by the growth of industrial towns. This deficiency was partially remedied by the network of canals engraved in the countryside following the pioneering work of the Duke of Bridgewater when, in 1761, he completed nearly eleven miles of waterway to link his coal mines at Worsley in Lancashire with Manchester. The motive power of the horse was increased fiftyfold and the price of coal in Manchester was halved. Thereafter canal building proceeded apace, was checked in the 80s, but reached a peak in the 1790s with a decade of canal 'rage'.

The turnpikes made for faster and more comfortable travel. Travellers carried with them information, knowledge and ideas, and it was the application of these which was characteristic of the age. The freedom to publish stimulated the production of books and periodicals; the greater ease and speed of their distribution further stimulated demand. By 1760 'a conscientious reader who kept abreast of new publications by scanning the advertisements and listings in newspapers, periodicals like *The Gentleman's Magazine* and reviews could collect a currently available title from the local bookseller within a week of having placed an order.'[6] (A situation rarely achieved today!)

Isaac Newton died in 1727. His achievements in astronomy, physics and mathematics underpinned many of the technical advances of the eighteenth century. The wide appreciation of this new knowledge is demonstrated by the popularity of Benjamin Martin's *Philosophical Grammar* which sought to bring Newtonian science to the public.[7] It was first published in 1733 and ran to 40 editions in as many years. For those who could not afford to buy books it had become common for provincial booksellers to lend them at a small fee, so further extending readership. By the end of the century there were a thousand of these 'circulating libraries' in the provinces and more than a hundred in London. For the better off there emerged the 'subscription library'; the first of these was founded, not in London, but in Liverpool in 1758. During the next twenty years they became a feature of ten more towns, all but one in the north of England.[8]

This developing interest in the acquisition of knowledge and its practical application inspired the formation of societies and clubs for these specific purposes. The Society for the Encouragement of Arts, Manufactures and Commerce, established in 1754, and later chartered as The Royal Society of Arts, was concerned with the practical application of science and rewarded successful practitioners with money prizes for specific projects. It set up committees on various disciplines (e.g., chemistry, mechanics, agriculture) to consider particular problems, and arranged competitions for their solution. The demand for better maps, stimulated by the improvement in communications, prompted the Society to offer £100 prizes for triangulation surveys and drawing of county maps at the one inch scale.

Although based in London the Royal Society of Arts made a serious effort to attract a provincial membership. However, it was not long before organisations with similar aims were being established in the northern and midland towns. Of these the Lunar Society of Birmingham exerted an influence quite disproportionate to its membership, which numbered no more than fourteen, but included Matthew Boulton, Joseph Priestley, James Watt and Josiah Wedgwood — names ever associated with the Industrial Revolution. 'They were men of broad interests and their discussions ranged widely, but their major mutual interest was the sciences, pure and applied — particularly as applied to the problems of industry.'[9]

Initially innovation was concerned with mechanical improvements which enhanced the productivity of the worker who still provided the power. The invention of the 'spinning jenny' by Hargreaves in the 1760s is a famous example. Water power and later the development of the steam engine accelerated the change from cottage and workshop manufacture to the concentration of men and machines into factories, the main hallmarks of the revolution. Nottingham and its neighbouring villages were early 'beneficiaries' of these changes. An important source of family income, already well established in the seventeenth century, was making stockings on the framework knitting machine. The new technologies were first applied to the preparation of the raw material for this occupation, i.e., in the spinning of linen and silk thread. The first mill in the county, at Bulwell on the river Leen, was built in 1738 by George Robinson who later built mills at Linby and Papplewick. It was here that the Arkwright inventions found early application and an interruption to the water supply at Papplewick led to the installation of the first Boulton and Watt steam engine there in 1784.[10]

There can be no better measure of the inventiveness of the period than the number of registered patents; no fewer than 776 over the years 1760–1785, an average of 31 per annum compared with the less than 5 per annum during the previous 140 years.[11] Landowners, professional men and educated farmers would be well aware of these developments and could hardly be unaffected by them — if only to question the assumptions that had hitherto determined their lives. Indeed many of them served on turnpike trusts and invested in the canal companies. Agriculture, the occupation of the majority, could not be immune from this spirit of inquiry.

Among those who sought to challenge the old ways and stimulate the new was Arthur Young who, for the 55 years from 1764 to 1819, produced a veritable blizzard of publications on agriculture. Notable among these were accounts of his tours through the English counties and the *Annals of Agriculture (1784–1815)*.[12] But perhaps his most important contribution was his successful advocacy of a Board of Agriculture established in 1793 under the chairmanship of Sir John Sinclair, with himself as its indefatigable secretary. It was the Board who commissioned Robert Lowe of Oxton to undertake the agricultural survey of Nottinghamshire published in 1796.

In the past most of lowland England had been cultivated by the open or common field system (see chapters 3 and 4). By 1700 however, some half of the country was already inclosed. The open fields survived largely in a broad swathe stretching from the coast of Dorset to that of Yorkshire, with the Midlands at its heart. We must assume that it survived because those engaged in it saw no sufficient reason for change and, where some might argue for it, the communal nature of open field farming militated against change. The impetus came from the increase in population, reinforced by urban growth, which occurred during the eighteenth century and required a concomitant rise in food production. This was achieved by a combination of the means available, namely by bringing more land into production, by more efficient farming methods and by innovation.

Already by the seventeenth century, English farming was amongst the most efficient in Europe — though one area surpassed it: The Netherlands and Flanders where population pressure was an even greater spur to raising production than it was in England. Many, but not all, of the improved farming methods that were introduced in the seventeenth century originated in these near neighbours. They included modifying traditional rotations by the introduction of sown (or ley) grasses, clover and sainfoin; their use in the development of 'alternate husbandry' (several years of traditional cropping alternating with periods under grass or clover leys); the use of a wider range of fertilisers; selective breeding of livestock; experimentation with unfamiliar crops, thereby varying rotations again; more systematic drainage of heavy land; spring flooding of water meadows. Of these, perhaps the most significant were the introduction of sown grasses and turnips, because they made it possible to dispense with fallow and provide more livestock fodder for winter. This not only increased the area under production but also freed farmers from the need to slaughter most of their animals in the autumn, which in turn allowed them to build up their flocks and herds, and so produce more manure to fertilise the arable fields.

Many of the most significant innovations of the period were first applied in East Anglia (an area close to the Netherlands), on large estates, on fields already inclosed, with light soils (turnips would not flourish in poorly drained clay), access to water-borne transport, and the proximity of a large market, namely London. One of the most far-reaching agricultural improvements however occurred not in arable farming but in livestock husbandry; not in East Anglia or the Netherlands but at Dishley Grange just north of Loughborough where Robert Bakewell (1725–95) developed the selective breeding of sheep and cattle. Prior to his work, meat for human consumption was largely derived from animals no longer fit for other purposes. His best known contribution was the development of the New Leicester whose genes have entered most breeds of British sheep. His interest in breeding extended to cattle, in particular to the improvement of the Longhorn breed. The practical effect of his work was a staggering increase in the weights of animals offered for sale at Smithfield. The average weight of sheep rose from 38lbs in 1710 to 80lbs in 1795; over the same period cattle weights increased from 370lbs to 800lbs.[13]

By the late eighteenth century English agriculture, as well as its industry, was admired by continental neighbours. Two young French aristocrats with their tutor came to England in 1784, spent a year in Suffolk and, in the following year, several months travelling as far north as Manchester and as far west as Plymouth.[14] Their diaries give a vivid account of all they saw. Apart from the entry, 'Is there anything in the world so boring as a Sunday in England?', they are full of admiration for both urban and rural enterprise. François de la Rochefoucauld, the author of these diaries, regarded almost everything he saw and experienced as superior to its French counterpart: farming practice, quality of livestock, the inns (particularly in the small towns), general cleanliness. He noted the care with which horses, carts and carriages, were looked after: 'The wagons, ploughs, harness, etc., are always in good condition. Their horses always groomed carefully ...'[15]

The widespread adoption of the best practice only became feasible with the mid-century road improvements which, as discussed above, facilitated both their diffusion and the trade in the products of their application. There remained the constraints of the open field system, the removal of which would entail embracing a wholly new way of life.

Imagine yourself a farmer, tenant or proprietor, cultivating a hundred acres or more, but the only piece of property which you can identify as 'belonging' to you and do with what you will is the house you live in and the small area adjacent to it separated from the rest of the parish by a wall or fence. Looking over this fence you see an open landscape of ridges and furrows patterned by their apparently random arrangement into furlongs; nothing interrupts the view until a mile away a hedge marks the parish boundary. You can point out where the strips are that you cultivate; however, what you grow is not your decision but a collective one — frustrating for the ambitious, a source of comfort for the majority. Inclosure would permit the former to embrace the 'new' methods, for the latter it would mean accepting an unlooked for, and unacceptable, responsibility. For both it would require (as a minimum) the expense of hedging, ditching and the construction of gates, perceived by the one as an investment and by the other as an unwarranted imposition.

It is not surprising, then, that the process of inclosure was slow and piecemeal. Rochefoucauld noted the existence of common land 'even at the gates of the capital' and commented on the difficulties of effecting inclosure. After citing the multiplicity of landowners and the high cost he wrote:

> Then the last and most persuasive reason is that the prime mover
> can always be sure of making himself unpopular, because the poor
> have, from time immemorial, the right to cut the bracken and brush-
> wood for firewoood. People in this country fear unpopularity more
> than anything else.[16]

This then was the England that was transformed by a spate of parliamentary acts of inclosure between 1760 and 1820. Inclosure of the open fields by a dominant landlord or by agreement between proprietors had been going on since time immemorial and would continue, but was increasingly seen as being open to abuse, and when achieved, open to question. By inclosing under the direction of an Act of Parliament and with commissioners appointed to control a process in which all the proprietors of land in the parish had a stake, the legal status of the outcome was beyond question.

The progress of parliamentary inclosure throughout the eighteenth and early nineteenth centuries was also affected by great matters of state — Britain's interests overseas. The Seven Years War (1756–63), the American War of Independence (1776–83) and the French wars at the end of the century all influenced, but in different ways, both the rate and nature of the process. The militarily successful Seven Years War caused no more than a brief interruption in the steady growth in the number of Inclosure Bills laid before parliament. On the other hand, the much greater costs associated with the conflict with our American colonies were met, firstly, by borrowing on such favourable terms that funds were diverted from agricultural investment; secondly, by increasing taxes which directly affected the landowning classes. Consequently there was a sharp fall in the number of inclosures which persisted at a low level for a decade until 1790, after which they resumed and exceeded their previous frequency. On the other hand, the increasing price of cereals prompted by the French wars had the effect of stimulating inclosure and was not inhibited by enhanced returns on financial investment; in real terms these declined as a consequence of inflation. The wars also affected the nature of inclosure. Wartime prices encouraged the cultivation of commons or waste; so we observe that the proportion of the total number of acts relating to their inclosure, in comparison with that of arable land, increased from the pre-1793 average level of 27% to 35% over the period 1793–1810.[17]

Nevertheless, the inclosure date of a particular parish depended upon local conditions, of which the number and inclinations of proprietors were determining factors. Obviously, in the case where there was only one proprietor, the decision would accord with his perception of his personal needs, but influenced by the attitude of his tenants. Where there existed several proprietors inclosure could be by mutual agreement, or where this was not possible, by 'buy-out' or coercion. What became the favoured procedure was to obtain an Act of Parliament which permitted inclosure where the owners of most of the land in the village wished it. This not clearly-defined majority was based on the value of land owned, not on the number of proprietors. The individual Acts set out the procedure to be adopted and provided for the results to be embodied in a document called an Inclosure Award. The procedure and its application to the inclosure of Keyworth at the end of the eighteenth century is dealt with in some detail in chapters 5 and 7.

The proprietors of land in Keyworth, whether they were resident, like Francis Eggleston, or absentee landlords as was Rev. Dr. Milnes, would have been conscious of the great changes that had taken place during their lifetime and of the benefits that could accrue if the improvements in agricultural practice could be implemented. Inclosure could mean more cultivated acres, better yields, better quality and better prices for Eggleston and higher rents for Milnes. It seems that as soon as the local conditions were favourable in the late 1790s the process was swiftly completed.

Notes

1. François de la Rochefoulcauld, 1784, Scarfe, 1988, p.146.
2. The population of Keyworth at the 1991 census was 8860.
3. Eric Hopkins, 'The Birmingham Economy during the Revolutionary and Napoleonic Wars', *Midland History* XXIII, 1998, pp.105–120.
4. Brewer, 1997, p.131.
5. Taylor, 1966, p.164.
6. Brewer, p.176.
7. Langford, 1989, p.279; Taylor, 1966, pp.184–5; Bendall, 1997, p.401 .
8. Brewer, 1997, p.180; Warrington (1760), Macclesfield (1770), Sheffield (1771), Bristol (1773), Bradford (1774), Whitby and Hull (1775) Leeds, Halifax and Carlisle (1778).
9. Schofield, 1963, p.2.
10. S.D.Chapman in Beckett, 1997, pp.319, 322.
11. Langford, 1989, p.655.
12. Arthur Young, *A Six Weeks' Tour through the Southern Counties of England and Wales (1768); A Six Months' Tour through the North of England (1770); The Farmer's Tour through the East of England (1771)*. For a list of the works of Arthur Young see Mingay 1975, Appendix, pp. 251–5.
13. Plumb, 1990, p.82.
14. Scarfe, 1988 and 1995.
15. Scarfe, 1988, p.155.
16. Scarfe, 1988: p.155.
17. Derived from Turner, 1980: table 11, p.71.

Chapter 2

Old Keyworth: a portrait

This chapter attempts to show what Keyworth was like in the decades leading up to inclosure: the landscape, the people, and how both were changing prior to that great upheaval. It provides the context for the following two chapters, which focus on farming: how the pre-inclosure open field system was conducted in Keyworth, and how it changed, particularly during the eighteenth century.

The landscape

Certain aspects of Keyworth's landscape have remained more or less unchanged from the eighteenth century to the present day. Except in areas subject to natural catastrophe, topography and terrain evolve almost imperceptibly. The gentle slopes leading down to the valleys of the Fairham and Willow Brooks and of Debdale (originally Deepdale), together with the spur of the Nottinghamshire Wolds on which the old part of the village lies, may be taken as constants in the time-frame in which we are interested. So can the heavy boulder clay soils with occasional patches of lighter sand and gravel which underlie most of the parish. The clay was deposited by an ice sheet several millennia ago, and the sand and gravel by melt-water, as the ice alternately shrank and expanded over our area in response to short-term climatic cycles. Interbedded clay and sand gave rise to the springs which probably attracted the original settlers to this hilltop location.

Another feature of the local landscape which has not changed much over the last two centuries is the lack of trees. At one time most of the parish of Keyworth, like its neighbours, was covered by dense forest. Long before the eighteenth century all the primeval woodland had been cleared; there were small clusters of trees near the village, many of them orchards, but nothing large enough even to be called a copse lay within the parish boundary. With the exception of Cotton's Plantation beyond the end of Debdale Lane, the same is true today. The much more substantial Bunny Woods and Rancliffe Wood are nearby, but both lie beyond the boundary.

In other respects, however, the landscape has changed dramatically, in part due to inclosure.

If we could stand on the church tower parapet and wind the clock back two hundred years, the scene confronting us would be very different from what we can see today. To the south we would look along Main Street, then called Town Street, a muddy lane bespattered with animal droppings. Many of the houses would be thatched, some made of mud, others half-timbered with limewashed

Figure 2 **View of pre-inclosure Keyworth from church tower looking south**

wattle and daub infilling. The newer and more substantial buildings would be of brick. We might be able to recognise some, like the two big barns (certainly) and two tall houses (possibly);[1] others would be more difficult to identify without the cement rendering and emulsion paint they have acquired in the last fifty years, though they would include what are now numbers 2, 3 and 4 Main Street. We would see numerous farmhouses with their yards, haystacks and outbuildings, interspersed with pasture paddocks, orchards and kitchen gardens (Figure 2).

Beyond the village, however, there were almost no houses or other buildings. Neither would we see many hedges. In place of today's rectangular fields, each devoted to a single crop or grass and bounded by ditches and hawthorn hedges, were huge arable fields, divided into hundreds of narrow strips, some separated from their neighbours by grassy paths or 'baulks'. For much of the time, however, it would not be possible to differentiate individual strips from a distance — for instance, if all in one field were growing the same crop, which was commonly the case, or if the field was fallow, the landscape would resemble a huge, uniform prairie. On a clear day, we might be able to see beyond the arable fields to what was called The Pasture — an area of rough grass and bushes being grazed by sheep and cattle, extending down to and beyond the Fairham Brook.

If we moved to the part of the parapet looking west, we would see, in The Square immediately below, the village pump, the remains of the village cross (we do not know whether it was a preacher's or a market cross), and the pinfold

Figure 3 **View of pre-inclosure Keyworth from church tower looking east**

where stray animals were kept until they were reclaimed by their owners after payment of a fine to the pinder. On fine days, this was a focal point of social life, where women met to gossip while filling their water pails, and old men grumbled about the young. Just beyond the pinfold, at the entrance to Blind Lane (now Commercial Road), was one of several beerhouses, The Hammer and Pincers, another focus of social life where cockfighting was reputed to be one of the entertainments. Also alongside The Square was Manor Farm: the farmhouse itself (once called the manor house but probably never lived in by a lord of the manor), together with its outbuildings, stack-yard where hay and straw were stored, and crew yard where livestock were held when not indoors or in the fields, and where their manure accumulated. Beyond, arable strips similar to those to the south of the village came right up to the farm complex.

A further move, to the north-facing side of the parapet, would again present us with a near-hedgeless prairie, though with practically no village in the foreground, for the church was located near its northern extremity. The only buildings to be seen would be the Independent chapel, now called The Hall, erected in 1768; the associated Manse, built soon after; and a collection of buildings — modest house, barns and byres — which constituted the rectory, but, with their yard and stacks, looking more like a farm than the sedate 'Old Rectory' and manicured garden occupying the site today.

Finally, looking east we would see the arable strips and intervening grass paths coming almost to the present Elm Avenue. A track to Stanton might be discerned, and a small collection of houses and farm buildings flanking a twisting extension of Town Street, subsequently renamed Selby Lane and Old Lane (now Elm Avenue). Only one of the buildings survives today: what must have been a farm outhouse opposite the present Methodist church, later used, among other things, as a butcher's premises. In the distance, beyond the strips of one of the open fields (Mill Field) we would see a windmill overlooking the valley along which Wolds Drive now runs — the only building outside the village at the time. (Figure 3, in which the mill has been somewhat enlarged.)

This was the landscape of medieval open fields and nucleated villages of the English Midlands, unaltered in its essentials for centuries. Not that it was like this everywhere, for while most parishes in south Nottinghamshire, like Keyworth, still operated the open field system through most of the eighteenth century, there were some that had inclosed their lands much earlier. Two of these were Keyworth's nearest neighbours, Stanton and Normanton, where field patterns then were similar to those of today.

Another feature for which we would search in vain two centuries ago is a network of clearly bounded and well-surfaced roads leading out of the village. Wide, ill-defined tracks across the open fields followed the approximate courses of today's Bunny Lane, Selby Lane, Lings Lane (but not Wysall Lane — see p.118–9) and Nottingham Road, but they were often quagmires in winter and deeply rutted in spring, discouraging journeys in and out of the village at these times of year, except on foot or horseback. The eighteenth century saw an increase in trade and travel, and with it greater pressure put on the roads and those responsible for their repair, under the Surveyor of the Highways (see below, p.35–6). On the other hand, turnpike roads came to within a few miles at Bradmore and Plumtree in the middle of the century, and these must have reduced the village's isolation — until they too deteriorated through overuse. The problems of the M25 are not new!

The People and how they lived

Keyworth's population in the eighteenth century was tiny compared with today. It is now over 8,000, although that includes more than 2,000 living outside the old parish boundary in what was, until 1984, part of Normanton. In 1801, the year of the first census, it was 325 and in 1700, probably about 250.[2] Through most of the century, births exceeded deaths, though there were considerable fluctuations, particularly in the number of deaths. Many people lived at the margin of subsistence, and any rise in food prices consequent on a poor harvest led to hunger, vulnerability to disease and sometimes starvation. In addition, there were periodic outbreaks of smallpox, measles, diphtheria, influenza and other epidemics — though bubonic plague seems to have disappeared in the seventeenth century, and cholera did not visit Britain until the nineteenth. Life expectancy was less than half what it is today, and still less in the rapidly growing industrial towns.

Birth rates were high by present standards: most women between the ages of 20 and 45 were probably either pregnant or nursing a baby most of the time. But infant mortality was high also: in Keyworth, the registers show that about 15% of baptised children were buried within a year — a level associated with least-developed countries today.

The overall excess of births over deaths (natural increase) during the eighteenth century should have resulted in a greater growth of population than actually occurred.[3] The explanation of this shortfall is to be found in net outward migration — more people moving out of the village than moving in, presumably because Keyworth offered insufficient economic opportunities to absorb the natural increase. Agriculture was by far the largest employer, but demand for additional labour did not keep pace with additional supply. A limited range of crafts offered apprenticeships for a few youngsters to become blacksmith, wheelwright, cordwainer (shoemaker), carpenter, miller, etc.. But framework knitting, which became Keyworth's mainstay in the nineteenth century, employed relatively few at the end of the eighteenth, although it was already flourishing in Nottingham and its surrounding villages, Ruddington being a notable example. Also, there were few opportunities in Keyworth for domestic service because of the lack of wealthy residents, while many nearby villages, as well as Nottingham, could boast great houses requiring armies of servants. So it is likely that significant numbers of young men left the village to become framework knitters, framesmiths or farm labourers; and young women to enter domestic service. However, *net* outward (outward minus inward) migration was small — it averaged less than one a year; and even *gross* migration (outward plus inward) would have been limited by the laws of settlement which operated throughout the century (see p.35).

Social Structure

Several sources are used here to piece together a picture of Keyworth's social structure in the eighteenth century. They include some from before 1700 and others after 1800, to fill gaps in the data, on the reasonable assumption that village, as distinct from urban, life changed only slowly at that time.

A useful starting point in describing Keyworth's social structure in the eighteenth century is the Hearth Tax returns of 1674 — see Table 1. These list, by name, the occupiers of each residence and the number of hearths (chimneys) it contained, together with the names of those who were exempt from the tax through poverty. On the whole, the number of hearths can be taken to correspond to economic and social status, and Fieldhouse[4] has suggested the following equivalences:

1 hearth: labourers and poorer husbandmen (to which may be added those who were exempt from paying the tax, representing paupers and other very poor people)

2–3 hearths: craftsmen, traders and yeomen

4–7 hearths: richer craftsmen, professionals, larger farmers and merchants

> 7 hearths: gentry and nobility.

Table 1 **Hearth Tax Returns 1674, for part of Rushcliffe Hundred**
Numbers and percentages of dwellings in different categories

	number of hearths								
	X* and 1		2 and 3		4 to 7		8 plus		Total
	No.	%	No.	%	No.	%	No.	%	
Plumtree	28	65	14	**33**	0	**0**	1	**2**	**43**
Normanton	14	**70**	4	**20**	2	**10**	0	**0**	**20**
Keyworth	29	59	16	33	4	8	0	0	49
Widmerpool	23	**56**	17	**41**	1	**3**	0	**0**	**41**
Willoughby	42	**61**	26	**38**	1	**1**	0	**0**	**69**
Wysall (& Thorpe)	28	**60**	15	**32**	4	**8**	0	**0**	**47**
Bunny	32	**67**	15	**31**	0	**0**	1	**2**	**48**
Bradmore	15	**54**	10	**36**	2	**7**	1	**3**	**28**
Ruddington	52	**55**	42	**44**	1	**1**	0	**0**	**95**
Costock	26	**72**	7	**19**	3	**9**	0	**0**	**36**
Stanton	6	**86**	0	**0**	1	**14**	0	**0**	**7**

X* means exempt from the tax

Fieldhouse's classification has been used in Table 1, which enables us to compare Keyworth with some of its nearest neighbours shortly before the beginning of the eighteenth century. What is perhaps most notable is how very ordinary Keyworth was, not standing among the top or bottom three in any column. It was the fourth largest village out of eleven; like all but three, it had no resident gentry or nobility; it was fourth in the percentage of rich craftsmen, etc., fifth in the percentage of ordinary craftsmen, traders and yeomen, and eighth in the percentage of the poorest category. In other words, it had proportionately fewer at the two extremes of affluence and poverty, and more in the middle; but neither to a remarkable degree.

It will be seen that the social structure in the mid 1670s was everywhere 'bottom-heavy'. The proportion living in houses with one hearth, or who were exempt from the hearth tax on grounds of poverty, was everywhere over half and in three parishes over two-thirds, with a median (midway) value of 61%. Nearly all the rest lived in two- and three-hearth houses. Out of 483 houses counted in the eleven parishes, only 22 (under 5%) had more than three hearths, and could be regarded as 'richer craftsmen, etc.', gentry or nobility. In modern parlance, only one in twenty might be considered 'middle class' economically, and probably fewer socially. In these respects, Keyworth and its neighbouring parishes were not unusual. Gregory King, in a survey of how income was distributed among the various classes of England's population at the end of the seventeenth century, estimated that over 60% of families earned less than they spent, implying that the difference was made up by begging, stealing or from Poor Law relief[5] — 'bottom-heavy' indeed!

Although there was doubtless some social and economic mobility during the century and a quarter following these hearth tax returns, the proportional distribution of prosperity, poverty and social status altered little; nor did the standards of living enjoyed or endured by the people in each social group. Or, to be more precise, living standards for the majority fluctuated violently in the short run, isolated as villages were by poor communications and therefore directly dependent on local harvests and bread prices; and tended to rise or decline imperceptibly in the long run.[6]

In most cases the one-hearth house had only one or two rooms, perhaps with an attic; many were built of mud, had leaky thatched roofs and no glazed windows in the late seventeenth century, only shutters. Floors were often of compacted mud, perhaps covered with rushes. With the exception of the shutters, which would mostly have been replaced by glass over the next hundred years, these were the conditions in which well over half of Keyworth people lived throughout the next century, mainly cottagers, farm labourers and those who, through age, infirmity or inadequacy, had no job and were paupers, supported by the parish poor-rate. They probably had enough to eat most of the time, but their diet would be monotonous, with only water or ale to drink. Fuel (tree branches, brushwood, furze, even cowdung) from the common pasture was not plentiful and clothing was often threadbare, so they suffered badly in cold winters. It also put a premium on cooking, reducing daily fare to little more than bread and cheese when times were hard. Packed in their tiny homes and underfed, they were then more likely to catch each other's infections.

A grim picture of life in the early eighteenth century is drawn by Fussell: 'The hardness of living is shown by the poor variety in the diet *of all classes* and the badly preserved meat and bacon, or the continuous diet of heavy bread and puddings or cheese, not mitigated by fruit or vegetables in the winter months, which led to serious disorders of the blood, while the casual but almost complete lack of sex morals led to an appallingly high incidence of venereal disease. Scrofula and scurvy were diseases caused by the food, sores and other unpleasant things were caused by dirt, and smallpox was as natural to the people as catching a cold is to us, but was more unpleasant.'[7] If that was the lot of 'all classes', it must have been much worse for those at the bottom of the social pyramid. However, Fussell may have exaggerated, or generalised from particular regions and localities: there were great disparities of wealth and well-being then, as there are today, and at least a minority must have lived comfortably in most parts of the country.

A different view of the poor is given by Robert Lowe[8] over a century after the hearth tax returns were made and 70 years after the period Fussell was describing, when he commented, referring to Nottinghamshire: 'There are few counties in England where they will be found better lodged, cloathed (*sic*) or fed, or better provided with fuel. Most cottages have a garden and potato garth and few are without a web of cloth of their own spinning... many, particularly in the Clay District (which includes Keyworth) have a few acres of land annexed to their cottages to keep a cow or two and pigs. The poor may be said to be industrious: they may be often seen, or their children, collecting the horse dung casually dropped on the road, for their gardens or to sell.' This is a reminder that we should try to see the past through the eyes of contemporaries; poverty is to a degree relative, and what would be intolerable today was considered acceptable two hundred years ago. On the other hand, Lowe may have underestimated the hardships and insecurity endured by the poor, which he had not himself experienced personally.

At the other extreme, as far as Keyworth was concerned, were the two houses recorded in the Hearth Tax with five hearths. We know one was the Manor Farm house which stood on the corner of The Square and Bunny Lane until 1970. The seventeenth century part of that house[9] was of brick on stone footings and a layer of slate for damp course. It had four spacious rooms (two upstairs and two down) together with a scullery and small 'boxroom' (to use a modern term). The boxroom and probably one other upstairs room would be used to store wool or food (cheese, grain, bacon, etc.). Each room except the boxroom had a fireplace. Downstairs, the floor was of brick, upstairs of plaster. All the windows were glazed. The only features it had in common with most one-hearth houses were the outside privies, and the lack of what we today regard as basic amenities — electricity, gas and running water. There would always be adequate clothing and fuel to keep warm; food would be plentiful and varied; there would be servants to perform some of the drudgery; but luxuries were few. Indeed, the house, though large, might be crowded, because, in addition to a living-in domestic servant, the farmer might employ one or more 'farm servants' who also lived in and were usually employed on annual contracts, in contrast to 'farm labourers', taken on by the day or week.

In between, many of the two-, three- and four-hearth houses were probably half-timbered, resting on stone bases to retard wood-rot and act as a damp course. They would be occupied by farmers and the better-off craftsmen and professionals. According to the first census (1801), people whose main occupation was *not* farming accounted for about a third of the workforce — 67 out of 197, though this would probably have included children as young as ten. Of the 67 some may have been framework knitters and seamers,[10] who were proverbially poor. But others would have provided the services that any relatively self-sufficient community required, many of whom enjoyed modest prosperity, including somewhat better housing than the worst-off. Among them we could expect to find a miller, joiner, blacksmith and wheelwright, while bricklaying seems to have been a part-time job engaged in by many when demand offered work. In addition, the digging, collection and transportation of local limestone (quarrying probably implies too large a scale) was of some importance in providing floors for houses and the crew yards of farms, and, perhaps more importantly, for paving streets in Nottingham.[11] Many of these occupations were followed by several people. For instance, there were seven shoemakers and an apprentice in Keyworth in 1841 — we have no figure for an earlier date.

Two other sources tell us quite a lot about social structure in eighteenth century Keyworth: probate inventories and land tax returns. The first is a collection of 33 surviving probate inventories, made between 1691 and 1783, which give estimates of the value of the possessions (exclusive of land and houses) of people who had recently died. Prosperous people were more likely to make wills and have their possessions valued than the poor, so there are more farmers than labourers represented in the collection. Nevertheless, it shows some striking contrasts in the value of property ownership:

a) 18 **farmers** range from £7 to £1948, with a median of £250;
b) 7 **craftsmen** range from £18 to £98, with a median of £40;
c) 8 **labourers** range from £4 to £40, with a median of £12.

Clearly, farmers seem to have been generally much better off than craftsmen, who were in turn better off than labourers, but there was some overlap, depending upon individual skills, size of enterprise (especially in the case of farmers) and how much individuals saved and spent. In particular, the smaller farmers are probably seriously under-represented in the sample. Arthur Young, writing in 1767, contends that 'a day labourer...is as well fed, as well clothed, and as well lodged as he would be, was he fixed in one of these little farms; with this difference, that he does not work nearly so hard...these small occupiers [the farmers] are a set of very miserable men.'[12] Much would have depended on the prices of bread and other farm produce. In the first half of the century they were generally depressed, which benefitted the labourer but hurt the farmer; in the latter half, and particularly in the last decade, prices rose, benefitting the farmer but hurting the labourer.

Also, while the overall proportions of rich, middling and poor probably changed little through the eighteenth century, individuals could move from one category to another, sometimes quite spectacularly. A notable example was that of Richard Hazelwood who in the Hearth Tax returns is recorded as living in a two-hearth house, indicating a position at the lower end of the middling category. Twenty years later his probate inventory shows him to have become a man of considerable substance — he was the one whose property was valued at £1948, four times more than any one else in Keyworth of whom we have records. Furthermore, his will shows that by then he owned a house similar in size to the Manor Farm house — perhaps he had bought the other five-hearth dwelling listed in the Hearth Tax returns.

A further point of interest revealed by the inventories is that most craftsmen and labourers grew some crops and kept a few animals — they had small plots of land and/or access to the common pasture for grazing their stock. In other words, they had more than one occupation: many craftsmen also ran small holdings, while many of the smaller farmers supplemented the family income by working some days for a larger neighbour, especially at harvest time, when labour was in demand and wages higher.

The probate inventories also indicate considerable variation within each of the three categories of farmer, craftsman and labourer. In the case of farmers, this is further demonstrated by the annual land tax returns. In 1797 for instance, the year before Keyworth's Inclosure Act was passed, 32 people were listed as occupiers of taxable land, the quarterly tax payable varying from 48 shillings to threepence. And although the tax was not exactly proportional to the amount of land occupied, it gives an approximate idea of the contrast between, on the one hand, a moderately large farm of perhaps 100 acres (48 shillings was about one-ninth of the total tax paid by the parish, which contained, before inclosure, some 900 acres of individually worked land), and on the other, of a small holding comprising a fraction of one acre. From these returns, there appear to have been just five farmers in the village with more than forty acres, who could be regarded as comfortably off by the standards of the time, and another five with between 20 and 40 acres. The other 22 were small holders or cottagers who would certainly need to supplement their income by other work, and whose living standards were fairly basic. But they were not the worst off. According to the 1801 census, there were some 65 households in the village at that time — twice as many as paid land tax — so half held practically no land at all. No doubt many of these were the households of full-time craftsmen — the blacksmith, framework knitter, wheelwright, miller, etc., already mentioned — but others would be those of labourers or paupers, living precariously on the margins of subsistence and often dependent on parish handouts. A parish of small and moderate-sized farms would offer few jobs for full-time labourers other than specialists like shepherd or dairyman. The general labourer would be required at haymaking and harvest time, and for threshing after harvest, but over much of the year he would have to find a living as Jack-of-all-trades, doing odd jobs, cultivating his potato patch or tending his few pigs or geese on the common pasture.

Another factor differentiating between farmers was tenure. Nearly half the land in Keyworth was owned by absentee landlords, of whom the largest, just prior to inclosure, were Samuel Smith of the Nottingham banking family, the rector who lived in Costock, and Sir Thomas Parkyns of Bunny. Of the ten largest farms, only two were worked by their owners. On the other hand, the majority of the smaller holdings were owner-occupied. But the distinction between owner-occupants and tenants was not always clearcut: the second largest farmer in the village, John Shepperson, rented most of the land he farmed from three different owners, but also owned three small 'plots' (each probably consisting of several strips in the open fields), one of which he cultivated himself while he let the other two out to tenants.

Furthermore, ownership of land was not necessarily an advantage over a secure tenancy from a benign, enlightened and substantial landowner. While tenants had to pay rents, owners often had to pay mortgage interest payments. Maintenance of buildings was usually undertaken by the owner so that fixed costs were shared between owner and tenant. And at a time when market prices of farm produce fluctuated wildly, as they did for much of the eighteenth and nineteenth centuries, owners frequently cushioned their impact on tenants. We have already noted that when prices were high, farmers of all kinds prospered, while those without land, who had to buy their food, felt the pinch. The reverse obtained when prices were low, but under those circumstances, tenants were often able to negotiate lower rents. Nevertheless, owner-occupiers had three advantages over tenants. First, they enjoyed complete security of tenure so long as they remained solvent, while some tenancies were on short-term leases which could be ended quite arbitrarily by imperious landowners — for instance if they disapproved of a tenant's religious affiliation. Second, if the value of land or other property rose, as it invariably did after inclosure, the owner gained, while the tenant probably found his rent increased. And third, landownership carried with it social and political status, though this applied in the main to large landowners only, and was a reason why so many industrialists and businessmen — like Samuel Smith, the banker — bought land in Keyworth and elsewhere.

Social Organisation

There is little in the records relating specifically to Keyworth which tells us how the village community was organised in the eighteenth century, so we have to rely more on secondary sources — books and papers written by historians about how rural England in general functioned at that time. Society was then strongly hierarchical, with people knowing, and mostly accepting without question, their place in it. Villages like Keyworth were fairly isolated from the rest of the country, and from London in particular, so they enjoyed a good deal of local autonomy. Authority rested with two people, and below them, two groups: the Lord of the Manor or Squire, who was usually also the local Justice of the Peace; the Rector; the parish Vestry Meeting; and a number of unpaid parish officers — church wardens, constables, overseers of the poor, surveyor of highways, and holders of lesser offices like that of pinder. We shall consider each in turn.

Lord of the Manor

Keyworth had only two Lords of the Manor throughout the century: Sir Thomas Parkyns II, the wrestling baronet of Bunny, who inherited the position at the age of 21, when his father, Thomas Parkyns I, died in 1684, and held it until his own death in 1741; and Sir Thomas Parkyns III, who succeeded his father at the age of twelve and remained Lord for the next 65 years until his death in 1806.

Although the parish had taken over most of the functions of the medieval manor by the eighteenth century, the Court Baron, which regulated the cultivation of the open fields, still functioned. Records survive[13] of courts for the manor of Keyworth, presided over by Sir Thomas Parkyns II in 1707 and a few years after that, in which fines are listed for minor transgressions of open field regulations, and which illustrate the kind of problems associated with open field farming:

	£	s	d
Robert Knight for [ploughing] two baulks on flatland		1	0
John Mee no baulk between two lans (*sic*)			6
William Shepperson for ploughing up greensward		1	3
Thomas Smith & son for keeping sheep in ye cornfield		1	0
etc.			

Similar courts may have been held, and fines imposed, until inclosure at the end of the century, but we have no later record. It became increasingly common for JPs to take over some of the functions of the manor court, while others were assumed by the Vestry Meeting and parish officers. Much depended on the personalities involved. Sir Thomas II was an exceptionally vigorous man who took his duties very seriously. His son seems to have been a more private individual and may have left the conduct of the manor court to a steward, or been content to see its functions taken over by other authorities.

Lords of the Manor frequently, but not invariably, were also patrons of the parish church and its living, and Justices of the Peace. This was the case in eighteenth century Keyworth. As patrons, they had the right and duty to appoint the rectors, which gave them an indirect hold on the spiritual affairs of the parish. Although once appointed rectors were accountable to the bishop, they must have felt under an obligation to the patron, though how constrained they were by this varied with the people concerned. As neither Parkyns II nor III lived in Keyworth, they would rarely come to the church, letting the rector get on undisturbed. There was room for nepotism here, as when Parkyns III appointed his 23 year-old son as rector in 1794, easing out the previous incumbent to make way for him, but this seems to have been an acceptable way of doing things in those days.

The Parkyns' role as JP was much wider than it would be today. First was their role as lay magistrate, adjudicating in disputes, conducting trials and pronouncing sentence. In trivial cases, they could act on their own and in private. Bearing in mind that most JPs had no legal training and were in these cases answerable to no-one, justice, if swift, must often have been rough. More serious cases would have to be dealt with at quarter sessions, where two or more JPs would act together, with the help of a legally trained clerk, as they are today.

Unlike today however, Justices of the Peace were also responsible for administration in the parishes in their district, which involved overseeing the appointment of parish officers, monitoring the way they did their work, and if necessary, fining them for dereliction of duty. In this respect, they undertook duties which are today the province of County and District Councils, but did so with no remuneration and no paid assistance.

The Lord of the Manor's other major role in village life was simply that of being Squire, the top man in a very hierarchical community, in which who you were mattered more than what you were like. His opinions would be treated with great respect, openly at least. When he visited the village, hats would be doffed and people would be on their best behaviour. He might throw the occasional garden party or other treat for them, but would normally mix only with people of his own class, which in Keyworth meant the rector and practically no-one else. Although the Parkyns family did not own all the land, as they did in Bunny and Bradmore, they were significant landowners in Keyworth, who would meet on more than equal terms with other leading proprietors, when matters such as inclosure were discussed.

The Rector

The rector's primary role was, of course, to look after the spiritual and moral welfare of his parishioners. At a minimum, this meant holding or making provision for at least one service of worship each Sunday, four services of holy communion a year, and the conduct of baptisms, weddings and marriages. In the latter half of the eighteenth century, the rectors of Keyworth were also rectors of Costock, and they all preferred to live in Costock.[14] Some appointed a curate to look after Keyworth, others managed both parishes by themselves, though one suspects that in those cases Keyworth was somewhat neglected. (Earlier in the century the boot was on the other foot: the rector of Keyworth from 1728 to 1751 was Edward Moises; he was also vicar of Wysall, but lived in Keyworth.)

Rectors had other duties. They were obliged by law to keep the parish registers, recording all baptisms, weddings and funerals taking place in their church, which are now such a valuable source for the reconstruction of demographic and family history before the census and civil registration were introduced in the nineteenth century. They were responsible for the upkeep of the chancel of the parish church, the rest of the building being the responsibility of their parishioners. They also had to look after a rectory in which, in the case of Keyworth, they did not live. They owned glebe land, which was normally rented out, and had to collect tithes from other farmers — in kind early in the century, in cash later on (see Appendix I). This was an unpopular tax, but rectors were obliged to collect it because their income depended upon it. They were also responsible for the conduct of the Vestry meeting, of which more is said below.

In addition to these obligations, the dedicated rector might undertake further activities. He might provide a village school, as Mr. Moises did in the 1740s, when it was probably conducted at the back of the church. (Keyworth had no wealthy residents to endow a school like those founded by Peacock in Ruddington, Parkyns in Bunny and Bley in East Leake.) After the launch of the Sunday School movement nationally in the 1780s, he probably felt obliged, and was perhaps eager, to start a Sunday School in the village, again held in the church. He might visit his parishioners in their homes, to urge attendance at Sunday services, and to offer comfort and encouragement to the sick and bereaved. Towards the end of the century, with competition threatened from a growing Independent congregation and an incipient Methodist movement in surrounding areas,[15] it might be thought that rectors would feel under pressure to undertake some of these extras, if only for the preservation of their own position. On this there is no direct evidence either way for Keyworth, although Stretton in 1815 commented on the state of the church thus: 'The lantern and spire are in miserable repair, to the great disgrace of the parish.'[16] Rectors during this period must have spent most of their time in their other parish (Costock) where they lived, so that Keyworth was probably neglected. On the other hand, nearly half the village's brides and bridegrooms were able to sign the marriage registers (women 41%, men 53%), indicating that many had achieved a basic level of literacy at least, for which the church can probably take some of the credit.

The Parish Officers

These were the men (and occasionally women) on whom the day-to-day running of the affairs of the village depended. In theory, all the office-holders served for one year, they were appointed by either the Justice of the Peace or the Vestry Meeting (see below), they were unpaid but could claim expenses, and they could not refuse to serve unless they could find an acceptable substitute. The principal offices were those of Churchwarden, Constable, Overseer of the Poor and Surveyor of Highways. The first was primarily an ecclesiastical responsibility, the others secular. This was of some significance in Keyworth because the village contained an enclave which was legally in the parish of Bunny. One George Martyn, builder of the timber-framed barn still standing on Main Street, successfully objected in 1654 to his appointment as churchwarden of Keyworth on the grounds that his farmhouse (adjoining the barn) was in the parish of Bunny; parishioners were told to find another churchwarden. No such objection could be made to other appointments, for which residents in the enclave were counted as belonging to Keyworth.

None of the offices was particularly sought after. To quote the Webbs:[17]

> The little farmers or innkeepers, jobbing craftsmen or shopkeepers who found themselves arbitrarily called upon to undertake arduous and complicated duties and financial responsibilities; ordered about during the year by Archdeacon, Incumbent or Squire; at the beck and call of every inhabitant; losing time and money, and sometimes reputation and health over their work; with no legal way of obtaining any remuneration...often felt themselves to be, not the rulers but the beasts of burden of the parish.

On the other hand, the poorer folk who were excluded from these offices, thought otherwise. They had no say in the appointment of the officials who were, again to quote the Webbs from the same passage, 'clothed with power over their fellow parishioners which we would now deem inconsistent with civil liberty...an uncontrollable parish oligarchy'. However, a key word in this quotation is 'now', the 1920s when the Webbs were writing. It is doubtful whether eighteenth century people thought in these terms, however much they may have resented the occasional overbearing parish officer. And it should be remembered that, in a small community, no-one could afford to fall foul of public opinion, which might be the price paid for officiousness. For all its limitations the system provided an effective form of local government for several centuries, with no serious breakdown.

There is limited documentary evidence relating to any of these offices in Keyworth. One source is the **Churchwardens'** accounts, though the earliest surviving date from 1820.[18] They show that churchwardens were concerned with the physical infrastructure of the church and churchyard, leaving the clergy free to concentrate directly on their ministry. But they were also spokesmen for the congregation. They were required to report annually to the archdeacon on the state of affairs in the church When one curate, who was supposed to be carrying out duties on behalf of an absentee rector (Edward Thompson) in the 1840s, also absented himself from the parish for weeks on end, it was the churchwardens who wrote to the Archdeacon of Nottingham, who in turn contacted the Bishop of Lincoln. The result was the dismissal of the curate and resignation of the rector.

Not all churchwardens' duties were strictly ecclesiastical, however. They also worked with the Overseers in regulating 'settlements' in the parish (see below, p.35); and with the Constables in bringing offenders to the magistrate's 'Court of Correction'.

The duties of the other officers were exclusively secular, and are implicit in their titles, though we have few references to their activities in Keyworth. **Constables** were, in effect, amateur policemen and tax collectors. If there was an affray in the village, send for the constable! If someone whose animals had strayed and been rounded up by the pinder, refused to pay the fine for their release from the pinfold, again call for the constable! He would also be called upon by the churchwardens and overseers to drive out vagrants or would-be migrants from other parishes, considered undesirable by the residents. And then there was tax collecting, which would have made him an unwelcome visitor to most households. All told, his were tasks requiring, on occasion, physical strength which he might not possess: to apprehend those deemed guilty of antisocial behaviour; to keep out or drive out unwelcome guests, as parish bouncer; and to parry the angry remarks of those who resented paying their taxes, often their social superiors.

The **Overseer of the Poor** was responsible for administering the Poor Law locally. This involved collecting the poor rate; distinguishing between the 'deserving' and 'undeserving' poor, helping the former to avoid destitution (especially the old and young, the sick and disabled); and denying help to the latter (those considered idle, who might include some we would now recognise as suffering from a psychiatric disorder), who would be threatened with the House of Correction or the Workhouse if they refused to work for their living and that of their dependants. It might also involve searching for deserting husbands and absconding fathers so that they could be required to discharge their responsibilities towards wives and children who would otherwise be a burden on the public purse.[19] We have already noted Gregory King's estimate that at the end of the seventeenth century over 60% of families in England needed to supplement their meagre income by begging, borrowing, stealing or applying for parish relief. The figure gives an idea of the scale of the Overseers' task (there were generally two in a parish).

Overseers had two other responsibilities which they shared with churchwardens. The first was to find 'apprenticeships' for pauper children — probably orphans. Five apprenticeship indentures relating to Keyworth have survived[20] and are in the Nottinghamshire County archives, the earliest dated 1731 and the latest 1801, of which four involve 'a poor child'. Of the four, three were sent to neighbouring parishes and the fourth stayed in Keyworth. Ages are given for two of the children: they were 'seven and upwards' and eight-and-a-half.

The apprentices were placed with 'masters' who undertook to house, feed and clothe them until they were 21 (or, in the case of girls, until they were married if that happened before they were 21), and to teach them skills to enable them to earn a livelihood. One boy was to be trained as a framework knitter, and a girl 'in the business of a housewife' (presumably by the master's wife). In return, the apprentices were at the complete disposal of their masters. In theory, the arrangement ensured a home, upbringing and training to otherwise destitute children, and on occasions it no doubt worked reasonably well. But often the apprentices were mercilessly exploited and treated like slaves all their waking hours, until they grew old enough to run away and fend for themselves. We do not know how the Keyworth children fared.

The other responsibility of overseers — again together with churchwardens — was the administration of the law of settlement. The Poor Law turned parishes into miniature welfare states, by laying on them the responsibility for ensuring that no parishioner starved — the apprenticeship arrangements just described were part of the system. The costs involved were paid for by the raising of a parish rate from those who were not themselves destitute. These ratepayers were anxious to minimise their burden, and therefore looked with suspicion or hostility on any incomer who might become a charge on the rates. Poor people generally (over half the population), and particularly those with many children, widows, single mothers and pregnant girls, came into this category. They therefore found it exceedingly difficult to migrate to another parish from where their settlement right was established but where they might not be able to find work, or might have difficult social relations from which they wished to escape.

It was the churchwardens and overseers who regulated what migration there was among poor people. Those of a parish from which someone wished to move could issue a 'settlement certificate' to their opposite numbers in the parish to which the person wished to go, guaranteeing to take him/her (and the family) back or pay maintenance if the need arose. On arriving at the new village, the migrant would hand the certificate over to the overseer or churchwarden, who would keep it safe (probably in the parish chest) in case the migrant became destitute and a claim had to be made at some future date. The County Archives possess 53 settlement certificates[21] addressed to the churchwardens and overseers of Keyworth, covering a period of over a hundred years, beginning in 1720. If they represent the complete collection received, less than one poor family in every two years succeeded in obtaining legal settlement in Keyworth from outside during that period. Perhaps Keyworth's churchwardens and overseers would have issued similar numbers for people who wished to leave the village; or slightly more, because, as already noted, there seems to have been a net outward migration of about one person (not family) a year. We do not know how often a person applying for a certificate was refused, but receiving and issuing settlement certificates was not an arduous task. The system did, however, severely restrict the movement of the poor, and put considerable power in the hands of parish officers.

The last of the principal parish officers was the **Surveyor of the Highways**. An Act of 1555 made parishes responsible for the upkeep of the roads passing through them, and parishioners were required to work for several days each year filling in ruts and potholes and spreading stone or gravel to improve drainage. It was the surveyor's job to organise and supervise this work. Some parishioners probably preferred bad roads to turning out in their own time to repair them without remuneration, so it could be difficult to persuade them to do their stint. In some cases, the statutory time spent under the surveyor's supervision was regarded as a social occasion rather than a working day. But if the work was not done and the roads deteriorated to the point where important people began to complain, the surveyor would be called in front of the magistrate to explain himself and perhaps face a fine.

These offices have sometimes been presented in romantic terms. 'Centuries before universal suffrage was ever dreamt of, we were governing ourselves... Every householder had to serve his year as an administrator of the nation's business... For a year the mantle of authority rested on his humble and unlettered shoulders.'[22] This is not strictly true however. Very poor householders, as already noted, were excluded from holding democratic office — at least those who were incapable of keeping accounts.

But some jobs were more prestigious, and some more onerous than others, and their allocation reflected the nuances of social structure.

> Churchwardens in rural parishes were drawn from local worthies, substantial farmers, inn-keepers, millers, while the overseers, whose office had slightly less dignity and more tiresome duties attached to it, came from a social layer just slightly below that of the churchwarden: small farmer, small trader, the skilled artisan. Below them still ranked the constable, a bothersome, unpopular position that no one wanted to fill, and which was, therefore assigned to those members of the community whose place in the social structure left them with little opportunity of protesting.[23]

Complicating the picture was church allegiance. In Keyworth, several of the leading farmers in the late eighteenth century (Thomas Hemsley, William and John Shepperson) were members of the Independent chapel and would have had to settle for an office less prestigious than that of churchwarden when their turn to do duty came round. The churchwardens' accounts from the 1820s already cited identify the churchwardens of that period as all being among the more prosperous farmers: the names Belshaw, Eggleston, Hebb and Cook keep cropping up. More surprising, in view of what has just been said about Independents, is Thomas Hemsley, but he is from a different generation to the one named earlier and may have changed his church allegiance.

Also complicating the picture is the fact that the same person seemed, on occasion, to hold two offices simultaneously. Thus, the constable's account books for both Bradmore (1772 to 1820) and Willoughby (1795 to 1811) contain entries showing that they distributed dole money, food and clothing to paupers, and also payment for some kinds of work — e.g., killing sparrows (Bradmore) and spinning cotton (Willoughby).[24]

The Vestry Meeting

Although the word 'vestry' implies a connection with the church, and although the incumbent traditionally chaired its meetings, it was open to all village residents, including dissenters. Its relations with parish officers has been likened to that between parliament and government, but only if a powerful Crown is included in the comparison, because the Justice of the Peace had authority generally overriding that of both vestry meeting and parish officers, as Tudor monarchs had over all their subjects, parliament and ministers included. Nevertheless, in addition to its rather vague statutory powers, the vestry meeting acted as a sounding board for local opinion and grievances, to which most JPs and officers paid attention most of the time. It would, for instance, nominate people to hold the parish offices, and the JP who had formal power to appoint but knew few of the people concerned, would normally follow its advice.

The scope of the vestry meeting's authority is indicated by the Webbs:[25] 'an undefined right to make by-laws on matters of parish concern...to make the Church Rate, to settle the assessment on which this should be levied, to impose fines for non-acceptance of parish office, to administer the pound [pinfold for stray animals], the common pasture and the wastes of the parish and generally to perform all the miscellaneous services of public utility...'. In many parishes they had taken over the role of the manor courts, but we do not know if this was the case in Keyworth around the time of inclosure, because the only vestry meeting minutes for the parish that have survived date from the late nineteenth century, while manorial records do not extend beyond the early eighteenth.

Social Change

While the eighteenth century saw relatively little change in village social structure (class distinctions and proportions in each class) or in formal social organisation (village government), there was considerable change in the day-to-day lives of people, though not on the scale experienced in the two subsequent centuries. Again, we have only fragmentary data relating specifically to Keyworth, so it is necessary to draw on more general information and infer from this how Keyworth was affected.

There were a number of underlying factors which brought about social change in the village, of which the following were perhaps the most important: transport improvements and industrialisation; fluctuations and trends in the price of farm produce; and an incipient humanitarianism arising out of religious revival and the Enlightenment. Each of these will be considered in turn.

Transport improvements and industrialisation

Nationwide developments in communications were referred to in Chapter 1. Probably the most significant improvement affecting eighteenth century

Keyworth was the turnpiking of the Loughborough Road (now the A60) in 1737/8 and Melton Road (A606) in 1753/4. Although neither road passed through the village, they both came within two miles at Bradmore and Plumtree respectively, improving Keyworth's access to the outside world, and particularly to Nottingham. The 'main road' to Nottingham had been a track over the open fields, via Debdale Lane and Flawforth; now people could go via one of the turnpikes, especially in winter, when the old tracks were muddiest — unless they wished to avoid the tolls. But we must not imagine that the turnpikes were always that much of an improvement, at least not until road engineers like Macadam and Telford changed the method of surfacing in the early nineteenth century. Some suffered from overuse. William Marshall, writing of the turnpike between Trent Bridge and Bunny Hill in 1790, called it 'one of the worst kept roads in the kingdom'.[26] Nevertheless, they were, with exceptions, a significant improvement: tolls provided more money for their upkeep than was available to parish surveyors; carts replaced packhorses for the transport of most merchandise, and fewer horses were now required to pull carriages.

The latter half of the century also saw a rapid increase in Nottingham's population — from just under 11,000 in 1750 to nearly 30,000 in 1800. It needed, and turnpikes enabled it, to spread its net for food supplies to encompass previously remote parishes like Keyworth, enabling villagers to dispose of surpluses more easily when they occurred, thereby steadying prices farmers could command. It also stimulated a greater emphasis on commercial, as opposed to subsistence farming, increasing the amount of money in circulation. And, as farm produce was sold out of the village, a reciprocal inward movement of goods occurred, providing people who could afford them with a greater variety of food, clothing and other goods. Some began to drink tea from China instead of, or in addition to, locally brewed ale. The pedlar had long been a familiar sight. With 'his pack on his back or leading a packhorse, [he] visited all the villages and farms. Not only did he sell scissors and spectacles, coloured handkerchiefs and calendars, but stuffs, fancy leather goods and watches and clocks, in fact everything the village wheelwright and blacksmith could not make.'[27] His visits continued and his trade may have grown for a time; but some people now preferred to go on shopping expeditions to Nottingham market, where there was greater choice. And, as more people travelled to town (Nottingham was not then a city) they came back with news of the outside world, some carrying newspapers. Nottingham hosiers began to consider Keyworth within range for putting out work which could be done more cheaply in villages than in town, where wages were higher.

But it was not only the nearby turnpikes that increased commerce into and out of Keyworth. The whole national network of improved roads, and towards the end of the century of canals also, resulted in a vastly increased amount of traffic in goods and ideas throughout the kingdom. The increasing trade that focused on Nottingham from afar also radiated from there to nearby villages. Metalware from Birmingham, cutlery from Sheffield, pottery from Staffordshire, calicos from Lancashire, carpets from Kidderminster, worsted from Bradford, and timber coming possibly from as far away as Scandinavia via Hull and the river Trent: the industrial revolution was on its way with its cornucopia of goods, many of which most villagers had never seen or even heard of before.

One item was of particular significance: coal, a commodity where a high proportion of its doorstep price was the cost of transport from the pits. We have already noted the shortage of firewood in the parish. Coal would have to be brought through Nottingham — originally from pits at Wollaton and Strelley and later from the Erewash valley. Turnpike roads had led to reduced prices, but canals brought them down further. The 1790s was a decade of canal mania and barges rapidly took over the long distance hauls from packhorses and carts. The Grantham Canal, opened in 1797, came to within four miles of Keyworth at Cotgrave, offering an alternative supply line to the turnpikes, at least for bulk cargoes.

Developments in transport and in industry paralleled and depended upon each other. New materials or familiar materials in far greater supply and at lower costs were coming onto the market. Three of the most important examples affecting everyday life were bricks, tiles and cotton. In the early eighteenth century, bricks and tiles were handmade and expensive. Only the well-off could afford them; the poor lived in hovels made of mud or timber, wattle and daub, with thatched roofs. By the end of the century, nearly all new houses were being made of brick and tiles. Wattle and daub infilling of some timber-framed buildings was replaced by brick - the old barns on Main Street are examples, in one of which the original timber frame is now almost entirely hidden from the outside by later brickwork. The new materials made houses stronger, less susceptible to fire, more waterproof, and were less likely to become breeding grounds for insects. Indeed, it has been suggested that the disappearance of bubonic plague already noted, may have been due, at least in part, to the new building materials and generally cleaner environment which they facilitated, contributing as they did to the extinction in Britain of the black rat which carried the plague-bearing flea.[28]

Cotton cloth was also, at the beginning of the eighteenth century, expensive and the preserve of the rich — handmade in India. By its end, cheap cotton cloth and clothing were being mass-produced in factories in Nottingham, the Leen Valley, and, on a far greater scale, in Lancashire, so that most people could afford them. Being lighter and washing better than wool or even linen, cotton promoted cleanliness, better health and greater comfort, at least in warm weather. People probably smelt sweeter at the end of the century than at its beginning — in summer, at least. They doubtless continued to wear wool in winter.

Price trends and fluctuation

Since most people in eighteenth century Keyworth depended either directly or indirectly for their livelihood upon farming, it was the price of farm produce that particularly affected their levels of poverty and prosperity. Variations in prices were of two kinds: long term trends reflecting the balance between the productive capacity of English agriculture and availability of food imports on the one hand, and demand on the other; and short term fluctuations in output resulting from variable weather conditions and pest infestation or disease affecting crops and livestock.

The long term price movements during the eighteenth century fall into three parts. The first half of the century was one of falling food prices, mainly brought about by a combination of increased agricultural productivity and little or no population growth. Average wheat prices fell from 34 shillings per quarter between 1700 and 1709 to 27 shillings between 1740 and 1749.[29] Everybody benefited except farmers and landowners; living standards of many of the poor rose and it was during this period that the wheaten loaf became the staple food, replacing the much heavier and less palatable one made from a mixture of barley and rye. But it was not only their diet that improved. 'Go into one of these poor men's houses,' wrote a 'real farmer' in 1768; 'it is more than an equal chance but we shall find a clock, pewter, chairs, tables, feather beds, quilts, hangings, etc., etc., all in regular decent order; there we shall also see hung beef and bacon, cheese, bread and butter in their pantries; all this is the fruits of good living — the result of hard work.'[30] Poverty is, however, relative: one suspects this does not describe the conditions of the very poor, who may have comprised much of the village population at that time.

In any case, by the 1760s the 'good' life of the poor was already coming to an end. The second of our three periods ran from mid-century until the early 1790s, which experienced a reversal of the previous fifty years: population began to rise faster than food production, there was a food deficit only partly made up for by imports, and prices rose. Wheat prices reached an average of 46 shillings per quarter in the 1780s. Because food in general and grain in particular is such a basic necessity, its price is very sensitive to shifts in the balance of supply and demand. Gregory King pointed out in 1696 that 'one tenth the deficit in harvest may raise the price three tenths'[31] and the same was still true three-quarters of a century later. It was now the farmers and landowners who benefited, encouraging investment in farming and leading, among other things, to the inclosure of thousands of parishes between 1760 and 1820, and the building of new farmhouses. 'The Midland countryside is strewn with evidence of a building boom that affected every social grade at this period ... (1760 to 1800), and the discerning eye can see in ornamental brickwork, string courses and fanlights a reflection in the village of conspicuous consumption in the Hall.'[32] Unfortunately not many buildings of this period survive in Keyworth, and those that do (e.g., Nos. 2, 3 and 4 Main Street) have had their brickwork covered with cement rendering. The three tall houses (Nos. 17, 19 and 45 Main Street) are of a slightly later date but represent the fruits of the same farm prosperity. Those who were not farmers or landowners may have benefited where they were able to occupy, at affordable rents, houses vacated by farmers moving into their new properties, though with most farmers rebuilding in the village alongside or on the foundations of their old houses, such opportunities were limited. Most non-farmers would have felt the pinch of prices rising faster than wages.

The wars with France, from 1793 to 1815, covered the third period, one of almost runaway inflation. Average wheat prices doubled, and in some years when harvests were poor, they went even higher. By this time, population increase had outstripped growth in agricultural output to the extent that England had become a regular importer of grain, and the war cut off supplies. Farmers and large landowners prospered as never before, but the landless, whose wages did not keep up with inflation, suffered severe deprivation. 'The crisis through which England was passing had wiped out all distinctions between the poor and the destitute.'[34] People who normally lived close to the bread line could only be saved from starvation by Poor Law relief, and overseers' account books (e.g., those of Bradmore and Willoughby — that of Keyworth has not survived) show expenditure more than doubling over these years. The plight of many was exacerbated by a decline of cottage industries like spinning, in face of competition from newly established factories; and, in recently inclosed parishes, by the loss of commons. Both cottage industries and commons had provided subsidiary sources of livelihood which were now gone. We are here straying into the post-inclosure period of Keyworth's history however, and this subject will be taken up again in a later chapter.

In addition to the long-term price changes just outlined, there were violent short-term fluctuations caused by bad harvests or temporary interruptions in food supplies from overseas, which could cause acute distress to people living near the margins and with no reserves to fall back on. These were at their worst during the Revolutionary and Napoleonic wars with France, as illustrated by the following sequence of wheat prices in shillings per quarter in 1793, 1795, 1797, 1799 and 1801 respectively: 50, 108, 62, 76, 128.[35] The years 1795 and 1801 must have been particularly grim for the poor without land.

Humanitarianism

It may seem strange to associate the age of slavery abroad, and of merciless exploitation of child labour at home with humanitarianism, but there was a growing current of opinion that was opposed to these and other abominations. Its influence began to be felt in the eighteenth century, but became much more significant in the nineteenth, with the abolition of slavery in the British Empire in 1807, and a succession of factory acts limiting and finally prohibiting child labour. To quote Harold Perkins: 'Between 1780 and 1850, the English ceased to be one of the most aggressive, brutal, rowdy, outspoken, riotous, cruel and blood-thirsty nations in the world and became one of the most inhibited, polite, orderly, tender-minded, prudish and hypocritical.'[36] Allowing for a degree of hyperbole in this assertion, it seems likely that life in Keyworth was affected by the changes in values and social norms that it implies. Without direct local evidence, it may seem inappropriate to outline these national trends, but it is reasonable to assume that their impact on the lives of local people was at least as great as other developments that are better documented. The final paragraphs in this chapter therefore set out some of the legislation and currents of opinion which did much to determine the way in which élites exercised their power and influence on humble villagers during the eighteenth century.

Changing attitudes on the part of the well-off towards poverty and the poor are the most important manifestation of this trend, at least as it affected village life. The Poor Law, as conceived by the Tudors, was itself a humanitarian measure, in that it sought to protect the needy from complete destitution by requiring individual parishes to raise a poor rate to provide for those who, through age or infirmity, could not earn their own living; and to find work for those who had none. As this latter group grew, it became increasingly difficult to find work for them; they became a growing burden as the poor rate had to be raised to cover their needs as well. Humanity was eclipsed by resentment on the part of those in work towards those who seemed idle spongers — a familiar attitude among some of today's 'haves' towards the 'have-nots'.

This resentment found particular expression in two laws: the Law of Settlement, enacted in 1662, and an act of 1723 requiring local authorities to build workhouses and refuse relief to any not willing to work in them. We have already referred to the former: everybody had a statutory right to be supported by the parish in which they were legally settled should they fall on hard times, but only in that one parish. Settlement rights belonged to those born in the parish, women married to 'settled' men (but not men married to 'settled' women), people who had worked in the parish for a year or been apprenticed in the parish for at least 40 days. Anyone without settlement rights who threatened to become a charge on the rates would be driven out, often with a whipping, 'until his back be bloody'. Unmarried pregnant women were a particular target, since their children, if born in the parish, would become an automatic charge on the rates. They would sometimes be driven out and simply dumped beyond the boundary, just before the baby was due, whence they might be picked up and taken to yet another unwelcoming parish, and so on until the baby was born or the woman died of exhaustion. Economy got the better of humanity.

The act of 1723 was a more direct response to those who blamed the poor on their own idleness. People who could not find work in the normal way were to be virtually imprisoned in workhouses. Outdoor relief (i.e., financial help outside workhouses) was no longer to be given, except to the very old or obviously disabled. In practice, the workhouses were in many places not built — there is no record of Keyworth or its neighbouring parishes having one[37] — so paupers were now reduced to beggary, theft, or starvation.

But by mid-century voices were being raised against the often brutal treatment or neglect of the destitute. One of the most influential was that of the novelist Henry Fielding, who was also a magistrate. One of his more telling statements on the subject, penned in 1753, read: 'The sufferings of the poor are less known than their misdeeds, and therefore we are less apt to pity them. They starve and freeze and rot among themselves, but they beg and steal and rob among their betters.'[38] If the suffering was out of sight it was, for most, also out of mind, and it required articulate men of compassion to confront people with harsh truths. Others whose influence contributed to more humane attitudes from very different standpoints included the Wesleys, with their call for Christian compassion, and disciples of the French idealist Rousseau, including Tom Paine, author of *The Rights of Man*.

A change in the law came in 1782, when outdoor relief was once again allowed for able bodied people. A further improvement came in 1795, when people could no longer be expelled from a parish because they might become a charge on the rates, but only when they actually needed relief, in which case they either had to return to, or receive relief from their parish of settlement. But perhaps most remarkable was a decision taken by the parish of Speenhamland in Berkshire, to subsidise the low-paid out of the poor rate. This was also initiated in 1795 — a year of very high grain prices, as we have seen — and may owe something to fear of hunger leading to unrest and revolution, as had occurred so recently in France. Whatever the reason, a precedent was set which was followed over much of England. It had some unfortunate consequences, but these belong to Keyworth's post-inclosure period. In any case, with so many self-employed people on small farms and as framework knitters and other craftsmen, there was not a huge surfeit of casual labourers in Keyworth, to be underpaid by employers and have their wages topped up by a Speenhamland subsidy.

However, two factors were producing a counter current to the rising tide of humanitarianism. The French Revolution and subsequent 'Terror', together with growing unrest associated with rising food prices, loss of common rights resulting from inclosure and the growth of an urban proletariat, led to fear among many of the spread of revolution to this country. Law-breaking in general and attacks on property in particular were treated with growing severity throughout the century, with the number of offences for which the death penalty could be imposed increasing from about 50 to around 200.[39] After 1789 they were applied with greater ferocity, while spring guns and man-traps were set by estate owners to kill, maim or catch poachers as if they were vermin.

Meanwhile economists like Adam Smith were arguing that wages should be determined by supply and demand — a popular doctrine among employers at a time when population and therefore labour supply was growing, especially in the countryside — rather than by the traditional notion of 'the just wage'.[40] Another economist, the Rev. Robert Malthus, came to a similar conclusion by a different route: he contended that poverty for the majority was inevitable, being determined by the available means of subsistence; that relief of poverty, or wages above the bare minimum, would result in a growth in population (presumably because fewer would die of malnutrition or starvation) which would therefore outstrip the means of subsistence; and that poverty relief or wages above the minimum were therefore useless in the long run — again, a popular proposition among employers.

How these changes and cross-currents in attitude and in the law were manifested in Keyworth can only be guessed at. It is to be hoped that the people benefited more from the more humane attitudes and enactments that have been described in preceding paragraphs than from counter tendencies. But improvements came about slowly and unevenly — not soon enough for George Benson who was sentenced to transportation in 1787 for stealing a hen worth 10 pence from Thomas Hemsley — he must have been among the first convicts to be dispatched to the new colony of New South Wales, to work as virtual slaves if they survived the journey. Heavily pregnant girls were still being expelled from parishes in various parts of the country at the end of the century and into the next, to prevent their children becoming a charge on the rates: one authority cites examples from Oxfordshire, Dorset and Pembrokeshire.[41] In 1800, as in 1700, child labour was still regarded as normal, even desirable — both as training in application, and as a way to supplement family income. The early success of Sunday Schools after 1780 owed much to the fact that they did not take children away from their work to be taught basic literacy. Apprenticeships were diminishing in number with the introduction of machinery and the decline of craft guilds, but where they existed in the late eighteenth century they could be no less harsh than they had been earlier on. Indeed, Blackstone, writing at the end of the century, justified slavery on the grounds that it was no worse than the apprenticeship system[42] — in which respect he was accurate, at least for many orphans or bastards sold into apprenticeships by the parish (if one discounts the horrors suffered by slaves during the 'middle passage' across the Atlantic). There is no reason to believe that pregnant girls, orphans or bastard children were treated any better or any worse in Keyworth than elsewhere (outside the often brutalising and impersonal environments of newly developing factories and towns). The poor were almost invariably illiterate and left little record of their experiences. In Keyworth, they left none.

Yet, however harsh conditions were in villages like Keyworth, they were, towards the end of the century, becoming far worse in mushrooming industrial towns like Nottingham, with their 'dark satanic mills'. Urban congestion, polluted air and drinking water, stinking drains and open sewers exacted a terrible toll in sickness and death; the stresses of a strange and alien environment felt by new migrants were almost as hard to bear. Those who stayed in Keyworth were probably spared the worst horrors of the early industrial revolution.

Notes

1. There are two copies of the original Inclosure Award map, one held by the Central Record Office in London, the other by the Nottinghamshire Archives. They differ from each other in the village buildings they show; Figures 2 and 3 are based on the former, which shows houses that could be the present 17 and 19 Main Street; the latter does not.
2. Keyworth's Hearth Tax returns of 1674 recorded 49 households; at an average of 4.5 people per household — a widely recognised figure — this would give a population of around 220. By 1700 it might have reached 250.
3. Keyworth parish registers record 585 baptisms and 438 burials in the 18th. century. Though by no means precise measures of births and deaths, the figures suggest a natural increase of the order of 150, about twice the actual increase.
4. Quoted in Webster, 1988, introduction.
5. George, 1953, pp.150–1.
6. Deane, 1979, p.20.
7. Fussell, 1947, p.72.
8. Lowe, 1798, p.140.
9. It is uncertain whether the old part of the house that survived until 1970 did date from the seventeenth century: all-brick houses of modest size were a rarity at that time; most were supported by a timber frame.

10. The earliest references to framework knitting in Keyworth were the occupations of John Hall and Isaac Bowley, mentioned on their Settlement Certificates of 1723 and 1733 respectively. Hall then disappears from the local records and may have moved on, but Bowley remained in Keyworth until his death over fifty years later: he crops up in the account book of the Independent Chapel as a tenant of property owned by the chapel (in the 1760s) and in the church burial register (1789). He may therefore have introduced the industry to Keyworth. Early next century, 17 fathers are listed as framework knitters in the baptismal registers between 1813 and 1822, including five Pikes, but no Bowley.

11. 'Paving stone, which formerly used to be got out of the Trent, is now plentifully brought from Keyworth and other parts not far distant.' (Deering, 1751, p.88.)

12. George, 1953, p.87.

13. UNMD PaM21 1707

14. The first absentee rector of the period, Richard Barnard (1751 to 1783), lived in York for the first part of his incumbency, until he obtained and moved into the rectory of Costock in 1768.

15. Methodism does not appear to have established a foothold in Keyworth until 1804.

16. Quoted in Godfrey, 1887, p.129.

17. Webbs, 1924, p.40.

18. NA PR1141

19. Examples are mentioned in Johnston, P: 'The Management of the Poor Law in Seven Parishes of West Lincolnshire, 1790–1834' in *East Midland Historian*, Vol. 8, 1998, p. 15.

20. NA PR1928/1–5.

21. NA PR1926/1–53.

22. Arthur Bryant, quoted in Tate, 1983, p.9.

23. Marshall, 1956, p.93.

24. NA Bradmore PR7090; Willoughby PR804.

25. Webbs, 1924, pp.39–41.

26. Cossons, 1934, p.13.

27. Mantoux, 1961, p.111.

28. Deane, 1979, p.29.

29. Matthias, 1969, p.474.

30. Quoted in Chambers, 1957, p.46.

31. ibid, p.39.

32. ibid, p.49.

33. A 1914 survey of properties describes No. 2 & 4 Main Street as being built of 'cement and tile' with no mention of bricks. PRO IR58 63599.

34. Mantoux, 1961, p.437.

35. ibid, p.427.

36. cited by May, 1987, p.208.

37. The Poor Law Amendment Act of 1834 established Poor Law Unions, each with its workhouse, out of groups of parishes. Keyworth was assigned to the Bingham Union.

38. quoted in Mantoux, 1961, p.453.

39. Horn, 1980, p.165.

40. Thompson, 1968, p.244.

41. Horn, 1980, p.100.

42. George, 1953, p.126.

Chapter 3

Working the Open fields

In those parts of England where the medieval open field system remained substantially intact until the passing of a parliamentary Inclosure Act in the eighteenth or nineteenth centuries, there followed a dramatic transformation, not only of the landscape but also of village economy and society. To understand these changes, we first need to know something of the open field system in general and of its manifestation in Keyworth. Comparison with neighbouring parishes will also be useful, to illustrate the degree to which Keyworth typified conditions in South Nottinghamshire and perhaps a wider area. This chapter outlines some of the general characteristics of the open field system, while the next addresses the specific context in which they operated in Keyworth, and the changes the system underwent before being terminated by inclosure.

Perhaps the most obvious difference between an open field landscape and that of present-day England is the lack of hedges in the former. People who today complain about the rooting out of hedges and the destruction of the traditional English countryside should remember that, in the Midlands at least, much of the hedged landscape is only two hundred years old and was preceded by an older tradition stretching back for perhaps a thousand years. In this, hedges were largely confined to the crofts (garden-sized plots) adjoining farmsteads in the villages, though they may also have been used to demarcate parish boundaries and to enclose areas of common pasture. Other than that, the parish fields were virtually hedgeless. Even some of the few pre-inclosure hedges were little older than those associated with inclosure — for instance, according to manorial court records, an agreement was made in 1741 to plant a quickset hedge and make a ditch along the boundary of Bradmore and Keyworth, nearly forty and sixty years respectively before those parishes were inclosed.[1]

There were, however, many other features of the open field system which distinguished it from the modern countryside. One authority[2] argues that there were four essential elements in the system:

- arable land was divided into strips which were individually cultivated by their owners or tenants;
- this arable, together with meadow land, was open to livestock under communal supervision when there were no crops or hay growing;
- an area of pasture and/or waste was open to livestock at all times, again under communal supervision;
- all these activities were organised by a manorial court or village assembly made up of all farmers and landowners in the manor or parish.

Figure 4 **Map of Keyworth's open fields immediately before inclosure**

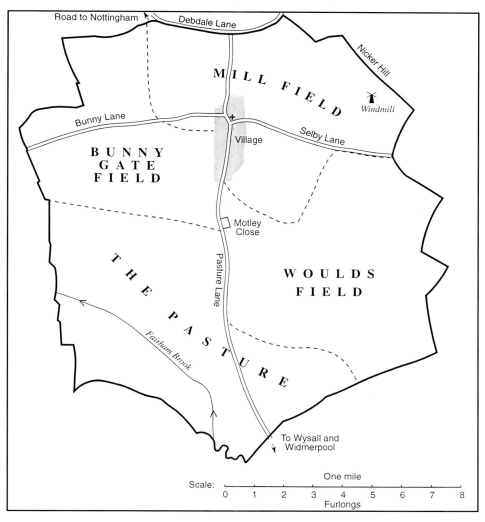

Scholars have drawn a distinction between the first of these elements, which characterised open fields in general, and the other three, which are associated with the common field system, the distribution of which was less extensive but included most of the Midlands.[3] All four elements are now discussed in further detail.

Arable Strips

Arable land is land that is ploughed and used for growing crops. In the open field system, the arable part of a manor or parish normally comprised two, three

Figure 5a **Meaning of terms used in open field farming** Figure 5b **How ridge-and-furrow was formed**

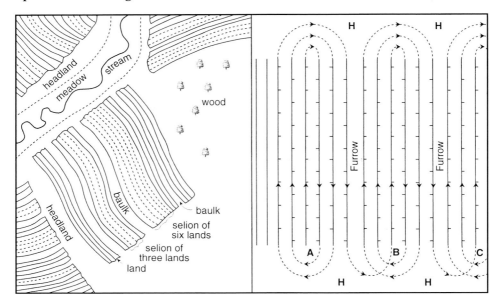

One whole and part of several other furlongs with intervening headlands, meadow and wood.

H = headland, where plough turns.
Starting from **A**, plough moves in direction of arrows. The mouldboard throws earth to right, indicated by the ticks on plough-lines.
A, **B** and **C** are the ends of ridges.
NB The length of ridges and furrows relative to their width has been reduced.

or four large fields of several hundred acres each. Keyworth, just before inclosure, had three, called the Woulds (the usual spelling at the time), Mill and Bunny Gate Fields, and occupying respectively the south-east, north-east and north-west quarters of the parish. (The south-west quarter was The Pasture — see Figure 4). The arable fields were divided into 'furlongs' (also called 'shotts' or 'wongs'), which in turn were subdivided into strips, otherwise known as 'selions', the basic elements of landownership and cultivation. These might be further subdivided for ploughing as described below. All the strips in a furlong were aligned parallel to each other and were ploughed lengthwise, usually up and down any slope, to assist drainage, at least on heavy land. A furlong was, therefore, the length of one furrow of the plough. (See Figure 5a.)

It should be noted that the term furlong referred to an area or cluster of parallel strips, each of which was a furrow long: it had a double meaning, as both area and length. But neither the area of the cluster, nor the length of indi-

Figure 6 **Map of Keyworth Rector's Glebe in 1752**

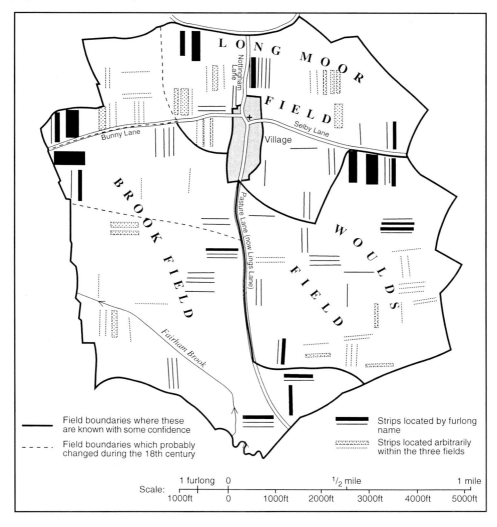

Note: The location of some furlongs named in the Rector's terrier of 1752 can be deduced fairly precisely from post-inclosure field names, where these are known and correspond — see those asterisked in Appendix III. The strips in these furlongs can therefore be located more exactly than the rest, where we only know which of the three large open fields they occupied. The approximate orientation of all the strips is indicated in the terrier by its identification of neighbouring strips being either to the north and south — in which case the orientation can be assumed to be roughly east-west; or to the east and west, in which case the orientation would be north-south.

vidual strips was of standard size. The modern furlong of 220 yards probably represented an average or common furrow length, which tended to be shorter on heavy than on light land. Indeed, the Orwins suggest that it was nearer the maximum furrow length than its average.[4]

The ploughing units were called 'lands', and while many strips consisted of several adjacent lands, others were of only one land's width. For instance, in Keyworth the Rector's glebe in one of the big fields (Woulds Field) comprised 46 strips, of which 36 were of only one land's width, 4 of two, 3 of three, 2 of five and 1 of fifteen lands' width — see Figure 6.[5]

However wide his strip, a farmer generally ploughed units of between 5 and 22 yards width at a time, working from the centre towards the outside, with the mouldboard throwing the turned-over soil towards the centre — see Figure 5b.[6] On heavy clay soil like that of most of Keyworth, these units were much nearer 5 yards, so that furrows, which acted as drainage channels, would be close together. The effect of repeating this process, perhaps over several centuries, was to create a series of ridges and furrows which can still be seen today — for instance, on Keyworth's recreation ground — where modern methods of ploughing have not flattened them. The ridges therefore represent individual lands, not necessarily strips or selions which might encompass several parallel ridges and furrows.

Individual strips might abut directly onto those of neighbours, separated by no more than a double furrow which had to be cleared regularly to facilitate drainage; or they might be separated by 'baulks' (unploughed strips of ground, otherwise called 'meers') which also provided access to land without trespass. At the end of the strips in a furlong were 'headlands' where plough teams could turn round. Furlongs and their strips were often slightly curved into the shape of a reverse S, to make it easier for the plough team, which might consist of six or more oxen or horses, to turn round when it reached a headland.

Although the strips were cultivated by their owners or tenants, this did not preclude cooperation. For instance, small farmers would have insufficient animals to pull a plough and may not have had a plough anyway, so they helped each other in informal arrangements. Also, it usually took more than one person to control the plough and the animals pulling it, as the following description indicates: 'Ploughing required a mixture of skill, experience and brute strength, and to control so many uneasily yoked animals (four on heavy soil, and up to eight on virgin soil) was something no novice could attempt. As many as four men might be at work on the job: one, the ploughman himself, holding and steering the plough; another to goad and encourage the oxen, walking backwards in front of them; another to plod beside the plough, adjusting the plough beam and helping to guide it; and perhaps another to ride on the plough to weigh it down and keep it steady in the ground. So ploughing was a matter of shouting and struggle — men against beasts and both against the soil.'[7] While this quotation refers to the medieval scene, it was probably much the same in the eighteenth century except that horses, pulling at perhaps two mph, would have replaced one-mph oxen, the whole operation therefore taking less time.

Communal supervision of arable and meadow land

The fields containing strips that were cultivated individually became 'commonable' after the harvest and until the next crop was sown. Poor families would glean the uncollected grain, and livestock belonging to the owners or tenants of the strips would be allowed onto them to graze the stubble, weeds and grassy baulks and headlands. They were often penned in by hurdles (movable fences) to ensure systematic grazing and dunging of the soil, but were not confined to the strips of their owners. The commonable periods were between harvest and preparation for autumn or spring sowing, except when a field was in fallow when they extended over most of the year, other than when the land was ploughed for weed control. One shepherd or cowherd might be responsible for supervising all the stock in a field.

The same arrangements applied to meadows used for hay. These were usually divided among the farmers into 'doles' during the hay-growing period (early summer) when no stock would be allowed on. After the hay harvest the meadows would become commonable, though they would be cleared during the coldest months to prevent the sward being churned up by animal feet. In Keyworth, their importance is hard to assess. The term 'Keyworth Meadow', denoting part of the nature reserve near Fairham Brook, is of modern origin: it is not found in old documents. In fact, floodable land (where meadows were often found) alongside Fairham Brook is not extensive, and the marshy backwaters give the area an unkempt appearance not associated with carefully managed meadows. Also, there are few mentions of meadows in the detailed terrier of land tithable to the rector (1752)[8] and no meadow is referred to in the inclosure award other than in the introduction, which is a standard form of words used for all awards at the time. On the other hand, a court inquisition of 1527[9] stated that the then lord of the manor of Keyworth, Thomas Barry, owned 8 bovates of meadow, 19 of (arable) land and 2 of pasture. A bovate was about 15 acres (the amount varied with the terrain) so that he alone — and he was not the only proprietor — owned about 120 acres of meadow in the parish; meadow, in his case at least, occupied nearly half as much land as did the arable. Again, a series of probate inventories between 1691 and 1772[10] estimate the average value of hay amounted to about 15% of that of all crops in the fields or in store belonging to the deceased to whom probate referred. Perhaps these items of apparently conflicting evidence can be resolved by suggesting that most of the hay came from tracts of grass, either on The Pasture, or on strips in the arable fields, which were fenced off in early summer to produce hay, before being thrown open to grazing. Whether or not these tracts were called meadow was not important.

The number of stock a farmer could put onto the commonable arable or meadow was generally 'stinted' — that is, rationed in proportion to the tenements he possessed or occupied, the amount of land he farmed and the grazing rights he possessed, expressed in medieval terms such as horsegates and cowgates.[11] This was to prevent overgrazing.

Pasture

Quite separate from the arable fields was an area of permanent pasture. This generally consisted of rough grass, bracken and various shrubs and trees, and provided not only grazing land throughout the growing season, but was also a source of wood for fuel and making or repairing household goods, free food like mushrooms, blackberries or rabbits, an assortment of extras such as rushes for making lamps, reeds for thatching or making baskets, peat or dung for fuel, and space for recreation. Again, livestock grazing would be supervised by one shepherd or cowherd and their number was usually stinted. But people who owned or rented no land in the arable fields often had common rights to use the pasture, either statutory or enshrined by custom; and as they were usually the poorest in the community, these rights were a vital part of their household economy. The right to graze one cow and collect what the pasture had to offer might make the difference between living above and below subsistence level.

Communal Regulation

The system so far outlined required communal regulation and this was carried out by a manorial court or other village meeting in which all farmers and land-owners took part. There were several issues needing regulation, the most important being:

a. the crops to be grown in the arable and the timing of seedtime and harvest — as the arable fields were turned over to grazing between harvest and the next sowing, these activities had to be synchronised among those working individual strips, which in turn meant selecting crops that required the same amount of time to grow and ripen;
b. marking boundaries between strips — there were usually no obvious landmarks by which to demarcate strips, and especially after a year of fallow precise boundaries needed to be reconfirmed and indicated to avoid disputes;
c. enforcing stints — ensuring that people were not grazing more than their allotted number of stock on the commonable lands;
d. devising and enforcing additional rules to facilitate the smooth running of the system, and making communal appointments — e.g., setting fines for the retrieval of stray animals from the pinfold, and appointing the pinder;
e. ensuring that strip owners maintain stretches of drainage ditch bordering their land and erect temporary barriers against livestock incursion onto the arable fields if their strips bordered a recognised track along which animals were driven;
f. adjudicating and settling of farmers' disputes.

Here was local democracy and participation at work in a way that has largely disappeared today. It was reinforced by the appointment or election of local men (and very occasionally women) to be village officers with power and responsibility — overseer of the poor, surveyor of the highways, constables, churchwardens and others, whose responsibilities are outlined on pp.33–6.

Other features of the open field system

While the foregoing may describe what Taylor considers the essential ingredients of the open field system (perhaps it should be called the common field system, as so much depended on communal management) as it operated over a large part of the English lowlands and a great deal of western Europe for much of the past millennium, there were other features associated with the system, some agricultural and some relating to other aspects of the pre-inclosure countryside.

The agricultural features can be summarised in three words: rotation, fragmentation and subsistence. The first two refer to the arable fields only, the last to the whole system.

Crop rotation both helps to maintain soil fertility and to control disease and pests. In pre-inclosure times this was generally reinforced by including a fallow year into the rotation. Where soil was particularly rich or population pressure required it, the rotation would be longer and therefore the fallow less frequent than elsewhere. In Keyworth, where there were three arable fields, a third of that land would not be growing any crop in a given year, while Ruddington had four fields and presumably fallow would only occupy a quarter of its arable land. At one time, all strips in a field, though cultivated individually, might be growing the same crop, in which case they would look like one almost unbroken field as the crop matured and obscured baulks between strips. The most common crops were cereals (autumn sown wheat or rye and spring sown barley or oats) and pulses (peas and beans, grown mainly for fodder). By the eighteenth century, however, experiment and improvement were afoot: new crops like turnips, potatoes, clover and sown grass were introduced, and the furlong rather than the large field often became the common unit of rotation.[12] Rotations themselves became of more variable length with fallows less frequent — the celebrated Norfolk four course (wheat, turnips, barley, clover), dispensing with fallow altogether, being a notable example. However, on heavy land like that of most of Keyworth, neither clovers nor turnips and other root crops were widely grown until undersoil drainage was introduced in the mid-nineteenth century.[13] On the other hand, by the mid-eighteenth century, sown grasses (leys) were of considerable significance in Keyworth — see p. 61 for a fuller discussion.

Because of the way fields and furlongs were subject to communally determined rotations, which included years of fallow, it was necessary for farmers to have their land distributed among all the fields and preferably most of the furlongs, so that they obtained regular annual harvests. This was one reason why their holdings were so fragmented. There were others. Many centuries earlier, when the open fields were being carved out of pre-existing scrub or forest, assarting (clearing) may have been carried out by a group who then divided the land won among themselves. Where there was marked variation in terrain and soil (which is not the case in Keyworth, though there are outcrops of sandy soil amid the more widespread boulder clay), it may have been considered fair to distribute land so that each had some of high, and some of inferior quality. Fragmentation might also be considered a way of spreading risk: if disaster (disease or a weather calamity) struck one part of the parish no individual whose strips were widely scattered would be as badly affected as one whose land was all concentrated in the disaster area. Yet another advantage — perhaps an effect rather than a cause of fragmentation — was that small units of land could more easily be bought and sold by people with few resources — 'retail, as it were', to use a phrase of R.H.Tawney. And although primogeniture was the usual way in which land was passed from one generation to the next (the eldest son got it all), partible inheritance (when the estate was divided between heirs) was not uncommon, particularly where there was no son and the heirs were daughters, and this inevitably increased fragmentation.

Whatever the reasons (and they are not mutually exclusive) individual holdings were split into very small units scattered throughout all the fields and many of the furlongs. The 46 strips comprising the Keyworth rector's glebe land in one field have already been mentioned and represented in Figure 6. From land tax returns for 1780, it appears that they, along with the rest of his glebe in the other two fields, were farmed by one tenant who must therefore have spent a great deal of his time simply walking to his scattered holding (though he would probably need to visit only a handful of strips in fairly close proximity on any one day). In the parish as a whole there were over 3,000 strips. If the average length of strip was half a modern furlong (many may have been a full furlong), this implied some 200 miles of property boundaries, often not clearly marked — a fertile source of dispute between neighbours!

Another example illustrating fragmentation of the open fields is given by Mark Pierce's 1635 map of Laxton in Nottinghamshire, part of which is shown in Figure 7. Laxton is widely known today as the only surviving example in England of the open field system, still run communally as a living museum. However, the narrow strips depicted by Pierce would be impossible to cultivate with modern machinery and have been amalgamated — up to ten adjacent strips joined together, to form broad, hedgeless swaths, more amenable to twentieth century farming. This was no doubt necessary for economic reasons, but one of the open field system's most typical (and inconvenient) characteristics — extreme fragmentation — has therefore been lost.

Until the transport revolution brought about by the advent of turnpike roads in the eighteenth century, followed by canals, railways and steam locomotion, most villages, if not individual farms, operated a largely subsistence economy, at least where food was concerned: they consumed most of what they produced and produced most of what they consumed. While trade within and between villages and nearby towns did occur, the presence of wind- or water-mills in most villages until recent times is a reminder of their level of self-sufficiency. This meant that farms were mixed crop and livestock enterprises: crops provided the bulk of food eaten by the people and some winter food for livestock,

Figure 7 **Part of Pierce's 1635 map of Laxton**

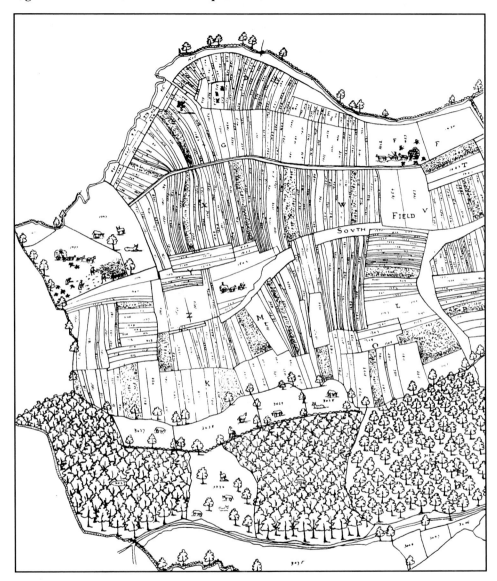

From Orwin, *The Open Fields* (1967) by permission of Oxford University Press.

while animals provided draft power and dung to cultivate the crops, as well as high protein food in the form of meat and dairy produce (and, of course, non-food products like leather, tallow and wool). The open field system served well in maintaining a necessary balance in the symbiotic relationship between crops and animals and could be adapted when this balance came under strain. If a growing population required more crops to be grown, the area of pasture or the amount of fallow could be reduced; if arable land showed signs of soil exhaustion, some could be put down to temporary grass (called leys), both to rest the soil and to increase the livestock-holding capacity and therefore the amount of dung available for fertilisation. The system worked less well when farming became more specialised, which was probably one reason why it was gradually abandoned in favour of inclosure when farming became more commercial.

The non-agricultural aspects of the pre-inclosure countryside can be dealt with briefly. First, we may mention tithes. All farmers had been obliged to pay one tenth of their produce to the established church since the tenth century,[14] at one time in kind, but by the late eighteenth century in cash, at any rate, in Nottinghamshire (see Appendix I). Although not intrinsic to the open field system, it invariably accompanied it and was the cause of much resentment, particularly among dissenters, who were numerous in Keyworth, the more so because tithes had to be paid not only to the rector of Keyworth, but also to Sir Thomas Parkyns of Bunny Hall, the vicar of Bunny, and the rectors of Gotham and Clifton. Of course, tithes on any single piece of land were only paid to one tithe owner, but having five tithe owners in one parish, all of them non-residents,[15] was highly unusual and no doubt correspondingly unpopular. Parliamentary inclosure was to bring tithes to an end in much of the country, including Keyworth.

Roads also received attention at inclosure and therefore deserve a brief mention here. Under the open field system, they were generally ill-defined tracks crossing or separating fields, their course being determined by custom rather than by statute. (Those used regularly by livestock would be flanked by temporary barriers of sticks to prevent the animals straying onto growing crops.) Apart from the turnpikes, none of which touched Keyworth, there was little provision for their maintenance — see pp.35–6 for the role of surveyor of the highways. The surfaces of roads were therefore appalling, particularly in winter, the more so on clay, and served to emphasise the isolation of villages like Keyworth and their need to be self-sufficient in bulk supplies such as food and fuel.

Finally, the pattern of settlement associated with open fields should be noted. With land holdings scattered throughout a parish or manor, it was not possible for a farmer to build his house and outbuildings in the middle of his farm. Instead, all farmers and other residents congregated into villages, so that scattered farm holdings led to a nucleated settlement pattern, typical of the East Midlands. (Conversely, where the open field system never operated, or had been abandoned many centuries ago, as in much of Devon and Cornwall, farms were compact [nucleated], and settlements dispersed as small hamlets and individual farmsteads.) Quite commonly, the only building outside an East Midland village before inclosure was the mill, situated to catch the maximum amount of wind; one of the open arable fields was often called Mill Field, as it was in Keyworth.[16] Other than that, and the occasional squatter's shack erected overnight on the common fields (one squatter was required to pull his down by a court order in 1656[17] because of the 'divers inconveniences occasioned to ye inhabitants'), settlement was confined to the farms and other dwellings lining Main Street, and a cluster surrounding the church and square. The open field landscape beyond was, therefore, not only one largely devoid of hedges but also of buildings — more like a prairie than the countryside with which we are familiar today.

Notes

1. NA PR1931
2. Taylor, 1975, p.71
3. see Thirsk in Preface to Orwin, 3rd ed., 1967, p.x.
4. Orwin, 3rd ed., 1967, pp.35–6.
5. Keyworth Church Terrier, 1752. NA PR1139.
6. ibid, pp. 32–3.
7. Derry & Blakeway, 1968, pp.89–90.
8. NA PR139
9. Thoroton, 1796, Vol.I pp.172–3.
10. NA Probate inventories on microfiche under Bingham Deanery.
11. One horsegate or cowgate was the right to graze one horse or cow on the common land.
12. Mingay, 1960, p.6.
13. Cantor, 1987, p.51.
14. Platt, 1995, p.4.
15. Keyworth had no resident rector between 1751 and 1859 — see p.32 for more detail.
16. For the location of Keyworth's mill, see p.23.
17. cited in Potter, 1935, p.35.

Chapter 4

Changes in Keyworth's
Open Fields

The previous chapter outlined the salient features of the open, or common field system as it was practised over much of England, including Keyworth and neighbouring parishes, for more than a thousand years. However, during that time there were substantial changes in the organisation of rural society in general, and in the operation of the open field system in particular, and it is with these that this chapter is concerned. Up to the mid-eighteenth century, there is little documentary evidence relating to Keyworth directly, so that local experience must be largely inferred from other sources. Five themes will be pursued: the extent and management of the arable open fields; the extent and management of non-arable areas; early engrossments and inclosures; land tenure; and a mid-eighteenth century reorganisation of the whole system in Keyworth.

The extent and management of the arable open fields

In the early middle ages only a fraction of the parish would have been under the plough and individually farmed. The Domesday Survey (1086) recorded Keyworth as having fifteen households, headed by villeins, bordars or cottars,[1] and may have represented a population of about 80. It seems that an average household at that time cultivated about twenty acres, being the amount of land from which an adequate subsistence could be obtained from a tolerable input of work. This would account for 300 parish acres of arable. But it is thought that at that time a two-field system prevailed: one field ploughed, the other fallow in any given year. So, of the 1500 acres constituting the whole parish, perhaps 600 were considered arable, the rest communally managed meadow, 'pasture' (rough grass with rushes, bracken, nettles and bushes) and 'waste' (woodland and scrub). It is likely that the arable fields, needing most attention, were nearest the village; the other land would be in the more remote parts of the parish, near Fairham Brook. This is borne out by the smooth southern parish boundary with Wysall and Widmerpool (except where it briefly follows the Fairham Brook), suggesting that it was demarcated, probably before the thirteenth century, through land which at the time was still waste, in contrast with the more irregular boundaries with Bradmore, Bunny and Stanton, where demarcation may have had to take account of property already occupied.

As population grew, more arable land was needed. To begin with this could be obtained by clearing pieces of waste or pasture to make fresh ploughland, a process known as 'assarting'. But some pasture was needed to graze the livestock that provided not only meat, milk, wool and skins, but also power to pull ploughs and carts, and manure to fertilise the soil; while 'waste' was the main source of firewood. So by the time population had doubled from its Domesday level, alternative ways of increasing crop output would need to be considered: either, turning from a two-field to a three-field system, so that the amount of fallow would be reduced from a half to a third of all the arable; or by increasing crop yields. One problem was that reducing the amount of fallow also tended to reduce soil fertility, as a field only had one year in three to recover from cultivation instead of one year in two. In some parishes like Ruddington, with soils of high natural fertility, a four-field system could be sustained, with fallow occupying only a quarter of the arable, but Keyworth does not seem to have been blessed with that advantage. Here, even a three-field rotation apparently threatened crop yields after repeated cycles.

This may account for what seems to have been a wholesale exchange of waste or pasture with arable land. At some time well before the eighteenth century, it appears that arable land extended all the way to the Fairham Brook, in what came to be known as Brook Field; while a stretch of waste was established flanking Debdale Lane and Nicker Hill, in what became Longmoor Field — the field alongside the 'moor'. (Later, when the 'moor' reverted to arable, and when a windmill was set up on the field, it was renamed Mill Field). This exchange would have been a major undertaking, involving the whole village in ploughing up a large tract of uncultivated land, and would not have been undertaken unless soils elsewhere were suffering from overcropping and needed a rest. We have only circumstantial evidence for this operation, but the reverse change in the mid-eighteenth century is documented and will be described more fully later in this chapter (pp.69–72). It is, of course, possible — indeed, likely — that there were other large-scale reorganisations of the layout of the fields during the centuries before we begin to have documentation: the geography of the open fields probably changed many times prior to inclosure.

We must not think of the evolution of the open field system as one of steady progress, with a gradual increase in arable at the expense of waste to support a steadily growing population. There were set-backs, the greatest being the Black Death (1348/9) and subsequent decades, when the population of England (and most of Europe) was reduced by between a third and a half. Although we have no evidence of its effects on Keyworth, we cannot assume that the village was unaffected. If its population was reduced by something like the national rate, much arable land would have been abandoned and allowed to revert to pasture or waste, until population recovered to its former level, perhaps in the sixteenth or seventeenth century.

The Black Death was indeed something of a watershed in English agrarian history. It hastened the decline of the manorial system, in which tenant farmers (villeins, etc.) paid for the right to cultivate their own strips in the open fields by working without wages on the demesne (or home farm) of the lord of the manor, who was the 'tenant in chief' or *de facto* landowner (the *de jure* owner was the monarch). By the fifteenth century this obligatory labour service (serfdom) had largely been replaced by rent, usually in kind — what is known as share-cropping, whereby the farmer handed over a share of his produce to the lord of the manor. This was later replaced by a cash rent. Not that the demise of serfdom was an inevitable consequence of the Black Death — rarely is historical change determined by a single factor, however catastrophic. In some continental countries such as Denmark, which were also struck by the Black Death, serfdom survived into the eighteenth century.

A further change precipitated by the Black Death and the demise of serfdom was the way in which the lord's own demesne was organised. In the early middle ages the lord of the manor had run the demesne himself or delegated the responsibility to a bailiff or steward, relying on serfs to do most of the manual work. But after the Black Death, with the disappearance of serfdom and with a general labour shortage, he usually found it easier to find a tenant to farm his demesne, which therefore became much like the other farms in the manor, though bigger.

We know little about early lords of the manor or demesne farms in Keyworth. The Manor Farm house, which stood on the corner of Bunny Lane and The Square until 1970, was also known as The Mansion House in the sixteenth century,[2] and may have been the centre from which a demesne was farmed some centuries earlier. On the other hand, there is no record of Keyworth ever having had a resident lord of the manor, so the Manor Farm, consisting of strips scattered throughout the two or three arable fields, was more probably cultivated throughout the middle ages by a bailiff or tenant than by the lord himself. By the time of inclosure in 1799, it was an owner-occupied farm of modest size, bought a few years before by Thomas Hemsley,[3] whose forebears had worked it as tenants for the previous hundred years when it was the property of a banking family, the Smiths of Nottingham.

Other changes affecting the management of the arable were improvement in farming methods, the introduction of new crops and variations in the supply and demand of different kinds of farm produce. Improved farming methods included the application of fertilisers to supplement animal manure — night-soil, wood ash, lime and marl; on heavy land like that of most of Keyworth, the digging of drainage ditches; and the introduction of nitrogen-fixing legumes like clover and pulses into the rotation. The result was increasing crop yields. In the middle ages, the ratio of yield to seed for wheat in England averaged only about four to one, so that a quarter of each year's crop had to be set aside as seedcorn for the following season; by the eighteenth century it was often over ten to one.[4] Much of this improvement was achieved in the previous hundred years[5] and coincided with two other trends: a slackening in population growth, and increased commercialisation of the national and regional economies, leading to an expanding urban middle class. The net effects of these trends on supply and demand was to depress the price of cereals (eaten, and in the form of gin and beer, drunk in increasing amounts by all) and to boost that of high-grade food like meat (mostly eaten by the more affluent). This in turn put a premium on keeping livestock — cattle and sheep — at the expense of cultivating crops. The shift in balance was given further impetus by a growing demand for horses both in commerce and for personal mobility by the well-heeled; by the improved fodder supply from clovers and improved grasses, reducing the need to cull the herds in autumn and half-starve those not culled during the winter; and by selective stock breeding (in which Robert Bakewell of Dishley, near Loughborough was a pioneer) which enhanced the profitability of live-stock husbandry — as already noted on p.16, the average weight of cattle sold at Smithfield more than doubled in the eighteenth century.[6]

One might expect these changes to be reflected in one or more of three ways in the open fields of Keyworth and parishes like it: a shift in the balance between wheat or rye (for human consumption), oats (for animal consumption) and barley (for gin and beer); the introduction of grasses, clovers and root crops into arable rotations, to provide more animal fodder; and an overall reduction of the amount of arable in favour of pasture or hay-meadow. Any shift from crops to grass might be expected to be greater on heavy soils like those underlying most of Keyworth, where ploughing was more difficult, and grass survived summer droughts better than on light soils. Under a purely subsistence system, each settlement had to produce all its own needs; growing commercialisation would encourage a degree of local and regional specialisation.

Unfortunately there are few data for Keyworth before the mid-eighteenth century to indicate how far these developments had affected farming in the parish. In 1752, a church terrier[7] listing all the strips in the open fields tithable to, or in the glebe of the rector of Keyworth, which amounted to about half the parish, recorded that some 15% of the individually worked open fields were under 'leys', and a further 1% were classed as 'doles' (meadow). It has already been suggested that leys might have been used to produce hay: they would require fencing, or beasts would have to be tethered if the leys were to be grazed during periods when neighbouring strips were growing corn. Although the modern use of the word 'ley' means a temporary stretch of grass, perhaps laid down for three or four years as part of an arable rotation, it was also sometimes used in the seventeenth and eighteenth centuries to indicate semi-permanent pasture.[8] Its importance may therefore have been greater than the 15% implies, because a third of the rest of the arable would have been fallow in any one season, while the ley would not.

Cultivated grass therefore, whether in long or short leys, became a significant element in 'convertible husbandry', whereby land that had yielded cereals or pulses for several years was converted, or put down to grass or clover for several more years, restoring the soil's fertility by a combination of rest and manure from grazing beasts, once the grass was established. It seems that by the mid-eighteenth century grass formed a major part of the arable fields as well as nearly a third of the parish in the (uncultivated) pasture, indicating the importance of livestock in the village economy. Though we have no earlier figures from which to infer trends, thirteen probate inventories between 1691 and 1772 confirm the picture: 15% of the value of crops in the field or in store was hay, a figure that accords with the amount of ley in the arable; and the total value of livestock (£1695) is considerably greater than the corresponding value of crops (£1175).

It is unlikely that root crops were important at this time on the heavy and poorly-drained soils of Keyworth and the Nottinghamshire Wolds. Turnips and the associated 'Norfolk Four Course' rotation, which dispensed with fallow, were largely confined to sandy soils until the introduction of underground mole drains and of the more tolerant Swedish turnip (swede) in the nineteenth century. On the other hand, potatoes were becoming an important food crop to supplement grain, though they seem to have been grown, along with other vegetables, in 'garths' or kitchen gardens attached to cottages rather than in the open fields.

It is clear therefore that the simple rotation conventionally associated with the three-field system (autumn-sown cereal; spring sown cereal or pulse; fallow) was being modified by the eighteenth century. Instead of each field being under a single crop, or perhaps two crops, it might contain a patchwork of crops and grass, or fallow and grass. Furlongs (clusters of parallel adjoining strips) may have been more uniform, but even these could contain variety. Strips were individually worked, and the only constraint put on the farmer was the date by which his crops had to be harvested to allow first the gleaners and then the village beasts onto his land.

The extent and management of the waste and pasture

Arable fields were individually owned and worked (but not necessarily worked by the owner) and only became 'commonable' during the seasons when they were not under crops. The waste and pasture, on the other hand, were used and managed by the community at all times, though the Lord of the Manor was, in theory, the owner (or tenant-in-chief) of the soil — as was recognised in the Inclosure Award (see p. 81).

We have seen that in the early middle ages, much of Keyworth would have been waste; that this would have been reduced as the population grew, and expanded again with population decline; that the waste survived longest in the more remote south of the parish; but that it appears to have occupied different areas as arable soils became exhausted through overuse and were allowed to revert to rough pasture while new lands were cleared for the plough — echoes of a much earlier system of shifting agriculture. It is also likely that the waste itself would have been improved over time, so that the word 'pasture' became a more appropriate term to describe it. Certainly the inclosure award makes no mention of 'waste': all the land not in the open arable fields and in village crofts (paddocks and kitchen gardens) is referred to as pasture. It was also then located in the south, near the Fairham Brook.

As Keyworth's population grew, there was pressure to make better use of the waste or pasture. When that area was plentiful for the needs of Keyworth's population and their livestock, people would have been allowed to keep as many animals as they wished, or could afford to overwinter, on the pasture. As their numbers grew, overgrazing would become a problem, both on the pasture and on the commonable arable after harvest and during fallow periods. It therefore became necessary to introduce 'stinting', whereby each householder in the parish was rationed in the number of beasts that could be kept on the pasture in proportion to the size of property he or she owned. Thus, in the 1752 terrier mentioned above, Mr. Smith, owner of Manor Farm, is listed as having eight horsegates and nine cowgates (he or his tenant could graze eight horses and nine cows) as well as an unspecified number of sheep — presumably sheep were not stinted in Keyworth at that time, though they were elsewhere (e.g., East Leake). The degree to which these stints were enforced depended on the amount of pressure there was on the land, how much the stints were abused, and on the efficiency (or officiousness) of the manor court. Sometimes farmers put more stock onto the pasture than they were entitled to, or rented out their stints to farmers from neighbouring parishes. Gross violations attracted fines from the court but minor infringements were often overlooked. Smallholders or cottagers with no statutory rights to pasture were normally allowed to keep the odd cow or pair of geese according to 'ancient custom', which often helped to keep them just above the bread line.

A further result of population pressure would be a steady improvement of the pasture. Part might have been fenced off for hay during early summer and let out as 'doles' to individual farmers, as already suggested; unwanted shrubs would be removed for firewood and there may have been communal working parties to get rid of nettles and other unwanted weeds. Gregory King, writing in the 1690s, estimated the average value of pasture and meadow (at 8s 8d per acre) to be considerably higher than that of arable land (at 5s 6d).[9] While this is only an educated guess, and is an average applied to the whole country, it is a reminder that pasture, even though not for the most part individually managed, should not all be regarded as only one grade better than waste. The term covered a wide range of usage and productivity.

Early Inclosures

Some parts of England — most of Cornwall and Kent for example — had probably never been farmed under the open field system. In others, open fields had disappeared by the early middle ages. In yet others, including the English Midlands, a long process of piecemeal inclosure of individual parishes or parts of parishes took place from at least the time of the Black Death in 1348/9, leaving a sea of predominantly open field agriculture interspersed with steadily increasing islands of inclosed land. It was this 'sea', of which Keyworth was a part, that was transformed during the period of parliamentary inclosure in the eighteenth and nineteenth centuries.

Pre-parliamentary inclosure sometimes involved whole parishes or manors, at other times much smaller areas. The former occurred when all the land was owned by a single proprietor, or by a small number who agreed among themselves that inclosure would be to their advantage. The latter was more common when smaller farmers opted out of the open field system which continued to be operated among their neighbours. Neither was of much significance in Keyworth, but it was in nearby parishes, so it needs to be discussed here to demonstrate the distinctiveness and context of Keyworth's position by the eighteenth century.

Two main factors provided the impetus for wholesale early inclosure: labour shortage and the growing market for wool in the late middle ages. The Black Death wiped out whole communities or left them so decimated that landowners could not find the labour they needed to maintain arable routines, while the demand for food crops was also limited. Meanwhile, and particularly during the fifteenth and sixteenth centuries, there was a growing demand for wool to satisfy, first, the Flemish textile industry, and later expanding English cloth manufacture. On counts of both labour scarcity and the relative prices of wool and grain, therefore, it made sense from the landowner's point of view to turn arable land over to sheep pasture. And to minimise the need for shepherds, land was inclosed to control sheep movement without much supervision. Many villages became unviable, either because most of their inhabitants had succumbed to plague; or because, with their labour no longer needed, they had left in search of work elsewhere. Buildings were abandoned, and only their footings remain today as rectangular mounds, visible for instance at Thorpe-in-the-Glebe. It is possible that Stanton-on-the-Wolds suffered a similar fate at this time, though no traces of the medieval village, other than the church and manor farm, have been found.

These inclosures, of the period 1350 to 1550, were opposed by church and government (in marked contrast to later parliamentary inclosures) because of the suffering and social problems to which they gave rise. They were responsible for a growth in the number of 'sturdy beggars', vagrants and vagabonds, and ultimately for the enactments constituting the Poor Law.

After the mid-sixteenth century, demand for wool slackened, while that for grain increased as population was again pressing on resources. Subsequent inclosures were therefore primarily aimed at increasing corn production and involved an intensification of land use rather than the reverse. Sometimes whole parishes were inclosed— Normanton-on-the-Wolds was an example,[10] already inclosed when Thoroton wrote his county history in 1677. If the arable holdings had previously been scattered among the open fields and owned by several proprietors, as seems likely from the later pattern of landownership (e.g., as revealed in the 1840 Tithe Award), inclosure would have involved considerable exchanges of land to create more consolidated units, a process known as engrossment.

In other cases, inclosure took place on a smaller scale. Exchange of strips would occur with a view to individuals assembling enough adjoining strips to make a compact unit that could be inclosed. They were then no longer subject to the constraints of the open field system: the owner or his tenant could grow what he pleased, sow and harvest at dates to suit himself, or put the field down to grass and graze his beasts if he saw fit. The Plumtree inclosure award map (1807) shows numerous early inclosures of this sort, and most parishes had some inclosed land before the main (parliamentary) inclosure took place in the eighteenth or nineteenth centuries. Keyworth was unusual in having practically none: apart from the crofts on which the village houses stood, the only pre-parliamentary inclosure closes were the rectory field and other nearby paddocks which could be regarded as crofts at the northern extremity of the village, Motley Close at its southern extremity off Lings Lane, and one or two others — e.g., Gorssie Close, mentioned in the 1752 terrier and in the inclosure award, whose precise location is not known. The distinctiveness of Keyworth is brought out by Table 2, based on figures derived from inclosure awards. With the exception of Ruddington, none of its neighbouring parishes were based on villages significantly bigger than Keyworth, so the difference in areas inclosed before the parliamentary inclosure is accounted for almost entirely by land outside the village and its crofts.

Table 2 **Acreages inclosed before parliamentary inclosure in Keyworth and neighbouring parishes**

	Total Acreage of parish	Acreage inclosed by Act of parliament	Acreage inclosed before Act (& %)	
Keyworth	1438	1373	65	(4.5)
Bunny	2135	>1000	c.1000*	(47.8)
Plumtree (with Clipston)**	2797	1228	1569	(56.1)
Ruddington	2987	2781	206	(6.9)
Tollerton	1211	435	776	(64.1)
Widmerpool	2102	1795	307	(14.6)
Willoughby	2103	1695	408	(19.4)
Wysall	1553	1375	178	(11.5)

*Mostly Bunny Park
** The (ecclesiastical) parish of Plumtree included the townships of Normanton, entirely inclosed by agreement before the rest of the parish and not therefore covered by the Plumtree Inclosure Act, and Clipston which was covered by it.
(Source: J.D.Chambers, 1962: Appendix II by W.E.Tate)

Land Tenure

With the exception of an occasional convulsion like the changeover from a two- to a three-field rotation, or the wholesale ploughing up of pasture in one part of the parish and the conversion of arable to pasture in another, the open field system changed little over the centuries. Crop rotations were modified, new crops and grasses were introduced, and improved methods of cultivation were adopted — e.g., the replacement of the ox by the horse to pull the plough, and of the sickle by the scythe for harvesting. But these developments were absorbed by a system which barely altered in its routines over the centuries.

Land tenure was subject to more change, particularly after the Black Death. Landowners had difficulty in finding tenants or labourers to work their properties; compulsory service on demesnes was replaced by rents and wages, which were high, reflecting labour scarcity. Money became a more important element in the economy, and quite humble people found themselves making much more use of it. This led to an increase in social mobility. On the one hand, land came on to the market, either from owners who could no longer manage their estates in the changed circumstances, or in the normal course of events when a landed family ran out of male heirs; while on the other, some tenants and even labourers were able to prosper to the point where they could afford to buy land, as could townspeople (e.g., lawyers, merchants or manufacturers) who wished to invest their earnings in real estate, which they perceived to enhance both their status and their security. Land changed hands much more frequently, either in large amounts or small — one of the advantages of the fragmentation of the open fields was that small men could buy and sell individual strips 'retail'; they did not have to deal in whole farms.[11]

The fluidity of the land market seems to have continued into the seventeenth century at least. Peyton,[12] referring particularly to south Nottinghamshire, notes that the majority of freeholders held their land for less than two generations and comments that 'the population of Notts between the years 1558 and 1641 was in a highly mobile condition'.

In Keyworth we have references to two significant land transactions in this period. Until the late sixteenth century much of Keyworth seems to have been owned by successive lords of the manor, first the Barrys, and then the Pendocks. According to Thoroton,[13] William Pendock and his son John 'sold their interest here [in Keyworth] to divers freeholders and the advowson of the church to Sir George Parkyns', after which there ceased to be a single dominant landowner in the village. The date of the sale is not certain, but Parkyns made his first appointment (William Smyth) to the rectory of Keyworth in 1619; the previous incumbent, William Barker, was appointed in 1585, so one assumes the sale took place between these two dates. From that time until well beyond inclosure, Keyworth was a parish of small and medium-sized properties, in marked contrast to many of its neighbours (and the power to appoint its rectors was in the hands of the Parkyns family for the next two centuries).

The second transaction concerns the Manor Farm. It was bought some time during the 1580s by John Lowth, Archdeacon of Nottingham, who lived in the 'Mansion House' on the corner of Bunny Lane and The Square until his death in 1590.[14] It seems unlikely that a man of his status farmed the associated land himself, or that the bailiff or tenant who did lived in the Mansion House with him. More probably the land (i.e., strips scattered in the three fields) was cultivated along with other strips associated with another farm house in the village, occupied by a tenant who managed both sets of strips. It is also unclear whether Lowth was one of the 'divers freeholders' to whom Pendock sold his interests in

Keyworth — the lord of the manor did not necessarily own the manor farm; two centuries later, when Sir Thomas Parkyns was lord of the manor, his land in Keyworth did not include it.

By the end of the eighteenth century, immediately before inclosure, the farm land in Keyworth was shared among 34 owners, only one of whom (Samuel Smith, the Nottingham banker) had more than 100 acres. After inclosure the size of all holdings increased as each proprietor was allotted some of the pasture which had previously been owned communally, while the rector and other tithe holders were given yet more land as compensation for loss of tithes. But even after inclosure, there was only one holding (the rector's) with more than 200 acres. Among its neighbours, the larger parish of Willoughby had a similar distribution of ownership, with a total of 51 post-inclosure holdings and only one above 200 acres. By contrast, all of Bunny belonged to the Parkyns family and the vicar; Plumtree-with-Clipston had seven holdings of which three exceeded 400 acres (which may explain the large proportion of early piecemeal inclosure here already referred to) and the other four were under 10 acres; Widmerpool had four holdings, two of which were over 400 acres, and Wysall had twelve holdings including one of over 400 acres.

Despite the relative equality of ownership distribution in Keyworth however, land tax returns indicate that about 45% of the land was held by nine absentee landowners before inclosure, a proportion that rose to 55% after inclosure because of awards in lieu of tithes. (The absentees included a succession of rectors who all lived in their other parishes between 1751 and 1859 — mostly in Costock, but also in York, London, and Risley Park, Derbyshire.) These holdings were mainly worked as tenant farms — e.g., Samuel Smith let all his land to William Belshaw, who also rented additional strips from two other owners and, with close on 150 acres, was easily the largest farmer, as opposed to owner, in the parish. Most holdings in Keyworth were small however — less than ten acres — and were worked by their owners, who often regarded themselves as 'cottagers' (smallholders); the only owner-occupied farms well above ten acres were those of Thomas Hemsley (Manor Farm, about 55 acres before inclosure) and Richard Tookey (about 60 acres), both of whom also owned land in other parishes.

The Smiths' stake in Keyworth is worth a paragraph. The banking family acquired Manor Farm in 1692 in the name of Thomas Smith and his wife Fortune, and let it to successive generations of Hemsleys until 1793, when Thomas Hemsley bought it. But the connection between the Smiths and Keyworth was renewed only three years later when another descendant of Thomas and Fortune Smith — a great grandson, Samuel — bought a different and larger holding in the parish, perhaps in anticipation of profits to be made after inclosure. The Inclosure Award shows him in possession of what later came to be known as Shaw's Farm (36 Main Street). He continued to own the farm until his death in 1834, and it was still owned by the Smith family well into the twentieth century. Samuel Smith was MP for Leicester for many years. Among his relations were a son, Abel Smith, the leading landowner in Normanton at the time of the tithe award (1840); and a brother, Robert Smith, who became the first Lord Carrington.

The Smith case illustrates two more general points: first, the way in which business men in the eighteenth century often invested their profits in land; and second, how land can change hands between individuals while the same extended family retains its interest in the parish.

If ownership of land in Keyworth was distributed among a large number of proprietors, so was its occupation and cultivation. The land tax returns for 1797 record 33 occupiers, of whom seventeen were tenant farmers and sixteen owner-occupiers. The former group included most of the larger farms, and comprised more than three-quarters of all Keyworth's strips in the open fields. But eight holdings of under twenty acres were also numbered among the tenancies, together with thirteen which were owner-occupied. Many of these were so small that they must have provided no more than a supplementary living to their holders.

It is not possible to determine the precise form of tenure enjoyed by the seventeen tenant farmers. Many were probably 'customary tenants', which meant that the terms of their tenure — including the rent paid, inheritance rights and requirements to maintain buildings, ditches, etc., and soil fertility — were determined by manorial custom perhaps stretching back centuries. Where these customary rights could be supported by documentary proof in the form of a copy in the manor records, the tenants were known as copyholders, and were in a strong position to hold on to the land they occupied at fixed rents. Their security of tenure was as strong as that of freeholders. However, while some copyhold tenancies were heritable others were for life only, while for yet others the 'copies' supporting their rights had been lost. In these cases, owners were able to change the terms of the lease, either upon the death of the tenant, or even sooner. The inducements for owners to do this were not great during periods of agricultural depression and price deflation like the early eighteenth century, because fixed rents would then become more valuable while there were problems finding tenants. Indeed, some copyholds were converted to freeholds, as owners got into debt during such times. But in periods of expansion and inflation like the second half of the eighteenth century, owners were likely to adjust tenancy terms where they could, by substituting fixed term leases or 'tenancies-at-will' for copyhold. These enabled the owner to raise rents more easily, and in the case of tenancies-at-will, to get rid of unsatisfactory tenants at short notice. It is likely therefore that the position of some of Keyworth's tenant farmers changed during the half-century prior to inclosure.

In addition to absentee landlords, owner-occupiers and tenant farmers, there were two other categories with a direct stake in agriculture: the farm labourer, living with his family as a separate household; and the farm servant, living in his employer's household. Keyworth's 1801 population of 325 represented some 65 households, half of which were headed by the 33 farmers in the parish — some full-time, others part-time, supplementing their income by labouring for their larger neighbours or engaging in occupations like bricklaying. Trades requiring more capital or skill, like smithying or milling, would be undertaken by specialists, but these comprised only a small part of the population. Framework knitting occupied only a few families (see footnote, p.45). There must therefore have been a significant number of households with neither land nor a recognised craft to provide them with a regular living, who were dependent largely on labouring for others, with perhaps the customary (but not statutory) right to collect fuel and sustenance from the common pasture for themselves and their few animals. So although ownership and tenancy of land were more widely shared in Keyworth than in most of its neighbours, many had neither, and depended all the more on their precarious rights of common.

Wholesale reorganisation in the mid-eighteenth century

The church terrier of 1752, listing glebe land and all arable plots tithable to the rector of Keyworth has already been cited (pp.49 and 61). We will now examine further its numerous references to individually-owned strips in the (common) pasture, which imply a wholesale reorganisation of land use and ownership. A more detailed summary of the terrier's contents appears in Appendix II.

Nearly a third of all plots in what had been the three arable fields are said to be 'in the pasture', suggesting that a substantial proportion of the arable land of the parish had recently been put down to grass and transferred to common ownership. This is confirmed by other entries, listing 'New land being the equivalent to that which is in the pasture', allotted to former owners of the new pasture who needed to be compensated for their loss. What seems to have happened therefore was a wholesale exchange, so that an extensive area of individually-owned arable became common pasture in one part of the parish, with the reverse taking place in another. Indeed, the detailed terrier may have been drawn up so that the rector could evaluate the impact on his tithe income from this transformation of land use, particularly as he was new to the parish — the Rev. Richard Barnard was installed in 1751.

The locations of these transfers are partially indicated by the terrier which tells us that land turned into pasture all came out of the Woulds Field and Brook Field, while the new arable was all in the Longmoor Field (see Figure 8). Furthermore, Brook Field changed its name to Bunny Gate Field 'by reason of the pasture being taken out of it' so that it no longer reached down to the (Fairham) Brook, which points to the newly created pasture being the same as that referred to in the Inclosure Award of less than half a century later, also shown on Figure 8. It is evident that this area was not always pasture: ridge and furrow in grass fields near the brook presumably date back to the period before the mid-eighteenth century change, when the arable strips of the Brook Field did extend to the brook. With regard to the Longmoor Field, its name was also changed (to Mill Field) by the time of inclosure, perhaps because it no longer abutted onto an elongated moor. Among the names given in the terrier to new furlongs (groups of individually-owned strips or plots) whose approximate location can be identified today are Nicky Hill (*sic*) and Debdale, suggesting that the old 'long moor' was a tract running alongside the eastern and northern boundaries of the parish, which were then marked by Nicker Hill and Deepdale Lane.

The reorganisation of parish lands just outlined involved more than an ex-

Figure 8 **Map to show transformation of Keyworth's open fields, *c*.1750**

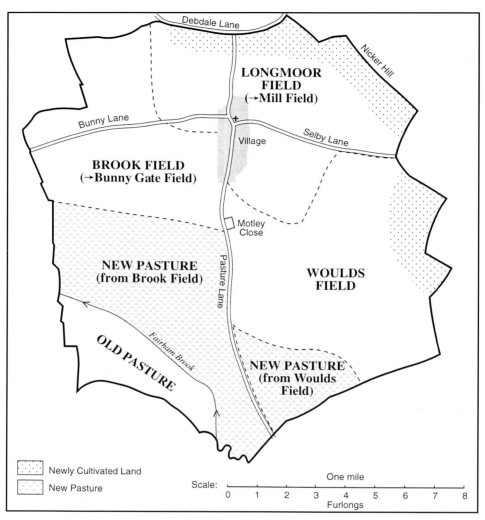

change of land use. There was also a significant, though limited element of engrossment, whereby the numerous scattered holdings of owners were consolidated into a smaller number of larger units. The former arable put down to pasture comprised 655 'lands' or other units, while 'new land being the *equivalent* of that which is in the pasture' and awarded as compensation comprised only 141 units. (Full details appear in Appendix II.) The figures do therefore suggest an important degree of consolidation throughout the parish with about a quarter less separate units scattered throughout the arable fields after the exchange than before. The number of separate plots in the rector's glebe, for instance, was reduced from 139 to 109 — still highly fragmented, but less so than before.

The questions arise: why and how was this transformation in land use and ownership undertaken? We can only speculate because there are no documents from the time explaining motivation. It occurred a few years before the much more fully documented movement towards parliamentary inclosure began in earnest in the 1760s, but may have been, in part, a response to similar pressures. They included a growing degree of commercialisation of farming, and the spread of new practices, which respectively called for and offered greater efficiency in production methods. Improved communication and the growth of Nottingham were bringing villages like Keyworth within range for the supply of meat and dairy produce to the city, while new crops and devices like Tull's seed drill were becoming known. Fragmentation of farmland was a long-standing difficulty: it wasted time in getting from one strip to another, which was particularly problematic if clumsy equipment was involved; efficiency tended to be determined by the lowest common denominator — unweeded strips and uncleared drainage ditches not only punished the offending farmers but their neighbours also; and there were frequent disputes over boundaries and encroachment onto baulks and headlands which provided access to farmers' strips. All these were, of course, reasons for inclosure, but presumably the time was not yet ripe for that even greater transformation, in a village of small landowners and tenants who could not afford the expense of ditching and hedging, and who, along with landless labourers, relied heavily upon the common pasture which, if inclosed, would deny them the right to graze livestock and gather firewood and other means of subsistence.

But there were probably two other factors precipitating the change which have already been mentioned: soil exhaustion, brought about by centuries of cultivation with limited fertilisers and, on a three-field rotation, inadequate fallow; and a change in the relative profitability of arable and livestock farming. The chief source of fertiliser was animal manure, the amount of which was limited by the small herds and flocks kept and the fact that the beasts were underfed during winter. In the early eighteenth century, the use of turnips to increase stock feed was difficult on heavy clay soils not yet improved by under-drainage, and this in turn limited manure output; while the systematic use of clover as a replenisher of nitrogen was not widely understood, even if the crop was grown by some.

Crop yields locally were therefore likely to have been low. Nationally however, they were increasing faster than demand, from a population which, for reasons not properly understood, had been growing only slowly since the mid-seventeenth century. Grain prices were therefore depressed, and this combination of low yields locally and low prices generally called for drastic action, to which Keyworth responded in the way outlined. The old pasture had, in effect, been in fallow for perhaps several centuries, allowing it to recover and then retain its fertility, while crop land turned to pasture would give it a protracted rest. Moreover, the new allocation of arable involved some consolidation of a multiplicity of small, scattered strips into fewer, larger 'flats', which in turn enabled farmers to fence off some of their new land and put it down to temporary grass, and thereby take advantage of the more favourable market for live-stock produce.

Keyworth was not unique in experiencing this drastic change in the distribution of land tenure and use. Barnes,[15] writing about Orston (SE Notts), details similar developments there in the early eighteenth century, and explains them in terms of changes in the relative price of grain and livestock produce. He comments that 'in many parishes this mainly involved the "gathering" of lands' — i.e., consolidating randomly distributed strips in the open fields, which were then temporarily enclosed (by stakes rather than hedges) to be grazed by untethered animals while neighbouring furlongs were under conventional arable routines. Subsequent awards associated with parliamentary inclosure, in Keyworth as elsewhere, include these temporary closes as part of the open arable fields, in contrast to the hedged inclosures dating from an earlier period, referred to under a previous heading.

Ironically, conditions changed in the latter half of the century: population, and therefore demand for grain began to grow rapidly, prices rose and encouraged landowners to inclose, thereby enabling them to increase rents. So a second, even greater transformation awaited Keyworth less than fifty years on. That is the story of the next section of this book.

Notes

1. A villein could cultivate one 'yardland', which averaged around 30 acres; bordars and cottars usually had less. (Stenton, 1962, p.138)
2. Hammond, 1997, p.6.
3. Hemsley owned land in Stanton and Cropwell Butler in addition to his Keyworth property — ibid p.13.
4. Slicher Van Bath, 1963, pp.328–30.
5. Kerridge, 1967 and Allen, 1992 are among scholars who have shown that many of the improvements associated with the agrarian revolution were pioneered before the era of parliamentary inclosure, and indeed before 1700.
6. Plumb, 1950, p.82.
7. NA PR 1139.
8. Hall, 1995, p.23.
9. Hoskins, 1970, pp.137–8.
10. Strictly, Normanton was a 'township' within the parish of Plumtree, but was focused on a distinct hamlet, and for many purposes, governed separately. The rest of Plumtree (with Clipston — another township) was subject to parliamentary inclosure in 1805.
11. Tawney, 1912, p.103.
12. Peyton, 1915, p.245 and following.
13. Thoroton, 1677, p.83.
14. Hammond, 1997, p.9.
15. Barnes, P: 'The Adaptation of Open Field Farming in an East Notts Parish, Orston, 1641–1793' in *Transactions of the Thoroton Society*, Vol. 101, 1997, pp.125-132.

PART II: PARLIAMENTARY INCLOSURE

Chapter 5

The Framework

The inclosure of land within fences, walls and ditches to define ownership boundaries or to minimise the destruction of crops or livestock by marauding animals pre-dates the written historical record. So why did it become necessary after so long a time to involve parliament in the process? The main reasons are to be found in the increasing dispersion of landownership coupled with the inability of the open field system of farming to make effective use of improved agricultural techniques. Proprietors, at a time when farming was moving from a subsistence activity toward one of trading beyond the immediate locality, were looking for a greater return on their investment.

Ironically, the fundamental objective of the inclosure acts was not the inclosure of the land itself, but reallocation and consolidation of landownership. The intention was to tie a particular piece of land to a specified owner. Furthermore this was to include land previously regarded as common property. Defining the new allocation on the ground by inclosing it, most often with the hawthorn hedges which for so long we have considered an indispensable component of the landscape, was a necessary consequence which gave the process its name. The advantages of inclosure, namely the increased efficiency, bringing common land into production and the ease of management leading to higher rents, were well recognised so that it was often possible to achieve inclosure by agreement between proprietors. However, the larger the number of proprietors the more difficult it was to secure this agreement, and where it was achieved cases of coercion were not unknown. Furthermore, such agreements were open to legal challenge. An Act of Parliament achieved legal status for the inclosure and ensured that the worst abuses of inclosure by agreement were mitigated. This route also ensured that a minority interest could not frustrate the wishes of the majority. Furthermore, a private act of parliament provided an opportunity to abolish the antiquated system of tithes by exchanging these payments for a once-and-for-all allocation of land in lieu. These advantages must have been perceived as worth having, for the cost of securing an act was not insignificant and the subsequent costs considerable.

The inclosure of the open fields of England was not achieved by a single piece of legislation, but by hundreds of private acts involving individual parishes over many years. This was a consequence of the diversity of conditions

Figure 9 **Number of Inclosure Acts for Open Field Arable Parishes 1730–1850**

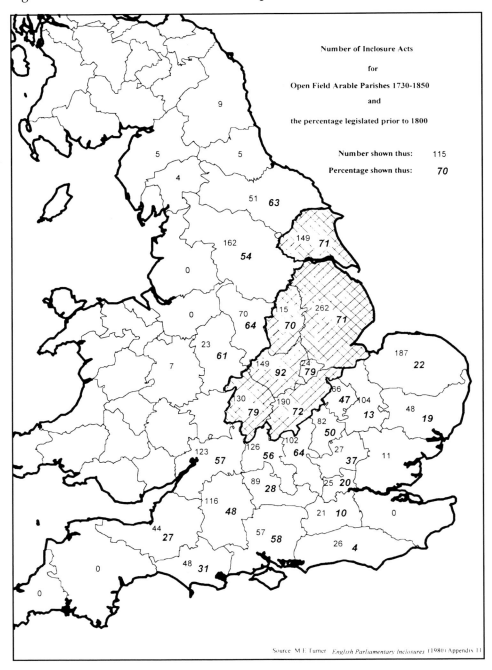

obtaining throughout the country. No two parishes were alike and only gradually during the eighteenth century with improvement in communications and the demands of new industries did there emerge something approaching a national economy. In the main, parish agriculture served local needs. Although the earliest act was in 1604 allowing the inclosure of Radipole in Dorset, it was in the eighteenth century that the procedure became increasingly common. Figure 9 shows the cumulative percentage of inclosure acts for open field arable parishes passed in each half decade from 1730 to 1850, for England and Wales and for Nottinghamshire. From it we can see that the number of inclosures increased during this period, though at an uneven rate: not only was there a hiatus around 1780 but a very rapid increase during the French wars at the turn of the century. At their start in 1793, less than half of Nottinghamshire's Inclosure Acts had been passed; by the time of the battle of Waterloo in 1815, over 90%. It was during this period that Keyworth and most of its neighbouring parishes were inclosed.

The requirements of the private act varied from case to case but there gradually evolved a standard procedure which became embodied in law. Thus in 1774 legislation was enacted requiring proper records of expenditure to be kept by those supervising the inclosure. A later act ensured that these supervisors (called commissioners) had no direct interest in the outcome of the inclosure — an example of parliament giving legal status to what was already recognised as best practice. Prior to this act (1801) it was not unusual for the steward or land agent of a major proprietor or Lord of the Manor to be a commissioner for the inclosure of lands which included those of his employer. Keyworth provides an example of this practice. Sir Thomas Parkyns was Lord of the Manor, major landowner and tithe holder; his steward and brother-in-law, Joseph Boultbee, was one of the three commissioners appointed in the Act for the inclosure of the parish. Later general acts, 1836 and 1845, simplified the procedures, eventually obviating the need for individual private acts. We can also observe changes in the number of commissioners engaged and the length of time between an Act being granted and its outcome as an Award. Thus the inclosure of Barton-in-Fabis, Notts., in 1759 involved eight commissioners and that of Coddington a year later, nine; but by the 1770s the number had settled to the customary three. The time taken for the commissioners to do their work and publish their decisions as an Award varied considerably. For Nottinghamshire's earlier inclosures (1760–1780) the interval between Act and Award was one to four years, but later there was much greater variability with, as extreme examples at the end of the century, Ordsall, thirteen years, and Normanton-on-Trent, eight years. The inclosures of Bunny and Keyworth, each completed within a year, appear to have been accomplished with almost indecent haste!

Inclosure did not proceed at the same pace in all parts of the country. The map in Figure 9 shows, for the period 1730–1849, the number of inclosure acts for each English county and the proportion passed by the end of the eighteenth century. Considerable variation is evident from county to county. For Leicestershire the process was practically complete by 1800, but for Cambridgeshire and Norfolk it had hardly begun. The later date for the bulk of inclosures in the

Figure 10 **Cumulative Percentage of Inclosure Acts for Open Field Arable Parishes in Nottinghamshire compared with the whole of England**

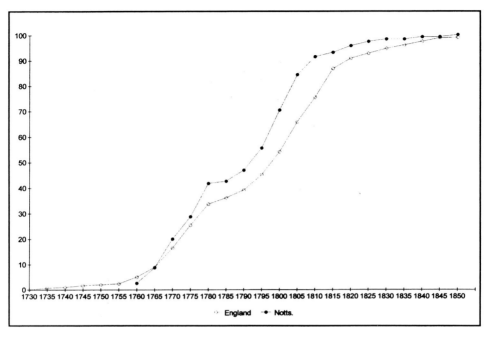

latter county contrasts with the county's association with pioneering agricultural improvement, but is attributable to the significant increase in the price of cereals, the county's major product, during the Napoleonic Wars. For Leicestershire and other Midland counties, where animal husbandry was important, the outbreak of cattle plague in midcentury and the consequent shortage of meat was a factor encouraging the earlier inclosure of their parishes. Nottinghamshire is among a group of counties adjacent to Leicestershire — the others being Warwickshire, Northamptonshire, Rutland, and Lincolnshire — together with East Yorkshire in which 70% or more of the inclosure Bills had been enacted prior to 1800. As we move away in any direction from this group, the proportion diminishes.

The progress of parliamentary inclosure in Nottinghamshire occurred at a similar rate as for England as a whole and experienced the same hiatus during the 1780s; but here it started later and, except for Laxton, finished earlier.[1] See Table 3 and Figure 10. However, a closer look at the distribution of the dates of inclosure indicates the effect of local factors.

It would be expected that one of these factors would be the character of the soil. At the time of the Keyworth inclosure Robert Lowe produced an account of the county's agriculture which included 'A Map of the Soil of Nottinghamshire'. This distinguished seven areas with different soil types. Examination of the dates of inclosure within those areas shows that in three of them which embrace the

Table 3 **Percentage of total number of Inclosure Acts by decade for Open Field Arable Parishes in Nottinghamshire 1730–1849**

Decade	per cent
–1759	3.0
1760–1769	17.9
1770–1779	21.4
1780–1789	5.4
1790–1799	24.0
1800–1809	20.5
1810–	9.0

Source: M.E.Turner, *English Parliamentary Enclosure*, Appendix 11

Trent Valley and the county north and west of the Trent, inclosure dates fall more or less equally between the two periods before and after the 1780s. However for the area of the Nottinghamshire Wolds which included Keyworth the dates are confined to the two decades straddling 1800. Lowe included within his 'Trent Bank District' land adjacent to the Soar extending to include East Leake. With the exception of East Leake, the other parishes in this small area of the county were inclosed prior to 1780. The differences between these adjacent areas bordering the southern boundary of the county remind us that other influences were at work which determined just when a particular parish was inclosed. They also are a reminder that county boundaries are artificial administrative concepts which take little account of topography or other factors which determine farming practice. The earlier inclosures in the south-west of the county along the Soar valley may well have been influenced by the same factors which account for the early inclosures of Leicestershire parishes. (See Figure 11.)

Of crucial importance was the attitude of the principal proprietor or the Lord of the Manor. The date of Keyworth's inclosure was almost certainly determined by the wishes of Sir Thomas Parkyns. Thus in 1781 proprietors in East Leake petitioned for an inclosure act which failed because of the opposition of Sir Thomas, a significant landowner who also claimed a manor in the parish. When in the mid-nineties he saw that it was in his interest to inclose, legislation in respect of Bunny, and of East Leake and Keyworth where he was a major proprietor and had manorial rights, followed in quick succession in 1797 and 1798!

Figure 11 Inclosures in South Nottinghamshire pre- and post-1790

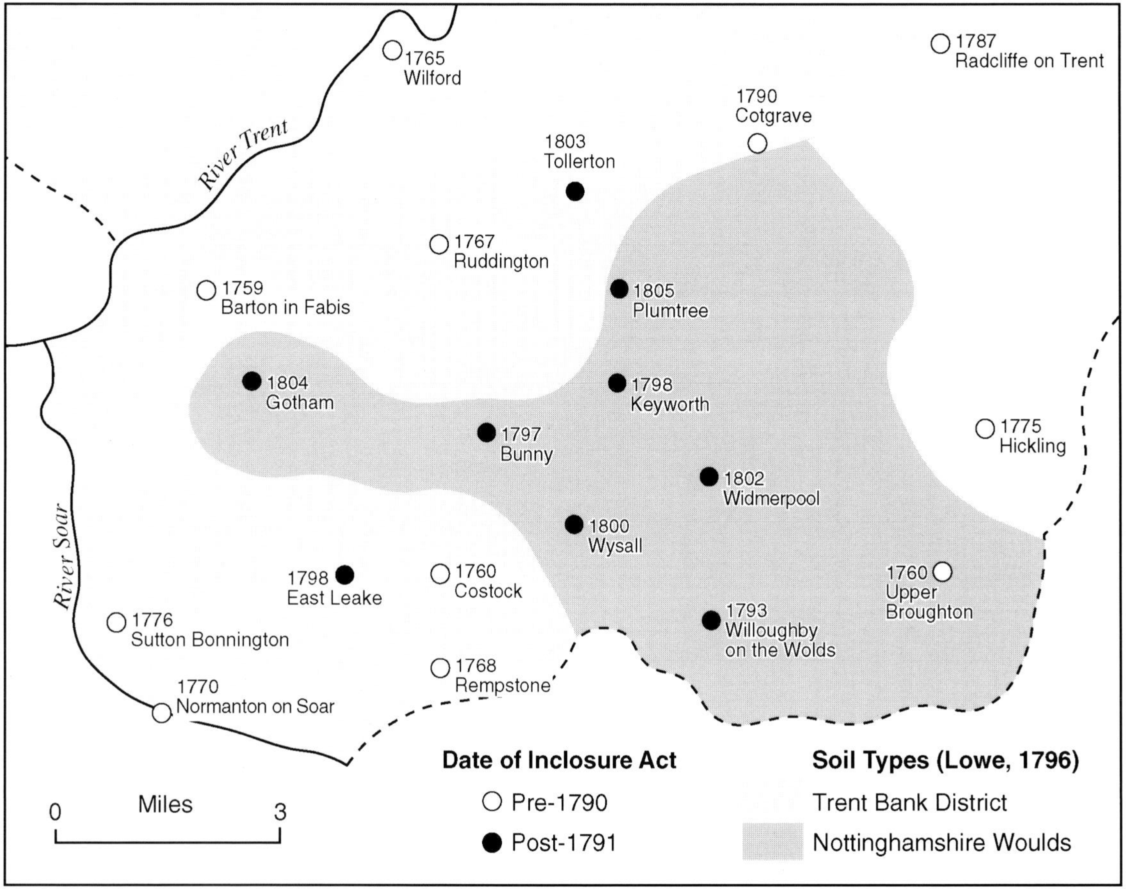

Date of Inclosure Act

○ Pre-1790
● Post-1791

Soil Types (Lowe, 1796)

Trent Bank District

Nottinghamshire Woulds

○ 1787 Radcliffe on Trent
○ 1775 Hickling
○ 1760 Upper Broughton
1790 Cotgrave ○
○ 1765 Wilford
1803 Tollerton ●
1805 Plumtree ●
1798 Keyworth ●
● 1802 Widmerpool
● 1793 Willoughby on the Wolds
○ 1767 Ruddington
1797 Bunny ●
● 1800 Wysall
○ 1760 Costock
○ 1768 Rempstone
○ 1759 Barton in Fabis
1804 Gotham ●
1798 East Leake ●
○ 1776 Sutton Bonnington
1770 Normanton on Soar ○

River Trent

River Soar

Miles

0   3

The Law

The legal framework of the Parliamentary Inclosure process may be appreciated by considering the procedure by which the Keyworth proprietors secured and implemented the Act of 1798.

Once the majority of landowners, calculated on the value of their holdings, agreed to a redistribution they petitioned parliament for leave to bring in a Bill which allowed their wishes to be realised.[2] In this it was stated that the lands which they possessed were 'intermixed and dispersed in small parcels and in their present situation are incapable of any considerable improvement, but if [these] were divided, inclosed and allotted it would be very much to the advantage of the said petitioners and of the public.' With these few words began the transformation of the parish. Leave was granted and two MPs were ordered to 'prepare and bring in' a Bill to this effect. These were the county MPs, Evelyn Pierrepont and Lord Rancliffe. While the former had no rights, proprietorial or family interest in Keyworth, the same cannot be said for Lord Rancliffe who was the eldest son and heir of Sir Thomas Parkyns, the Lord of the Manor and the principal petitioner. The appointment of the local members to perform this task made it probable that they would be friends or relatives of the petitioners, a practice which we would find wholly unacceptable, but was not considered strange in the eighteenth century. The petition was presented in November 1797 and the Bill, which had the unanimous approval of all the proprietors, was reported to Parliament by Mr. Pierrepont on 23rd February 1798 and agreed to by the Lords by the end of March. This rapidity suggests that the parliamentary procedure was little more than the application of a 'rubber stamp' to an arrangement already effected in the minds of the proprietors if not on the ground. Had the inclosure been opposed the petition would have been referred to a committee, and the Bill not ordered until the committee had made a satisfactory report.

It was frequently the case that the opportunity of Parliamentary Inclosure was used to deal with another and contentious matter, namely the payment of tithes. Over 60% of the Acts passed between 1757 and 1835 did so by the allocation to the tithe holder of land judged by the commissioners to have an annual value equivalent to that of the tithe about to be extinguished. Much of this land was found by the inclosure of the hitherto common pasture. In Keyworth there were, exceptionally, five tithe holders and the Act defined how they were to be compensated for their loss. The preamble to the Act names these tithe holders as *Sir Thomas Parkyns*, Baronet, as Lord of the Manor and Patron of the Rectory of Keyworth, the Reverend *Sampson Parkyns*, Rector of Keyworth; the Reverend *John Kirby*, Rector of Gotham, the Reverend *Abel Colin Launder,* Rector of Clifton, and the Reverend *William Beetham*, Vicar of Bunny. Sampson Parkyns also held certain glebe lands lying within Keyworth.

The proprietors named in the Act included Sir Thomas along with 'the Reverend *James Andrew Milnes*, Doctor in Divinity, *Samuel Smith, Langford Nevill, Samuel Greaves,* Esquires, and divers other Persons'. Having named the tithe holders and principal proprietors, the Act describes how its purposes are to be achieved. The work is to be undertaken by three commissioners, Joseph Boultbee, described as a gentleman of Bunny, Jonas Bettison, Esquire, of Holme Pierrepont and John Renshaw, Gentleman, of Owthorpe. Any two of them had the power 'to do and to perform every Act and Thing requisite to be done by virtue of this Act'. Commissioners had the authority of Parliament and were never afraid of using it. Although they acted in concert, the long section of the Act defining the procedure for the election of a new commissioner should one of them die prior to the completion of the task demonstrates that each had to heed a particular set of interests. For if Boultbee should die, then Sir Thomas Parkyns had the right to appoint a successor. Similarly a replacement for Jonas Bettison would be at the discretion of Sampson Parkyns. In the case that John Renshaw should die then the choice of replacement was that of the majority of the proprietors. This was not determined by a simple numerical count of those for and against a particular nominee, but according to the value of their holdings as indicated by the Land Tax Assessment. Sir Thomas and Sampson Parkyns were excluded from taking part in this election which would take place at a public meeting duly advertised by a notice on the church door and in the *Nottingham Journal*.

These means of keeping the public informed of the progress of the inclosure, in particular of the dates of meetings of the commissioners, was the standard procedure; but to avoid the expense and unnecessary reporting commissioners' meetings were usually adjourned rather than terminated! (This was specifically allowed for in the Act and the practice renders it impossible to use the *Nottingham Journal* as a means of assessing the number of *de facto* meetings required to complete the inclosure process.)

To aid the commissioners in their work the Act provided for the appointment of a surveyor who was to make a 'true and distinct Survey, Admeasurement and Plan' of the lands to be divided and inclosed and, at the discretion of the commissioners, of existing inclosures also. This survey was to 'be reduced into writing' and the area of each proprietor's land expressed in Acres, Roods, and Perches (statute measure). It was not always the case, but for the Keyworth inclosure the name of the surveyor, John Bailey, was stated in the Act. If he died, refused to act or failed to complete the survey then the commissioners could appoint a successor. To underline the importance and judicial nature of the work they were about to undertake the commissioners and surveyor were required to take and sign the following Oath:

> I do swear, That I will faithfully, impartially, and honestly, according to the best of my Skill and Judgement, execute the Trust reposed in me as a Commissioner [or Surveyor] by virtue of an Act for dividing and inclosing the Open Fields ... in the Township and Liberty of Keyworth in the County of Nottingham, without Favour or Affection to any Person whomsoever. So help me GOD.

These signed oaths, written on parchment, are included, as required by the Act, in the Award, the document setting out the results of the commissioners' deliberations.

The Act not only stated what had to be accomplished, but also the order in which the commissioners should address the different facets of the process. Clearly the survey had to be completed before land could be allotted and this had to precede the planting of hedges, but the sequence of allotment itself was governed by contemporary social convention. In practice, as we shall see in Chapter 7, it was probable that the sequence outlined below could not be followed as strictly as the Act presumed.

As soon as possible after their oath-taking, the commissioners were required to assume total responsibility for the agricultural activities in the open fields. They could 'order and direct what Course of Husbandry shall be used in the said Fields' and could 'set and impose such Penalties on every Person not conforming to such orders and Directions'. Thus the Act removed from the proprietors all control over the cultivation of their land while the reallocation of land was taking place. Following their first meeting the commissioners were required to invite proprietors to submit in writing their claims of 'Rights and Interests in and upon the Lands' to be inclosed. These claims were to be considered at an advertised meeting of the commissioners. Provision was made for a second meeting to deal with late claims, but if a proprietor failed to lodge a claim on this occasion the penalty was severe, for he would 'be excluded and totally barred of and from all Right and Title of ... the Lands so intended to be inclosed'. In short, he would be dispossessed.

The next task of the commissioners, which had to be done before they settled these claims, was the setting out of the roads they thought necessary. The Act defined the width of these and required the commissioners to appoint and pay a surveyor to construct and maintain them to an acceptable standard.[3] An allotment of land not exceeding four acres was to be made from which the surveyor could extract his road-building material. The commissioners could, at their discretion, set out and cause to be made public bridle roads and footways, and private roads and ways, as well as initiate such works as ditches, drains, watercourses, bridges and stiles.

Only when this framework was decided upon could they begin the allocation of land to the various claimants. The first to be considered was the Rector in respect of his Glebe lands, to be followed by the tithe holders. For the latter the basis of the allotment was quite specific. It was to be, in total, equivalent in value to two seventeenths of the already inclosed land and the common pasture plus two elevenths of the remainder of the land to be inclosed. This area of land was then to be divided between them in proportion to the tithes received hitherto. The next claimant to be considered was the Lord of the Manor in respect to his 'Right or Claim to the Soil' of any part of the land to be inclosed and also for his consent to its inclosure. He was to get the equivalent in value of one eighteenth part of the 'Commons and Waste Grounds only', but no portion of the open fields. These ancient rights having been abrogated and land exchanged for revenue, the commissioners could attend to the allocation of land to the 34 proprietors.

When allotted, the lands were to be inclosed by hedges, ditches and fences, but whereas proprietors had to bear the cost of fencing their own property, the tithe holders had their newly acquired holdings ring-fenced at the expense of these former tithe payers – the selfsame proprietors! Furthermore, the Act set out in some detail how this fencing was to be constructed, but leaving some discretion to the commissioners in respect of the proprietors' fencing.

Obtaining the Act, the surveying of the open fields, the allotting and staking out of land, the creation of roads and the administrative costs associated with the work of the commissioners all required money. Parliament granted power to the commissioners to raise this by a rate levied on the proprietors (but not the tithe holders) in proportion to the value of their land holdings.

There were a number of other provisions in the 29 pages of the Act, but these need not concern us here except for the one which required the commissioners to set out the results of their deliberations, in particular the quantity and location of land allotted to each proprietor, in a document called the Award. This was to be written on parchment and signed and sealed by them. Attached to it there had to be a 'correct Map or Plan' showing how the lands had been divided and allotted. The Award was, and remains, a legal document defining land ownership and the rights and responsibilities of the proprietors, former tithe holders, their heirs and successors. Arguably, it was one of the most significant documents to be deposited in the parish chest, affecting every man, woman and child in the village and all who came after them.

Notes

1. The interruption in the progress of inclosure coincided with the American War of Independence which necessitated an increase in borrowing and taxation. The favourable terms offered borrowers diverted funds which might otherwise have been invested in inclosure. Lord North, prime minister at the time, at first directed increased or new taxation toward the gentry, the very group likely to promote inclosure. Thus, in the first year of the war he increased land tax by a third, carriage tax was extended to stage coaches, stamp duty on deeds increased from 2s 6d to 3s 6d, newspaper tax by 1s 2d. Later a tax was imposed on manservants, stamp duty increased further to 5s, a tax imposed on auction sales of property, and wine tax increased. From 1774–1778 3% Consuls depreciated from 92 to 60. Robson, 1955, 147–8; Langford, 1989, 543.

2. This was not a simple majority by value. No particular majority was specified but was often three quarters or even four fifths. On the basis of these proportions the number of Keyworth proprietors (excluding tithe holders) required to sign the petition would be approximately one third of the total.

3. This surveyor was employed to construct and maintain the roads and should not be confused with the surveyor who had made the 'true and distinct survey'.

Chapter 6

The Principal Actors

In the last chapter we saw something of the legal and administrative framework of the Parliamentary Inclosure process; we now try to discover the nature of the people involved in bringing about the transformation of village life that the process engendered. Where it occurred, there was not a soul who was unaffected, but there were certain key people who played an indispensable part. The local Member of Parliament was one of these, so were the commissioners, surveyor and solicitor; they were the tools fashioning a new order. The material worked upon was the property and common rights of proprietors, tithe holders and cottagers. It has not proved possible to treat these different people in a standard way. We know little of the individual lives of those who owned land in Keyworth; in truth we know little about the lord of the manor, Sir Thomas Parkyns, and just about as much of Keyworth's Rector; so we shall consider their roles embellished by what meagre knowledge we have of their personal lives. On the other hand it is in the nature of these things that we can piece together the main features of the life of Charles Medows MP who was to inherit the estates of the Dukes of Kingston and so play an influential part in the lives of villagers in south Nottinghamshire.

Of the three commissioners who bore the responsibility for bringing about the changes, we have selected Jonas Bettison to represent a group of forward-looking men, who partly by birth, partly by patronage, but in the main by inclination combined with competence, concerned themselves with economic improvement. These men are to be found as turnpike trustees, investors in the canals, and if not themselves agricultural innovators, experimenters willing to introduce new crops or improved livestock. They were the leaders of the local community, in close touch with the major landed proprietors by virtue of their frequent contact with the latter's agents or stewards, themselves often progressive, constantly striving to improve the profitability of their employers' estates.

It will emerge that a key figure in the inclosure process was the surveyor. For the inclosures in southern Nottinghamshire, John Bailey was one of the most frequently appointed to this task. We know him only through his work, and it is the profession of land surveyor which we describe.

Finally, we examine the network of contacts which existed, and suggest that it was this unofficial unstructured intercourse which contributed significantly to the momentum to inclose which was a characteristic of the last decades of the eighteenth century.

The Members of Parliament

W.E.Tate, in his *Parliamentary Land Enclosures in the County of Nottingham, 1743– 1868,* published in 1935, listed the Members of Parliament and the inclosures with which they were concerned. The entry for Charles Medows on page 146 reads as follows:

> MR. MEDOWS *(Charles Me[a]dows, member for Notts.,1778 [b.e.], 1780, 1784, changing his name to Charles Pierrepont, member for Notts., 1790, 1801 [b.e.], 1802; later known as LordViscount Newark, member for Notts., 1806, 1807, 1812).*

The impression given is that all the inclosures which follow this introduction were steered through parliament by a single individual whose name and title changed over time. Not so — in fact they were handled by three men, a father and two sons. Here we tell of the events attending the name and title changes obscured in Tate's entry. Although this will show that Charles Medows had no direct involvement in the Keyworth inclosure, his importance as a major land-owner with property extending south of the Trent (including Radcliffe-on-Trent, Cotgrave, and Plumtree) and his contribution to agricultural improvement in the County suggest that he deserves more than a passing reference. Further-more, in succeeding chapters, we have drawn on correspondence and accounts from among his family papers to assist in understanding the inclosure process.

Charles was born in 1737, the second son of Philip and Frances Medows. His mother provided the Pierrepont connection, for she was the daughter of William Pierrepont, Earl of Kingston-upon-Hull, and the sister of Evelyn, second Duke of Kingston.[1] The combination of second son and matriarchal descent made it most unlikely that Charles would inherit the Kingston estates. He would have to make his own way in the world, but with his aristocratic connections that would not have been too difficult. His choice was the navy. At eighteen he was a Lieutenant and two years later, in 1757, held the rank of Commander. After a short spell commanding the sloop *Renown* he was appointed captain of the *Shannon*, a 36-gun frigate.[2] In this capacity Medows took part in one of the earliest of military and naval combined operations. This culminated in the capture of Louisbourg and prepared the way for the fall of Quebec and the establishment of British rule in Canada.[3] Among the dozen or so regiments engaged was the 45th, later known as the Sherwood Foresters. The French capitulated on 26th July 1758 and Medows (age 21) was entrusted with the task of conveying the messengers bearing the good news to the King.[4]

The following year he was promoted to Captain and continued his naval career in this rank for a further ten years. Thus, by the age of 32, when he retired to the naval reserve, he had gained considerable practical experience in one of the toughest schools in eighteenth century England.

Medow's inheritance of the Kingston estates was marred by a bizarre scan-dal thoroughly enjoyed in many an aristocratic salon. In 1769, the year Medows retired from active service, his uncle married Elizabeth Chudleigh. The marriage was childless, but also bigamous. In 1744 Elizabeth had secretly married Augustus John Harvey, but three years later they had separated. This state of affairs was not challenged until after the Duke's death in 1773. In accordance with his will the estate was to pass to the Duchess and on her death to his sister's second son, namely Charles Medows. Not unnaturally these dispositions were challenged by Charles' elder brother, Evelyn. Firstly he accused Elizabeth of bigamy. Elizabeth successfully petitioned to be tried by the House of Lords who found her guilty. Evelyn then contested the provisions of the Duke's will, but failed. Elizabeth exiled herself to the continent and died at Fontainebleau in August 1788. Charles claimed his inheritance and a month later, by Royal Licence dated 17th September 1788, assumed his mother's family surname and arms of Pierrepont.

By this time, Medows was well acquainted with the procedure of parliamentary inclosure, for in 1778 on the death of the Earl of Lincoln he replaced him as MP for Nottinghamshire, a position confirmed two years later at a general election. He continued to serve as MP for the county until 7th June 1796 when he was created Viscount Lord Newark. As an MP he had been involved in no fewer than 29 inclosure Bills.

From 1788, when he came into possession of the Kingston estates on the death of the Duchess, Pierrepont was actively involved in the practical aspects of inclosure. It is his experience as recorded in the correspondence of his estate managers (William Picken and William Sanday) and others upon which we draw in Chapter 7.

The transition from naval officer to a landowning Member of Parliament was now complete and he played a full part in the affairs of the county. For example, in 1797 when work was about to cease through lack of funds, he contributed £500 toward the completion of the Nottingham Flood Road.[5] Charles Pierrepont's interest in farming led to his appointment as an honorary member of the Board of Agriculture and he was instrumental in the appointment of Robert Lowe of Oxton to undertake a survey of agricultural practice in Nottinghamshire.[6] He seems to have had a particular interest in tree-planting. Robert Lowe in his *Agricultural Survey, 1796*, p.70, remarked that Charles Pierrepont had planted 981 acres with trees in and about Thoresby in the previous thirty years. The correspondence between Pierrepont and Sanday has many references to tree-planting and in the latter's 'Account of the Expenses attending the Inclosure of the Parish of Cotgrave in 1790, 91, 92, 93 & 94 ...' is an entry referring to the planting of 'young oaks & ash in the Quick Rows in Cotgrave new Inclosure'.[7] Perhaps this interest stemmed from his previous experience as a naval officer which would have impressed upon him the importance of an adequate supply of good timber for the maintenance of British supremacy at sea.

Referring to his political career, the *English Chronicle* wrote of him in 1781: 'Is an honest, upright, independent country gentleman ... He is not the *necessary* advocate for either side of the question, but votes from feeling and generally with the Opposition.' He voted for parliamentary reform in 1783 and 1785; and opposed Pitt until the French Revolution.[8]

When Charles Pierrepont became Viscount Lord Newark in 1796 he was succeeded as MP for Nottinghamshire by his son Evelyn. Therefore it was he, not
his father, who reported Keyworth's Inclosure Bill to Parliament on 23rd February 1798. Accounts of Evelyn Pierrepont's parliamentary career suggests that he
was a stickler for protocol and was reactionary in his views — for example, he
was a teller against the bills to abolish the slave trade, and was deputed in 1800
to help prepare a new anti-trade union bill. He was not held in high regard, at
least by the press, for 'the note takers in the gallery of the House of Commons
used to say of poor Pierrepont, that in a year more he would be so great a fool as
Robson'.[9] Neither the House of Commons nor his constituents suffered him for
long, for he died a bachelor on 22nd October 1801, to be succeeded by his younger
brother, Charles Herbert Pierrepont.

Charles Herbert was born on the 11th August 1778. Like his father, he em-
barked on a naval career with no thought that he would succeed to the management of the family's estates. By the time he retired from the navy on half pay in
1803, he had risen to the rank of Captain and had served with Nelson in the
Mediterranean. That he was returned unopposed as MP for Nottinghamshire to
make him the third Pierrepont in succession to occupy this seat gave rise to
some complaint and fear that the honour had become hereditary! In contrast to
his brother, he was thought sufficiently highly of by Canning to be considered as
a potential under-secretary at the foreign office.[10] When his father became Earl
Manvers, Charles Herbert assumed the unofficial style of Viscount Newark, but
remained in the House of Commons until his father's death in 1816. His elevation to the peerage brought to an end thirty years of Pierrepont representation
of Nottinghamshire at Westminster.

The Commissioners

While the commissioners as a group had complete responsibility and authority
in the allocation of land between the claimants, by implication (as we saw on
p. 80) each had a particular concern to secure a fair allocation to a particular
claimant or group of claimants. Thus, in Keyworth, Joseph Boultbee's first concern was the interest of Sir Thomas Parkyns, Lord of the Manor, Jonas Bettison's
that of Sampson Parkyns, the Rector, leaving John Renshaw to take care of the
requirements of the other proprietors.

While Boultbee only acted as a commissioner in the three parishes in which
his employer and brother-in-law had an interest, Renshaw and Bettison had
each acted in this capacity on ten or more occasions prior to the inclosure of
Keyworth and in five cases they had worked together. In this respect they dif-
fered from the majority of commissioners in Nottinghamshire of whom 82%
were engaged in no more than three inclosures up to that time.[11] Over the period
1760–1798, only ten men acted as commissioners on six or more occasions.[12]
However, they were by no means unique in the history of Parliamentary Inclosure
in England and Wales which records examples of men undertaking one hundred commissions or more.[13] Nor was the Nottinghamshire experience very dif-

ferent from that of other counties: of 328 commissioners engaged in Warwick-shire, Worcestershire and Staffordshire, 81% acted three or less times, while data for Buckinghamshire shows a similar pattern.[14] A listing of commissioners for Hampshire enclosures indicates threequarters of them were so engaged on not more than three occasions.[15]

What manner of men were these commissioners? What qualities did they bring to this role which had vested in it so much authority? Rather than attempt to answer this question, we here provide a brief account of the life of Jonas Bettison in the belief that he was not untypical of the knowledgeable, practical and trusted men who were chosen, time and time again, by proprietors to over-see the redistribution of parish lands.

Jonas Bettison was the fourth generation to have lived and farmed at Holme Pierrepont. He was born in 1748, the only son and second child of the Jonas Bettison who died in 1761. It may be that it was his uncle, William, a Notting-ham surgeon, who was responsible for the education of the young Jonas before his inheritance of the family's land. We know that at the time of its inclosure in 1787 he owned 90 acres in neighbouring Radcliffe-on-Trent and rented other land from Charles Pierrepont.[16] A late-eighteenth century directory which listed 'seats and villages in the neighbourhood of Nottingham' described Holme Pierrepont as being the seat of 'Jonas Bettison Esq'.[17] That he became a progres-sive and successful farmer is indicated by his advocacy of Robert Bakewell's methods of improving livestock, especially sheep.[18] Only a well-breeched farmer could afford Bakewell's charges! In due course he was to become a respected member, indeed a leader, in the local community. Thus when part of the steeple of Radcliffe church collapsed we find William Sanday, Charles Pierrepont's agent, writing to his employer, 'I am directed by Mr. Bettison and the other freeholders ... to acquaint you that it is necessary that something be considered upon as soon as possible.'[19] In an undated list of twenty of Pierrepont's tenants, Jonas Bettison is the only one referred to as Mr.[20] He was appointed Sheriff of Notting-hamshire in 1795, a clear indication both of his standing in the county and his personal wealth.[21] In the following year, he was listed as one of the principal signatories, after Charles Pierrepont, of the latter's Association created to ap-prehend and prosecute 'HORSE STEALERS and OTHERS who shall commit ROBBERY or other OFFENCE upon MEMBERS' of the Association.[22] When, in 1798, during the Napoleonic War, the Holme Pierrepont troop of Yeoman Cav-alry was recruited, it was Jonas Bettison who was gazetted as its Captain, a position he retained until his death.

Further examples illustrating his role in the local community and of his sup-port for improvement include his participation in an abortive attempt, supported Lords Chesterfield and Newark, to bridge the Trent at Gunthorpe and create a Turnpike Road to link the Vale of Belvoir with Sherwood Forest.[23] He was also on the boards of the Trent Navigation, Cromford Canal and Grantham Canal.[24] The high regard in which he was held by Lord Newark is well demonstrated by the latter's request in 1799 that Bettison should act as arbitrator in the valuation of tithes, a matter that was in dispute between Newark and the Rector, Mr Donnithorne.[25]

These facts taken together portray a man of high standing, not only in his immediate neighbourhood, but throughout the county, an impression confirmed by his role as inclosure commissioner. His first appointment as a Commissioner was in 1789 when he joined John Beighton and John Renshaw in the inclosure of Arnold. During the next nine years prior to the inclosure of Keyworth, he was to act as Commissioner on ten more occasions, four of them with Renshaw. Thus when Keyworth was inclosed Bettison was thoroughly experienced. He went on to act as a commissioner well into his sixties for a total of 24 occasions, including among these the inclosure of lands in which the Dukes of Newcastle and Portland had interests. In two cases (Annesley, 1808/9, and Eaton, 1809/14) he was the sole commissioner. The majority of the inclosures were in the southern half of the county, but he did venture to its northern tip, presumably at the request of the Duke of Newcastle, to join Jonathon Teal of Leeds and William Whitelock of Brotherton in the inclosure of Walkeringham. (See map, Figure 12, and Appendix IV for a full list of the inclosures for which he served as a commissioner, and the names of his colleagues and surveyors.)

Bettison's later life was marred by financial difficulties. In 1802, at a cost of £3450, he acquired the mortgage of Bromley House — later to become the home of the Nottingham Subscription Library — but on two occasions in the same year borrowed money from a Sara Storey. In 1805 having failed to pay off this debt of £1364 it was met by a Prisca Needham, who advanced him a further sum of £1636, the whole being secured by his Radcliffe property.[26] It must be presumed that he was able to liquidate this debt, for in 1816 he was in more serious trouble, this time involving the Duke of Newcastle. Exactly how he came to owe the Duke £7500 is not entirely clear. But in June 1814, Bettison replies to a letter from the Duke in a manner which shows that at this time he was employed by the Duke as a land agent or steward and failing to give satisfaction: 'Ever since I had the honour of your Grace's appointment to the superintendance of your Estates, my time hath been employed by due attention to your Grace's interest by every possible care for the improvement of your Estates ...' He goes on to say, 'I have to lament that your Grace should entertain doubt of my want of ability or inclination to serve your Grace, as to cause you to wish to superseed [sic] me in your employment ...' Two years later the whole of Bettison's property at Radcliffe was mortgaged to the Duke as security against the £7500 owing.[27]

Jonas Bettison married Sarah Wright of Burton Joyce on 25th October 1771, died without issue in February 1825 (age 77) and was buried at Holme Pierrepont on the 10th. The *Nottingham Journal* reported: 'The members of the Troop of Yeomanry Cavalry mustered on the occasion and attended the corpse of their deceased and highly respected Commander to the place of interment. At the close of the funeral service, the last sad honours were performed by the Troop firing three volleys over the grave.'[28]

Figure 12 Nottinghamshire Inclosures for which Jonas Bettison was a Commissioner

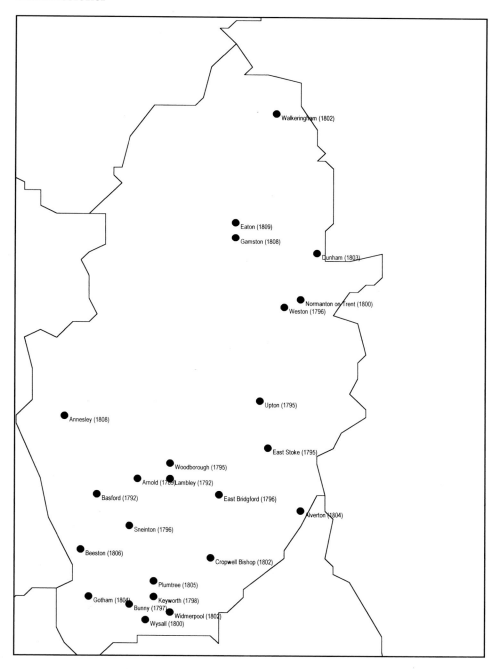

The Surveyor

It will become clear in the next chapter just how important was the role of the surveyor in the practical business of achieving the objects of an Act for the inclosure of the open fields. So it is appropriate to devote some space to considering both the practice and practitioner of this skill.

The oath of an inclosure surveyor required him to make a 'true and exact plan and admeasurement' of the land to be inclosed. Furthermore, a map would accompany the final Award providing a one-sheet summary of the commissioners' work; a welcome alternative to the many sheets of legal jargon which comprised the Award. 'Enclosure was a pre-eminently mappable activity.'[29] It contributed in no small measure to the notion of the late-eighteenth/early-nineteenth century as being the 'Golden Age' for land surveyors. Yet, at that time there was no formal surveying profession. Although incorporation of qualified surveyors was suggested some 250 years earlier, it was not until 1834 and the formation of the Land Surveyors' Club that an attempt was made to form a professional association. By then the days of the independent local land surveyor were numbered. The tithe surveys provided an extension of time but the existence of the Ordnance Survey (founded in 1791) and the slipshod work of the untrained during the railway boom caused terminal decline.

Even in their heyday few surveyors made a substantial living. Mostly they were self-made and depended on some other occupation to make ends meet. This might be as a schoolteacher, estate steward, farmer, carpenter, baker or even as a portrait painter.[30] There are examples of family businesses in which the skill was passed down from father to son — the Fairbanks of Sheffield being a notable and perhaps exceptional example of a successful business being conducted through four generations — but most must have learnt their trade assisting a practising surveyor.[31] They may have learnt the fundamentals at school. Charles Wilkinson, who had a school in Nottingham, almost certainly taught the subject, for in 1764 he proposed a survey of Nottinghamshire. The school at Bunny, founded in 1700, was endowed the rent from land in a neighbouring parish, the deed requiring that the money was 'for making provision for the training up of poor children in the knowledge of God and to teach them to read, write and cast accounts and so much of trigonometry as related to the mechanical and useful parts of mathematics'. Those useful parts would have included land measurement or elementary surveying. It would be a charming coincidence if John Bailey, the surveyor for the inclosures of Bunny (1797), East Leake (1798), Keyworth (1798), Wysall (1800), Widmerpool (1803), Tollerton (1803) and Plumtree & Clipston (1805) and many other local inclosures, could be linked with Bunny School, but we lack biographical detail and know Bailey only through his maps and a few references in the correspondence of contemporaries.

The earliest reference to him as an inclosure surveyor relates to the inclosure of Blidworth, 1769, in which he assisted Thomas Oldknow. He was again associated with Oldknow in 1775 doing similar work at Sutton Bonington. From then on he became the surveyor of choice for inclosures in South Nottinghamshire (see Figure 13 and Appendix V). He was closely associated with commis-

Figure 13 **Nottinghamshire Inclosures for which John Bailey was the Surveyor**

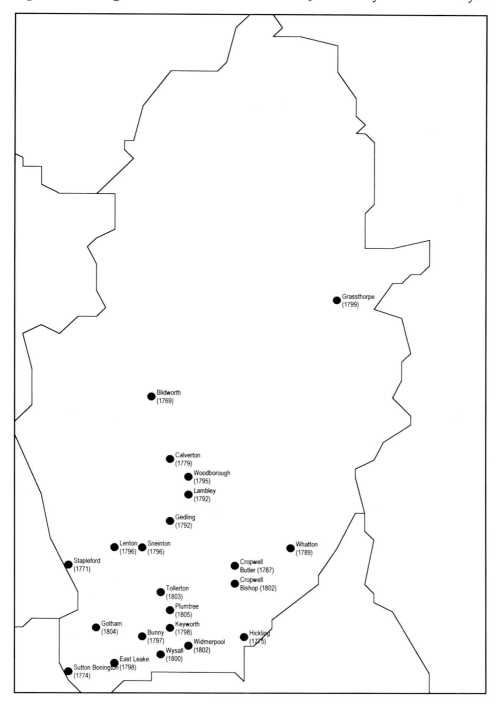

sioner Jonas Bettison, their names being jointly inscribed on no less than nine awards. Like many inclosure surveyors, Bailey later acted as a commissioner. In four cases — Woodborough, East Leake, Gotham, and Plumtree and Clipston — he filled both roles. In the latter two, which were the last of his Nottinghamshire inclosure surveys, he was assisted by John Brown, who was himself to become a notable surveyor. In total Bailey surveyed 39,000 acres in Nottinghamshire for 22 inclosures. Over the decade following 1795, which embraced the inclosure of Keyworth and its neighbouring parishes, he was the surveyor for 12, averaging 2300 acres per year.

When not surveying or map-making for inclosure commissioners, Bailey undertook work for a variety of clients including the Borough of Nottingham who engaged him for a number of projects over the period 1783–1802 (see Appendix VI). We lose sight of Bailey in Nottinghamshire after 1807; there is no mention of him in Sutton's Nottingham Directory of 1818, but the Public Record Office has two plans attributed to a John Bailey: Cheswick-in-Ancroft and Scremerston, Northumberland, dated 1811.[32]

Whatever kind of training he received we can be sure that Bailey made use of one or other of the current text books on the subject. At least a dozen books on the art of surveying were published during the eighteenth century, some running to many editions, notably those by Hammond, Wilson and Wyld.[33] These tended to be written to a standard pattern and assumed little prior knowledge by the reader. The first part was a straightforward treatise on arithmetic. There would be a section on instruments. Then came detailed instruction on how fields could be measured using them. Examples of increasing complexity made up this part of the book. From fields, discussion would move on to describe procedures appropriate to estates and even counties. Finally, instructions for the drawing of the map and its embellishment, including the preparation of ink and colours, would ensure the complete education of the would-be surveyor.

The most important and indispensable of the instruments available to the surveyor was the chain, introduced in 1620 by Edmund Gunter and named after him. Gunter's chain was 22 yards in length made up of 100 links, every tenth link being marked by a brass disc. (See Plate 1b.) During the eighteenth century its universal and often sole use branded the practitioners 'chain surveyors'. When the orientation of the resulting map was unimportant, a chain survey was adequate for use by estate managers or inclosure commissioners.

For long distances chaining was a slow and tedious process, but over easy ground a device called the 'waywiser' provided a rapid and simple alternative. This consisted of a wheel of 31.5 inches diameter so that 8 revolutions traversed a length of one chain. Gears transferred turns of the wheel to the rotation of pointers around graduated dials to permit the direct reading of distance travelled.[34] (See Plate 1a.) A less cumbersome development of this machine is frequently to be seen in use by survey teams along our highways today.

Most of John Bailey's Inclosure Award maps indicate the direction of north by including a simple compass rose, so we can assume that he had, at the very least, a compass to provide the orientation. Probably he possessed and used an instrument called a Circumferentor (see Plate 1c) which would permit him to

Plate 1 **Surveying instruments**

a

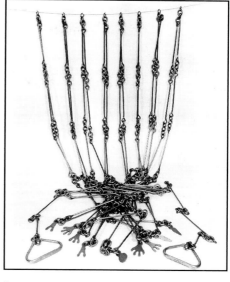

b

c

(a) Waywiser, by Wright and Wyeth, Museum of the History of Science, Oxford. Inv No: 93-3

(b) Gunter's Chain, mid-19th century, by Baker. Science Museum/Science & Society Pic Lib. Inv.No: 1872-0078.

(c) Circumferentor, 1763, by G. Adams. Science Museum/Science & Society Pic Lib. Inv. No: 1977-0755.

take bearings of prominent features (e.g., a church spire) or the bearing of a chained line from one feature to another.

But most of his work would be done with the chain alone. As far as possible, he would divide the spaces to be surveyed into suitably-sized triangles from which by the application of elementary geometry he would be able to calculate the area.

The text books described how the measurements should be entered into a 'Field Book'. These were usually variants of the example shown in Figure 14.[35] How widely these were used in practice is uncertain. But Fairbank's field books for the Eckington Survey are not in this form. Nor is it likely that Bailey used this system but followed Charles Hutton's recommendation in *A Treatise on Mensuration in Theory and Practice* where, having described the 'Form of the Field Book', he goes on to say, 'But in smaller surveys and measurements, a very good way of setting down the work, is to draw, by eye on a piece of paper, a figure resembling that which is to be measured; and so write the dimensions, as they are found against the corresponding parts of the figure. And this method may be practised to a considerable extent, even in the larger surveys.'[36] This common sense approach seems to have been the method preferred by the Fairbanks and by John Bailey. In the latter case we infer this from the following note made by Rev. S. P. Potter.[37] 'One of the few antiquarian "finds" which has come to the writer's hand is the Note Book of Mr Bailey the Surveyor who was engaged for the Survey of the Parish of East Leake with a view to carry out the Enclosures. *This is filled with sectional plans of every corner of the village and parish.'* (our italics) Sadly this notebook seems to have been lost.

So we can imagine Bailey in the early summer of 1798 walking or riding around the parish, conferring with the meresman to locate its boundaries, talking to the farmers whose strips he would be measuring, perhaps ascending the church tower to view the scene described in Chapter 2 and illustrated in Figures 2 and 3, before visiting the windmill that then existed near the eastern boundary of the parish to see another aspect of the Mill Field.[38] Now he would be ready to convert his mental map to the accurate paper map his oath required of him. Accompanied by at least one competent assistant, and armed with notebook and chain he would start the laborious process of measuring Town Street, Blind Lane, Old Lane, the Square and the farmsteads, barns and cottages and closes adjacent to them. Then he would turn his attention to the open fields, perhaps surveying the pasture before tackling the complex patterns of furlongs and their constituent strips — all 3000 of them. Plate 2 shows surveyors at work from an inclosure map of Henlow, Bedfordshire, 1798.

Until we know more about John Bailey's circumstances, it is reasonable to assume that like the majority of contemporary land surveyors he used for this purpose a combination of chain, circumferentor and waywiser. Similarly we can infer from other data what costs Bailey had to meet and what his remuneration could be.

In the 1790s a good quality chain could be bought for 11 shillings, a circumferentor for 4 guineas and a waywiser for 10 guineas. Labourers employed in staking out would be paid 1s 6d per day, a chain leader perhaps 2s 6d and

Figure 14 **A page from an eighteenth century text book on surveying**

The FORM of a FIELD-BOOK.

John Ancker's holding

Dairy-Field.

South Off-fet, &c.

At o————————— o
3.67————————— 17
4 90————————— 1.62
7.84————————— 74

Eaft Off-fet, &c.

Note, This Method of enter-tering Dimenfions, fhall be more fully explained in a proper Place.

REMARKS.
A Pond of Water on 6 Chains, Right-hand Perpendicular.

15 Timber Trees on South Side *Dairy-Field,* equal Dif-tance.

Thus expreffed, 15 T.T. eq. D.

Note, If you would diftin-guifh the Timber, you may obferve the following Charac-ters, *viz.*

a — Afh, A, large Afh.
o — fmall Oak : O, large ditto.
p — poplar, &c.

A few Days Practice in the Fields will render fuch Remarks both familiar and eafy.

More Directions to young Practitioners in the Fields.

Firft, In meafuring by the Chain only, or taking exactly the Dimenfions of any Field, or enclofed Piece of Ground, it is moft methodical to begin at fome remarkable Place, *viz.* Houfe, Gate, Style, Tree, &c. and for want of fuch, fix a Mark at your ftarting Place, as directed in the firft Section of this Chap-ter ; and from thence proceed orderly according to the Situation of the Field, *viz.* If a four-fided irregular Field, firft ftraighten the Boundaries thereof, by taking up the Off-fets, as hereafter taught ; and the Body of the Field you may take up in a Trape-zium, or Rect-angle, whichever feems convenient.

Secondly, It is not material in meafuring with the Chain, whether you go to the Right-hand or Left, that is to fay, with or againft the Sun.

Thirdly,

95

Plate 2 Eighteenth century surveyors at work

horse hire cost 4s per day.[39] He would pay 7s each for his field books and 15s per skin for the vellum on which he drew the map to accompany the award. Typically a surveyor was paid one guinea a day when 'attending on the commissioners', 6d per acre for the survey work and 1d per acre for drawing the finished map. On the basis of the detailed accounts of the inclosure of Eckington near Sheffield where the surveyors' total expenditure equated to 2s 6d per acre, Bailey probably presented to the commissioners a bill for £175 for his work in Keyworth.[40]

Bailey drew two maps from his survey data, one to accompany the Award and a second for the enrolled copy. They differ only in respect of the cartouche embracing the title. Bailey's maps, drawn on parchment approximately 25 x 22 inches wide, are simple, clear and designed for the specific purpose of showing the disposition, ownership and area of the allotments described in the Award. He showed in green the ancient closes centred on the church and extending on either side of what is now Main Street with their boundaries and pre-inclosure hedges/fences in black. With the exception of the church, which is shown in elevation from the south, the buildings are in plan, coloured red-brown and partly outlined in black. The boundaries of the new allotments are drawn in red, as are the allotment numbers; the names of the proprietors and the area of the land awarded them are shown in black. In the top right-hand corner is a simple eight-point compass rose. (For a more complete description see Appendix VII.)

Scale and accuracy are important characteristics of most maps and it is usual for the scale to be stated either diagrammatically or in words. No such indication exists on either map, nor, of course, is there any indication of the maps' accuracy, but we can get an estimate of both properties by comparison with other survey data. The best estimate would be obtained using modern satellite technology, but in its absence we can make use of the best modern maps we have, namely those of the Ordnance Survey. By measuring the distance between pairs of points on the two maps, we arrive at a scale of 1:5740 or 11 inches to the mile. But these measurements also show that the scale is not the same over the whole map. This small variation is of little practical importance; after all, Bailey was not engaged in making a topographical map, but one which depicted the location and area of each allotment of the award. More significant in assessing Bailey's work, therefore, is a comparison of the acreage of these allotments with those of the corresponding fields on the OS map. The area of 45 allotments identified on the OS map totalled 1171 acres compared with Bailey's 1162 acres. However, this difference of less than one per cent disguises the quite large variations shown in the scatter diagram, Figure 15, which also reveals a probable systematic error underestimating areas by about a fifth of an acre, a quite significant figure for the small proprietor.

As the evidence of commissioners' minutes confirms, there was more to the surveyor's job than map-making. He was the link between the commissioners and the farmers; he was pig in the middle and bore the brunt of any dissatisfaction there might be with the valuations. The commissioners would rely heavily on his knowledge, the farmers on his fairness.[41] We must conclude that John Bailey had secured the trust of both to have been employed so extensively in this business — a view confirmed by the following extract from a letter written by the solicitor involved in the proposed inclosure of Plumtree and Clipston: 'We all know him, his industry, ability & correctness....'[42]

The Lord of the Manor

Sir Thomas Parkyns (1728–1806) was lord of the manor in Keyworth, a tithe holder and major landowner at inclosure. Son of Sir Thomas Parkyns, 'the wrestling baronet', he inherited his title along with the Parkyns estate and the lordship of Keyworth and several other manors (Ruddington, Great Leake, Costock, Wysall, Thorpe-in-the-Glebe, Willoughby and parts of Barrow-on-Soar and Gotham) when he was 13, in 1741.[43] He also held the advowson of several parishes including Keyworth and appointed his own 23-year old son Sampson to be Rector of Keyworth and of Costock in 1793, obliging the then incumbent, Thomas Beaumont to find another post.

Unlike his flamboyant, energetic and eccentric father, this Sir Thomas seems to have been a quiet, unambitious and retiring personality. We know very little about his life except that it was long and prosperous. A.C.Wood remarks that he was 'seemingly content with the local station which his title, his land and a well-filled purse gave him'.[44] He raised a local volunteer defence group during the Napoleonic Wars which was based at Bunny Hall; otherwise we know nothing of his public role, except that he served, as did most men of his rank, as a Justice of the Peace. Given his stake in the land in Keyworth, he must have played an important part in its inclosure, but we have no record of what it was.

He married three times. His eldest son, Thomas Boothby Parkyns was given an Irish Barony to become the first Lord Rancliffe in 1795, but died in 1800, whereupon his son George Augustus, grandson of Sir Thomas, became the second Lord Rancliffe. When Sir Thomas died in 1806, George Augustus inherited his estate, valued at £21,000, together with the lordships of manors and advowsons held by his grandfather. However, he lived 'in the gay and extravagant circle which surrounded the heir to the throne'[45] and presumably squandered much of his wealth, so that his various lordships and advowsons, including those of Keyworth manor and rectory respectively, were sold and much of the 200-year-old connection between the Parkyns family and Keyworth was terminated, though they continued to own land in the parish for some decades.

Sir Thomas's second wife, whom he married in 1765, was reputed to be a servant at Bunny Hall. She bore him two sons and several daughters — one of the sons was Sampson who became rector of Keyworth. She died in 1796. His third wife was Jane Boultbee, a relation (sister?) of Joseph Boultbee, one of Keyworth's three Inclosure Commissioners.[46]

The proprietors

Of the 34 proprietors of land in the parish 18 were absentee landlords and only 16 farmed their own land. For the following account of one of the latter, Francis Eggleston, we are grateful to Alan Dexter, the author with Ben Eggleston of a history of the family.[47]

'Francis Eggleston (1732–1819) was the only surviving son of William Eggleston and the grandson of Francis Eggleston who arrived in Keyworth from Weston-on-Trent around 1700. They all left wills and all three were described as 'yeomen'. They were farmers, part of the village community which cooperatively cultivated the land according to the traditional ways of the ancient open field system. Francis was born in 1732 into this ancient village system, but one hundred years after his grandfather had arrived in the village it was inclosed and he had to adapt to the new ways which superseded the old. As a yeoman, Francis was a freeholder. This 'class' of villager ranked below the Lord of the Manor and consisted of a few large proprietors and more smaller ones. Of lesser standing were the copyholders, tenant farmers, cottagers, squatters and labourers.

'Such were the inhabitants of pre-inclosure Keyworth. Francis' status in the village and the extent of his holdings would be of crucial importance to him and his family when the common fields were inclosed by act of parliament in 1798/9. The lower one's status, the fewer the rights; but under the old system the village had an obligation to provide for even its poorest inhabitants and there was usually the opportunity to improve one's lot by dint of hard work and a thrifty nature, for holdings in the common fields could be bought and sold, and a cottage which had rights of common attached could be hired, as could strips of land.

'Like his father and grandfather before him, Francis was not at liberty to cultivate his strips of land as he pleased. Generally those aspects of village life which were not directly controlled by the local Justice of the Peace (often also the Lord of the Manor, as has already been mentioned) were organised by the 'Jury' of the Manor Court which went under different names in different villages. At various times and alongside other villagers Francis would have been a member of this Jury, the business of which was the management of the common fields, common pastures and the election of the village officers for the year. He no doubt took his turn in fulfilling some of these village roles, and he also served as churchwarden at times as had his father and uncle. There were restrictions on the number of animals which could be grazed according to the size of an individual holding, and the dates when they were allowed on the various pasture lands would be carefully prescribed. Fines at an agreed rate could be imposed on any transgressions of the agreements so made. Before the inclosure, Francis, alongside his neighbours, would have cultivated the strips of land allocated to him in the common arable field, cut hay from his allocated parcel of land on the common meadowfield, and made full use of his rights to the 'common' or waste, and to his rights of pasture on the meadowfield once the hay was cut.

Figure 15 **Scatter diagram illustrating the distribution of errors in Bailey's Award Map**

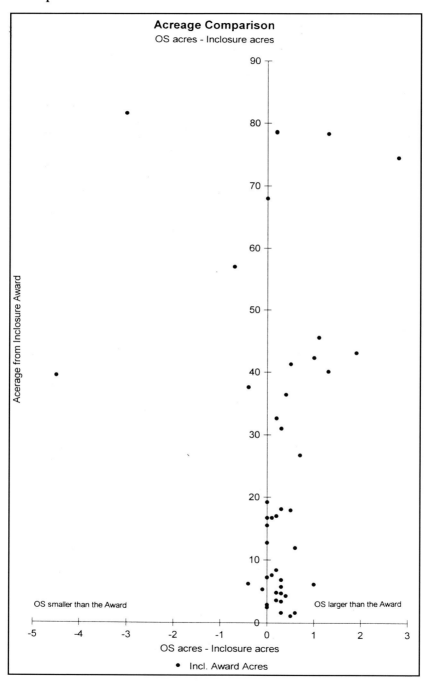

'Francis was typical of those yeomen whose farming inheritance would in the natural order of things be passed on to his own sons. His own five sons would have served as labourers on the farm as they grew up and his two surviving daughters no doubt would have helped with the animals as well as help their mother run the busy farmhouse. But the time would come when they would have families of their own which would need to be self-supporting, so provision had to be made. More farms and land would be needed for them and Francis appears to have acquired these, though to what extent he achieved this before the inclosure is not known.

'He would have been well aware of the upheaval caused by the inclosure of the common fields in different villages throughout the country, and he would have been an anxious man indeed when the Inclosure Commissioners arrived to announce how the fields were to be inclosed and what lands he would be allocated, and if these were to be greater or less in extent than his previous holdings or sufficient for his needs. Also some land would be better than other plots and may or may not be at a convenient distance from the farmhouse. There would be the loss of the rights of common, and he would need to ensure that essentials of fuel and water were available.

'There would be greater responsibility and risks in having to make independent decisions for the running of his own farms, decisions no longer being made by the village 'jury'. At the age of 67, he would have to move on with the times. Technical advances in farming methods called for investment in new equipment, and there would be the added expense of inclosing his new fields with fences or hedges.

'Francis was awarded lands. His new fields and other properties are clearly shown on the inclosure map and referred to in detail in the inclosure award. But, interestingly, he made, or remade his will in 1805 just after his third son died. This shows the extent of his possessions just a few years after the inclosure of the village. At this time he had a farm, including about 14 acres, at Wysall, occupied by his son-in-law Thomas Anabel who had married daughter Mary. This was now bequeathed to his son Joseph who was then occupying a farm including six and half acres of land at Willoughby. This was now to go to his son Thomas who then had, and was to retain, the bakehouse at Keyworth, next to which were some 'closes, lands, garden and yard in the tenure of Thomas Poulson' which were also to go to Thomas. Two other tenements next to the bakehouse in the tenure of Thomas Poulson and Samuel Brickley were to go to his son John, as was an orchard and cowhouse in the tenure of son Thomas. Some garden ground in the tenure of Samuel Brickley was also to be left to his son John. Some newly inclosed land, namely 'Martin Close' (about three acres) and 'Burrowgate Lees' (about eight acres) which Francis himself farmed was also to go to John, whilst his son William was to inherit Francis' own farm at Keyworth with its outbuildings and orchard, and 'Town End Close' of about two acres, 'Dockpool Close and the close above' totalling another nine acres.

'So Francis survived the inclosure of the open fields. He and his sons had to adapt to the new way of farming. The lands he held in total were not insignificant, but as we have seen these were split amongst his sons and were little more than a number of small holdings in today's terms. He probably ended his days happy in the knowledge that he had provided for his family in the traditional way, but perhaps not realizing that in the future farms would need to be much larger in order to survive.

'Francis died aged 87. Some of his descendants are still farming in Nottinghamshire and Leicestershire — and also in Queensland, Australia.'

A network of interests

The Keyworth commissioners and surveyor were part of a close network of similar men operating throughout the county and beyond. The collaboration of Bettison and Bailey has been dealt with on p.92. Here we look at the network itself, showing how its personalities were not only involved with each other but also in canal companies, the militia and other bodies in which they came to know and influence each other.

Throughout his career as an inclosure surveyor, John Bailey worked with no fewer than 34 different commissioners. Of these, we can pick out five of particular interest not simply to Bailey, but as major players in the inclosure of Nottinghamshire parishes in the eighteenth century. They were Thomas Oldknow, William Fillingham, John Renshaw, Jonas Bettison and James Dowland. Between them they were involved in over one hundred inclosures in Nottinghamshire and had been commissioners or surveyors for the inclosure of parishes in neighbouring counties, or even as far afield as Northamptonshire and Warwickshire.[48] Thus they can be regarded as the intersections or nodes in an influential network facilitating inclosure and the adoption of improved agricultural procedures. The following paragraphs examine some of the links in this web.

Figure 16 shows the extent of the careers of these five men as surveyors or inclosure commissioners, comparing them with the working life of John Bailey. Because their careers overlapped in time, they were often associated with one another in the inclosure of a particular parish. Thus, Oldknow and Fillingham worked together on four occasions; Fillingham and Renshaw on seven; Fillingham and Bettison, three; Renshaw and Bettison, six; Bettison and Dowland on three occasions. In the inclosure of Lambley, Fillingham, Renshaw and Bettison were the commissioners with Bailey as the surveyor. It is not unreasonable to suggest an evolution of the role of commissioner which would justify it being termed a profession. Indeed, these men could be considered as being members of a school of commissioners analogous to the groups of writers or artists for which this sense of the word is most frequently used. As will become apparent in subsequent chapters, the commissioners and surveyor would work closely together over significant periods of time and each would bring to their deliberations experience gained from a wide variety of sources, not least from their own lives as farmers, land agents or administrators.

If these men formed the main strand of the net, the other strands were their links with land surveyors, estate managers and other commissioners who in turn would be influenced by the knowledge and experience of their colleagues.

Figure 16 **Time-span of careers of John Bailey and principal Nottinghamshire Inclosure Commissioners**

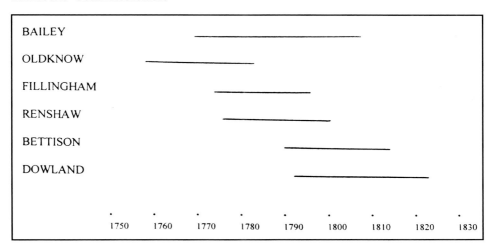

An example would be William Calvert, a surveyor and commissioner, who mapped Charles Pierrepont's estate at Cotgrave and whom Pierrepont once considered as a successor to the ageing William Sanday as his agent for his property in south Nottinghamshire. Further strands comprised men in other professions: legal, clerical and financial. Commissioners' minutes and estate papers record the role of the solicitor as an executive of the commissions, dealing with the paper work in a manner complementing the field and drawing-office work of the surveyor. The commutation of tithes inevitably created another link, and the commissioner could hardly escape the implications of the costs of his decisions, particularly if, as frequently was the case, he was also a land agent. The negotiations attending the abolition of tithes and their substitution by an allotment of land were far from easy, but in the process the commissioners used their net of contacts to find acceptable solutions. Thus when the commissioners Jonas Bettison, William Calvert and Samuel Wyatt were unable to resolve these matters at Sneinton, proposals put forward by William Fillingham were found to be acceptable.[49]

Of the five commissioners, three — Fillingham, Bettison and Dowland — are known to have been agents of aristocratic landowners; the importance of this link, especially when their employer's land was involved, can hardly be exaggerated. In the case of Bettison, as we have seen, employment by the Duke of Newcastle came late in life and after becoming a prominent figure in the county. On the other hand, Fillingham's service to the Duke of Rutland and the employment of Dowland by Earl Bathurst would have had, at the very least, a beneficial effect on their standing within the community and provided them with a range of contacts.

Thomas Oldknow, on the other hand, was a surveyor and businessman living in Nottingham. He was probably born in Heanor, Derbyshire, but was married at Strelley, Nottinghamshire, in 1731. Ten years later he is recorded as a maltster living on Long Row in Nottingham. He was sheriff of the town in 1746 and mayor in 1773 and 1778. He had a small estate in Calverton; it was here he died in March 1787, aged 78, and was buried the following month with his forbears in Heanor. It seems that he had some interest in Stanton-on-the-Wolds where his young daughter, Phoebe, was buried.[50] His public service to the corporation of Nottingham is an indication of his standing in the community; his career as an inclosure commissioner, a reminder to us of the interdependence of town and country — that in the eighteenth century urban business had an agricultural base.

We know little of Renshaw. He seems to have lived most of his life in Bakewell and may well have known Fillingham who made frequent visits to the Duke of Rutland's property in the neighbourhood. In 1788 he moved to Bilborough and later to Owthorpe, renting the Hall there. He was a man of substance, for on his death in 1802 while still working as a commissioner, he left in his will (witnessed by Jonas Bettison) an estate valued at £10,000. He was a commissioner for the inclosure of Gedling in 1792–6, working with Joseph Outram of Alfreton and Samuel Wyatt, a well known surveyor of Sinai Park, Burton-on-Trent. When this inclosure process was nearing its end, Outram and Renshaw were appointed commissioners for the inclosure of Eckington and worked with the surveyor William Fairbank and his sons. Outram is described as being an agriculturalist, auctioneer and valuer as well as being a surveyor. He was the father of Benjamin Outram who, with William Jessop, was one of the leaders in the development of iron railways in the pre-locomotive age and, at the time of these inclosures, the driving force behind Benjamin Outram & Co., renamed the Butterley Company in 1807. Thus our Nottinghamshire commissioners were not unaware of the industrial revolution and, indeed, played some part in its unfolding.

William Fillingham was baptised at Balderton on the 20th February 1735/6 and lived until 1795. In 1767, when he married, he was farming at Flawborough as a tenant of the Duke of Newcastle and was probably even then a land agent to the Duke of Rutland, a position he held for the rest of his life. In 1792 he bought the Syerston estate for £12,375 and on this built Syerston Hall, but died before it was completed. From 1774, when he was appointed commissioner for Sutton Bonington (Thomas Oldknow being one of his colleagues and John Bailey the surveyor), he was inclosure commissioner on a further 22 occasions in Nottinghamshire and a similar number in adjacent counties. Like Jonas Bettison he invested in canal companies; he was closely associated with the Nutbrook canal in Derbyshire in which the trustees of the Duke of Rutland as Lord of the Manor of Ilkeston had an interest. Both men had a practical interest in the Grantham canal due to its proximity to their property, and as canal board members would have had personal contact with William Jessop, the engineer responsible for the Cromford, Nottingham, Grantham and Nutbrook canals and for improvements of the Trent as a navigable waterway.[51]

The formation of troops of yeomanry cavalry during the French wars at the end of the eighteenth century provides a further illustration of the links that existed between some of these men. Both Charles Pierrepont and Sir Thomas

Parkyns raised troops; Jonas Bettison commanding the Holme Troop and Joseph Boultbee the Bunny Troop. Ichabod Wright, the Nottingham banker, commanded yet another. In due course the Nottingham and Holme Troops amalgamated as the 'The Nottinghamshire Yeomanry Cavalry'.

These few notes indicate the variety of influences experienced by the most active commissioners in Nottinghamshire and suggest that they were progressive men, part of a network of interests allied to those more directly concerned with the emerging industries which would remain dependent upon a productive agriculture.

If we accept the notion of a school of commissioners, then the school buildings were the inns and hostelries in the towns and villages. The principal establishment for the conduct of all sorts of business in the south of Nottinghamshire was the Black Moor's Head Inn situated on the corner of modern day Pelham Street and High Street in Nottingham. Not only did inclosure commissioners hold their meetings there: it was the place for land sales and the auction of properties; it was an important stopping point for the London coaches and the local canal companies held their board meetings on its premises. It was the place to meet people, to exchange news and gossip; it would be a place where views would be aired and opinions formed. It may well have been the centre of the network described above.

Notes

1. DNB.
2. Charnock, 1794, p. 269.
3. Clowes, 1900, p.183.
4. Admiral Boscowan's Journal, PRO, ADM 50 3.
5. NUMD, Manvers' Papers, Ma B 236/59.
6. ibid., MaB 244/3/1, MaB 244/4/1, MaB 244/7/1, correspondence between Sir John Sinclair and Charles Pierrepont.
7. ibid. MaB16/111.
8. Namier and Brooke, 1964, III, pp.128–9.
9. Thorne, 1986, pp.802–3.
10. ibid. p.801.
11. These figures ignore occasions on which a commissioner may have acted outside the county, but do suggest that relatively few individuals were engaged in inclosure on a 'professional' basis.
12. John Stone, (6), Geo. Mason, (7), Thos. Smith, (7), Geo. Smith, (9), Jonas Bettison, (11 prior to 1798), Henson Kikby, (11) , John Renshaw, (13) Geo. Kelk, (15), Wm. Fillingham, (18), Thos. Oldknow, (26).
13. M.W. Beresford, 'Commissioners of Enclosure', *Econ. Hist. Rev.* XVI (1946), p. 132. Michael Turner, 'Enclosure Commissioners and Buckinghamshire Parliamentary Enclosure', *Ag.Hist. Rev.* (25) 1977, pp.127–8.
14. Data from Beresford and Turner, ibid.
15. Chapman and Seeliger, 1997.
16. Priestland, 1990, p.35. 111 acres according to Wm. Attenburow in his 'Particulars of Mr Bettison's Property at Ratcliffe as in the open state at the time of Inclosure in

1787', BL, Eg. 3642 f 129. NUDM, MaB236/57: an undated account of Charles Pierrepont's old inclosures at Ratcliffe names 20 tenants including Jonas Bettison who rented a total of 9a-3r-11p.

17. *Universal British Directory of Trade, Commerce and Manufacture*, 1793, p.56.
18. Lowe, 1796, p.129.
19. William Sanday to Charles Pierrepont, Nov 1792, NUMD, MaB 240/11.
20. NUMD, MaB 236/25. Being undated we cannot be sure that this does not relate to his father, but even so it indicates the standing the Bettisons had in their community.
21. Dickinson, 1816, between pages 106–7; Bailey, 1852 Vol. IV, 157; François de la Rochefoulcauld describing the duties of Sheriff stated 'Generally you reckon that a Sheriff has to spend, on being Sheriff alone, £400 or £500 in the year', equivalent to over £22,000 in 1998. Scarfe, 1988, p. 91.
22. *Nottingham Journal*, 12th March 1796.
23. NUMD, MaB243/48/1&2, Wm. Sanday to Lord Newark 16th Oct. 1801, a letter inclosing a copy of the resolution of a meeting held at the Black Moor's Head Inn on 7th October.
24. Hadfield, 1966, p.62.
25. NUMD, M/3322/43, Wm. Picken to Jonas Bettison, Dec 21st. 1799, '... his Lordship will be very much obliged to you, if you will be kind enough to undertake the office of Arbitrator between them and settle and adjust by a valuation of the Tythes of the Parish, what annual sum shall be paid to Mr. Donnithorn in lieu of the Tythes thereof.'
26. Bromley House, Nottingham, was mortgaged by Sir George Smith (the second baronet) to Jonas Bettison. Neville Hoskins 'The best built house in town' in *Bromley House,* ed. Rosalys Coope and Jane Y. Corbett. BL, Eg. 3642 ff 137, 140 and 147. He was also in debt to the Thoresby estates. In a letter to William Pickin, dated 24th December 1804, William Sanday reports that for a second time he has asked Bettison to settle his account and writes, 'If I could but get his money I should be able to remit to Lord Newark's account Five or Six Hundred pounds.' NUMD, Ma B 236/68.
27. *Indenture between Jonas Bettison and Sarah his wife and the Most Noble Henry Pelham Duke of Newcastle,* 22nd June 1816, BL, Eg. 3642 f153. Gilbert Jones to Duke of Newcastle, 15th March 1816, NUMD Newcastle Papers NeC 6247.
28. Fellows & Freeman, 1928, p.43.
29. Thompson, 1968, p.32.
30. Bendall, 1992, pp.114–19; Mason, 1990, Table 1, p.6.
31. Bendall, 1992, p.129, 'Learning by apprenticeship and example was probably the most usual method...'
32. PRO, MP1 236. These plans are probably the work of John Bailey of Chillingham, Northumberland.
33. For a brief account based on the study of 33 surveying texts published between 1523 and 1827, see Bendall, 1992, pp.119–125.
34. Descriptions of the perambulator or waywiser are to be found in several eighteenth century surveying texts, e.g. *The practical Surveyor: ...*, John Hammond enlarged by Samuel Warner, 3rd ed., 1750; *Surveying improved ...*, 6th. ed., 1769, p.75.
35. Burns, 1771, p.91.
36. Hutton, 1802, p.394.
37. NUMD, Potter's papers, 1/3/55.
38. John Chapman's map of Nottinghamshire, 1776.
39. Horse hire seems to have varied considerably from on place to another, the Fairbanks were charged only 2s 6d per day at Sheffield.

40. A somewhat lower estimate of Bailey's charges for his work in Keyworth is given in Chapter 8.

41. Stephen Joyce in his study of the inclosure of parishes in the Soar valley remarked, 'One is left with the impression that it was the Surveyor who did much of the ground work.' ('The impact of external change in the locality of Barrow-upon-Soar, Quorndon, Sileby and Mount Sorrel North End, 1750–1801', p.51, MA Thesis, University of Nottingham, 1997.)

42. Mr Jamson to Wm. Picken Dec 8th 1801; NUMD, MaB243/61.

43. *Transactions of the Thoroton Society*, Vol. 6, 1902 in 'An account of a Spring Excursion'.

44. *Transactions of the Thoroton Society*, Vol. 58, 1944:A.C.Wood on George, Lord Rancliffe.

45. ibid.

46. Notes on the Parkyns Family by Beryl Cobbins; Bunny Parochial Church Council, 1992.

47. Dexter and Eggleston, 1996.

48. Bendall, 1997.

49. NUMD, MaB 248/7, Mr Jamson to Wm. Picken, 3rd February, 1796, 'I understand Mr. Pierrepont and Mr. Musters have closed this unpleasant business of the Sneinton Inclosure on the Terms offered by Mr. Fillingham...'

50. A. Bernard Clarke, 'Notes on the Mayors of Nottingham', *Transactions of the Thoroton Society*, 42 (1938), p 118.

51. For more information on William Fillingham see K.S.S. Train, 'The Fillinghams of Syerston Hall', *Transactions of the Thoroton Society*, 74 (1970) pp.22–30.

Chapter 7

Dividing the Parish

Whatever the parishioners of Keyworth may have known or thought about the likelihood of the inclosure of their open fields, they discovered it to be a certainty when they attended church on Sunday 29th April 1798, for there on the church door was a notice similar to one which had appeared in the *Nottingham Journal* the day before:

> The Commissioners appointed by an Act passed in the present Session of Parliament, intitled 'An Act for Dividing and Inclosing the Open Fields, Meadows, Pastures, Commons and Waste Grounds within the Township or Liberty of Keyworth in the County of Nottingham', do hereby give Notice that they intend to hold their first meeting for putting the said Act into execution, on Monday the 7th Day of May next, at 11 o'clock in the Forenoon, at the house of William Attenborrow, the Sign of the Nag's Head in Bradmore, in the Said County of Nottingham.
> Dated the 26th Day of April 1798.
> By order of the Commissioners, John Harrison, Solicitor

A day or so earlier Mr Harrison's clerk had ridden over from Derby carrying with him two copies of this notice one to be 'affixed' to the church door and the other for the Rector or his curate to read out during the Sunday morning service.

The Process

For the villagers this was the beginning of a process which was to change their lives for ever. In reality the process had begun much earlier: before — perhaps long before — the Act of Parliament which required this notice to be posted; and it would go on for some time after the Award was published.[1]

In this chapter we seek to describe the events which transformed the parish to the pattern of hedge-lined fields and roads which even today exert their influence on ownership and development (see Chapter 10). The inclosure process is readily divisible into three chronological stages, viz.:
(i)   Obtaining the authority of Parliament
(ii) Translating the requirements of the Act into the set of instructions which comprise the Award
(iii) Implementing these instructions.

The considerable costs involved will be examined in a later chapter.

The Commissioners appointed to oversee the inclosure were required to keep a record of their deliberations, a record that one might suppose would have been safely kept for future reference. Not so; relatively few of these documents are known to have survived, and the Commissioners' Minutes for Keyworth are not among them. However, those for East Leake, inclosed at the same time as Keyworth, reside in the Nottinghamshire Archives; even more fortunate, both the solicitor, John Harrison, and the surveyor, John Bailey, involved in the East Leake inclosure were employed in the same capacities at Keyworth.[2] This coincidence, together with other factors which will be discussed later, suggest that we can use the East Leake minutes as a good indicator of the sequence of events in Keyworth. These will be supplemented by information contained in the partial minutes of the Gedling commissioners and the detailed accounts of the surveyor for the inclosure of Eckington near Sheffield.

When we wish to discover what may have occurred prior to the Act, or subsequent to the Award, we have to rely on the existence of documents which by their very nature are far more likely to be destroyed than carefully filed away. Only letters between the major players in the move to inclose are likely to provide an insight into their motives or the difficulties that they had to overcome. It might be thought that the estate of Sir Thomas Parkyns would have maintained and preserved a record of estate business which we could draw upon to understand his role in the inclosure of Keyworth and Bunny. But the Parkyns papers held by the University of Nottingham contain little to help us. By way of contrast, the extensive papers of the Manvers estates include correspondence relating to the inclosure of Gedling, Cotgrave, Plumtree, and Sneinton which we will use to understand the problems facing proprietors both before the commissioners were appointed and after the embodiment of their decisions in the Award. Fortunately the solicitor's accounts for the inclosure of East Leake have survived and they cover the expenses associated not only with commissioners' deliberations, but also with those occasioned by the framing of the Bill and the petition to Parliament.

Securing the Act

We have seen that by the 1780s most major landowners had accepted that open field farming was outmoded; the move to inclose, irreversible as it always had been, was now irresistible. By the late 1790s the question in Keyworth and Bunny must have been not 'if', but 'when'.[3] Between 1779 and 1796, Charles Pierrepont, as member of parliament for Nottinghamshire, had been associated with 29 successful inclosure acts in the County. In addition, as heir to the estates of the Duke of Kingston, he had experienced the process as a major landowner. His status, his membership of the Board of Agriculture and his practical experience must have had a major effect on the attitude of 'lesser' men, if only to create a climate of favourable opinion toward inclosure.[4] But it would be wrong to believe that only the rich and powerful sought inclosure of the open fields, though without their support the process would not begin, or would founder if this support were withdrawn for some reason.[5] Thus in the case of Gedling and its associated hamlets of Stoke Bardolph and Carlton, it was one of the lesser freeholders, Thomas Smith, 'having long had a wish to promote such a measure, of his own accord consulted all the freeholders of that description who, approving the measure, delegated him to convey their wishes to Lord Chesterfield and Mr Pierrepont, well knowing that nothing could be done without them'.[6] In Cotgrave, Pierrepont was the major landowner and such was his authority that he, or his estate manager, William Sanday, was able to secure agreement to the new inclosures. In the event the Inclosure Act of 1790 merely endorsed the action already agreed to: no commissioners were needed and hence there was no award.[7] A year later when the inclosure of Gedling and its neighbouring villages was under consideration, Sanday was anxious to achieve it by the same successful procedure adopted at Cotgrave.[8] But the situation was quite different. There was another powerful landowner to reckon with, the Earl of Chesterfield. To make matters even more difficult, a long-standing dispute existed between the Earls of Chesterfield and the Dukes of Kingston over manorial rights.

The Earl of Chesterfield's London solicitors (with the unlikely name of Strong and Still) produced a document entitled *State of Facts &c Touching the intended application to Parliament for inclosing the Parish of Gedling and the Hamlets of Stoke & Carlton in the County of Nottingham*.[9] In this they summarised the ownership of land by Chesterfield, Pierrepont and 'Divers Freeholders' including 'Mr Smith's late purchases' and traced their clients' ownership and rights back to 1592. Sanday's adverse reaction to this document, Pierrepont's insensitivity and Chesterfield's arrogance all but wrecked the negotiations.[10] However, when the solicitors proposed a compromise in which Pierrepont's Thoresby estate agent, William Picken, would replace Sanday in the negotiations, Lord Chesterfield was happy to leave 'the whole matter of the inclosure to be finally adjusted between us'; he would ratify whatever was agreed by the solicitors.[11] The way was now clear for the preparation of the petition to Parliament.

The experiences of Gedling and Cotgrave are perhaps extreme cases. We are not aware of any high-level wranglings attending the inclosure of Keyworth or of its neighbouring parishes; on the other hand they were, unlike Cotgrave, subjected to the whole routine of the Parliamentary Inclosure process. It is probable that the experience at Keyworth was more akin to that of East Leake, or Great Leake as it was then called, which shows that even in a straightforward case there was much to be done before a petition could be submitted to Parliament.[12]

An essential preliminary, because their names had to appear in the Act, was the choice of Commissioners (see Chapter 6). We get a glimpse of this process in the case of the inclosure of Plumtree and Clipston. Lord Newark (Charles Pierrepont was elevated to the peerage in 1796 — see Chapter 6) was of the opinion that the fewer Commissioners the better, and if the other proprietors could agree on the choice of Mr Jonas Bettison, he would be perfectly satisfied.[13] The Messrs Elliotts, the other principal landowners in Plumtree, were agreeable, but Bettison, because of his health and his other commitments, requested a second commissioner to assist him. He proposed John Bailey who had worked with him before, mainly as a surveyor. Six years later Bettison and Bailey were duly named as commissioner in the Inclosure Act, and Bailey was the principal surveyor.

Before the General Inclosure Act of 1801 forbade the practice, it was frequently the case that the commissioners had a vested interest in the outcome of the process. Often they were the stewards or agents employed by the principal proprietors. Thus Joseph Boultbee, Sir Thomas Parkyns' steward and related to him by marriage, was a commissioner on only three occasions, each time in parishes where Sir Thomas was a major landowner or possessed manorial rights — Bunny, East Leake and Keyworth. On the other hand, neither Jonas Bettison nor John Renshaw had any proprietary interest in Keyworth and were chosen on the basis of their experience.

Another important player in the process, one who receives scant attention in the literature, was the solicitor who drew up the draft Bill and Petition and ultimately prepared the Award. It would be he, or his clerk, who would provide the communication between the different parties and negotiate the allotment of land in lieu of tithes. One of the main attractions of inclosure was the opportunity it afforded to eliminate these unpopular payments to the Lord of the Manor, Rector or others. As far as possible the basis on which this allotment was to be made was negotiated prior to the formal inclosure process. Thus we find William Sanday reporting to Charles Pierrepont on a meeting in which Sanday was arguing for one fifth of Field Land for tithes when the other party was only prepared to offer one sixth.[14] On another occasion the boot was on the other foot and we find William Picken, speaking for Pierrepont, only prepared to offer one sixth when the Rector of Gedling was proposing one fifth.[15] In the case of Plumtree and Clipston, Charles Pierrepont, now Lord Newark, agreed to the inclosure on the basis of an allotment of one seventh of the tithable acreage.[16] In Keyworth two seventeenths of the little existing inclosed land, a similar proportion of the common pasture and two elevenths of the remaining land to be inclosed was to be allotted to the five tithe holders. As these proportions appear in the Act it is apparent that much negotiation must have preceded its preparation.

Inclosure of the open fields would require that the proprietors had access to their new holdings and as provision for new roads appears in the Act it is reasonable to assume that the proprietors would have discussed possible locations when the Bill was being drafted.

Particular problems affecting a proprietor or the parish as a whole would be resolved at this stage. Thus in the case of East Leake, Harrison made a special visit to Boultbee to frame a clause which would ensure the allotment to Sir Thomas Parkyns of land containing a particular spring.[17]

Essential for the whole process was a competent surveyor acceptable to the commissioners and proprietors, for it would be he who would measure each man's holdings both in area and value. Without him the commissioners would be impotent, so it is not surprising that his name often appears along with those of the commissioners in the Act.

The drafting of the Bill could be quite prolonged. Even in the relatively straightforward inclosure of East Leake, Harrison's accounts open in February 1797, but it was a whole year before the draft Bill and Petition could receive parliamentary attention. It is clear that much of his time was spent making sure that Sir Thomas Parkyns, Theophilus Henry Hastings, Rector of East Leake, and his Patron, Earl Moira, were persuaded that there was a satisfactory basis on which to proceed.

Both the Bill and the Petition required the signatures of the proprietors. A meeting would be called for this purpose, one which could become a social occasion.[18] Notice of the meeting would appear in the local newspaper, and on the Church door which would assume the role of public notice board for the first of many occasions before the Award was completed. If not all the proprietors could attend, it was then the task of the solicitor or his clerk to visit each of these and secure their signature. Thus we find recorded in the East Leake accounts for the early part of January 1798, 'Mr. Harrison's Clerk's Journey to Gt. Leake and many other Places to get the Bill signed by Proprietors, out 3 days £4:14:6, horsehire 12s'.

In the case of Keyworth we know practically nothing about the preliminaries; however, we are aware of the existence of a potential source of conflict. We learn this from a letter between Lord Newark's two agents, Sanday and Picken.[19] On behalf of his employer, Sanday had attended a meeting of proprietors of land in Keyworth held to bring in a Bill for the inclosure of that Lordship during the current session of Parliament. He was present to claim on behalf of Lord Newark:

> a right of a Manor for his Lordship, stating that it was similar to that of Hickling; although the Kingston Family had no landed property there yet at the time of the inclosure it was allowed by the Commissioners for them to be Lord paramount notwithstanding there were three other Manors claimed ... this was because these Estates were within the Manor of St. John of [illegible] and paid Chief Rents at that Court yearly; it is true, there are no lands at Keyworth within the Manor of St. Johns, but there are several within the Manor of Holmepierrepont, and pays Chief Rent at that Court, to the amount of 17s a year, and Lord Newark has no more landed property in that Lordship than his family had in Hickling. The intended solicitor of the Bill and Sir Thomas Perkins's [sic] Steward declared they would not admit to any such claim, but insisted that Sir Thomas was the sole Lord of the Manor of Keyworth.

In an undated letter to Lord Newark, William Picken confirmed his belief in the legitimacy of the claim.[20] However, it seems that Lord Newark decided not to press the point.

Applying the Act

Once the bill became an Act the commissioners could get to work. The progress of the inclosure of East Leake is recorded in what seems to be a complete set of minutes of meetings extending from 15th May 1798 to 23rd December 1800.

Mostly the meetings were held at the Bull's Head Inn, Loughborough, but hostelries in East Leake (Windmill; Three Horseshoes), Kegworth (Flying Horse Inn) and Nottingham (Black Moor's Head Inn) were sometimes used either as meeting places or for the dissemination and collection of information. It would seem that these institutions were significant beneficiaries of Parliamentary Inclosure! A timetable for the submission of claims was decided at the first meeting and three weeks later the commissioners began their valuation. An alphabetical list of the claims was deposited at the Three Horseshoes; written objections to any of these claims had to be made to John Harrison, the solicitor, by the 21st July and ten days later the commissioners met with the objectors and listened to their evidence. It was at the latter meeting that the eleven proprietors whose claims were disputed had the chance to put their case. Among these were Lord Middleton and the Rev. Theophilus Henry Hastings, the eccentric rector of East Leake. The commissioners 'Judged and Determined' that Lord Middleton was not entitled to his claim, and 'also the said Rector is only Intitled to Three Horse Commons, Seven Cow Commons and an half and Seventy Sheep Commons'. Sir Thomas Parkyns claimed the whole of the allotment due to the Lord of the Manor. This was disputed by John Hardy. The commissioners concluded that there were three manors within the Lordship of East Leake, two of which belonged to Sir Thomas and the third to John Hardy. They reserved judgement as to their extent. Clearly, the powerful and influential did not always get their way. These decisions demonstrate the authority parliament had vested in the commissioners.[21]

At an early stage the Commissioners decided the location of the public roads. Their proposals were published in the *Nottingham Journal* and posted up on the church door. These notices invited comment or objection.[22] As the roads would be constructed from materials found within the parish, the Commissioners would instruct and give authority to a suitable person to enter any land intended to be inclosed and 'Bore, Dig, Delve or cut the same in order to find proper places' which would then be allotted for the getting of stone or other material for the making and repairing of roads. This person might subsequently be appointed as Surveyor of Highways.

By October the Commissioners were ready to set out 'the Allotments on the Plan'. This they did in the comfort of the Black Moor's Head Inn at Nottingham where they 'ordered Mr. Bailey as Surveyor to get the same adjusted and staked out forthwith Conformable or as near as may be to the Lines Drawn on the Plan'. The parishioners and proprietors learned of this decision from the notice 'affixed on the Principal Door of the Parish Church of Great Leake on Sunday the fourth of November next'. Bailey had to get the boundaries staked out by the 20th of that month and the Commissioners would hear objections at their next meeting on the 26th November at the Bull's Head Inn, Loughborough.

By this time considerable expense had been incurred. The solicitor had been engaged since February 1797, during which time he prepared the Bill and carried the cost of seeing it enacted, as well as undertaking all the negotiations and clerical work required under the Act. So, it was at this stage that the Commissioners set a rate on the proprietors to raise £2069 12s 6d towards defraying the general expenses of the inclosure. Of the 65 persons named eight were zero rated. About half the amount was raised from just four proprietors of whom Sir Thomas Parkyns was assessed at a total of £380 5s 6d.

The four-day meeting at the end of November put into effect all the deliberations of the past six months. Tithes were extinguished. Bailey was instructed to restake boundaries where the commissioners had agreed to late objections and prepare schedules of all the allotments. These had to be available to the proprietors on 7th December so that they could enter their allotments on the following day. He was also to make a survey and valuation of all old hedges standing in the boundaries to allotments not belonging to the owner of each allotment and prepare an account for the next meeting. When that was done he was to make 'an account of the Ploughing on each allotment in the Fallow Field and by whom the ploughing was done and the number of Tilts'. Finally, he was to employ 'person or persons' to level the route of the new roads, removing any obstructing gorse and thorns in the process.

The proprietors were directed that 'on or before the 25th of March [they] plant their respective Allotments with good Hawthorn Quicksets at least 4 feet within the Line of Stakes and properly guard the same and that convenient openings be left for the present in such fences at all the ancient roads heretofore used in and upon the said Fields'.[23] They were also allotted a share of the task of the ring-fencing.

All of this was to be communicated by the usual medium of the church door, and with the notice drafted the commissioners adjourned for three months. During this time Harrison prepared the draft of the Award. In this task he was assisted by John Bailey who, like William Fairbank in the case of the Eckington inclosure, prepared all the essential information which the solicitor transposed into the appropriate legal form. The East Leake accounts show that Harrison attended 'Mr Bailey' at his home on each of the three days 21st, 22nd and 23rd of January 1799 'taking Instructions for the Award'. The draft was 'perused, considered and settled' by the commissioners at the end of February 1799. This was no formality, for the meeting at the Bull's Head Inn, Loughborough, lasted five days. However, the Commissioners did not sign the Award until the following June, a full six months after its main provisions had been acted upon.

Only three other working meetings were held in 1799, of which the assessment of the remaining expenses of the inclosure and for making roads was the most important. A rate was imposed to raise £1326 which included the first instalment toward the road building to be paid by 10th June 1799. The second instalment of £614 became due on 1st January 1800. It was expected that the roads would be constructed in the spring of that year, but at the last recorded meeting in December 1800 an examination of the accounts of the Surveyor of Roads showed that 'owing to the high price of labour and the very bad season for making Roads ... they [had] expended nearly One hundred & eighty Pounds more than had been raised by the Rate already made ... and that £200 more [would] be wanting to Complete the said Roads'.

Overall, the inclosure of East Leake was accomplished in fourteen meetings occupying a total of 66 days.[24]

These extracts from the Minutes of meetings of the commissioners for Gedling and for East Leake show that the surveyor was the executive through whom the practical requirements of inclosure were accomplished. They also suggest the care that was taken to ensure that the interests of the different proprietors were properly considered. There is no reason to believe that the process of inclosure of Keyworth proceeded any differently from that of East Leake and it is probable that a similar pattern of meetings took place over roughly the same time span. Harrison and Bailey led very busy lives.[25]

East Leake inclosure was accomplished without serious difficulty and probably the same can be said for Keyworth and Bunny. In the latter case the dominant position of Sir Thomas Parkyns made the outcome of the process certain, but for Keyworth this conclusion is founded on two factors: firstly the short time between the Act and the Award and secondly that Bailey was engaged in both Keyworth and East Leake during the same year. Had serious difficulties arisen in either parish, surely one or other, if not both, would have taken longer.

Not all inclosures went so smoothly. In Gedling, where the interval between Act and Award was four years, there were difficulties of a serious kind. The commissioners involved were William Calvert, William Pearce, John Renshaw, Samuel Wyatt and Samuel Deverill. Pearce dropped out over an exchange made between two of the parties, with which he disagreed. Calvert, who had good grounds for complaint when the agent for Lord Chesterfield constructed an unauthorised road through land allotted to Charles Pierrepont, was excluded from the final signing of the Award. On 21st March 1796, Calvert learned that Messrs Renshaw and Wyatt would be meeting in Loughborough two days later to sign this document. Calvert wrote: 'I was surprised such a meeting should be called without consulting or informing me, however my surprise ceased when I was told by Mr. Bailey that a Mr. Deverill was called in and sworn to enable him to sign the Award tho. [sic] he had not attended a single meeting before.'[26] An example of the ruthless abuse of power.

The Keyworth Award

Bearing in mind that the Keyworth Bill had only been agreed to by the Lords on March 27th, the Commissioners, Jonas Bettison, Joseph Boultbee and John Renshaw (see Chapter 5) wasted very little time. Only Bettison and Boultbee were present at the first meeting on May 7th, and each administered the oath to the other. The surveyor, John Bailey, who had been named in the Act, took the oath at the second meeting held on June 12th and the Inclosure team was completed on the 20th of the same month when John Renshaw was present to take the oath.

The main provisions of the Act for inclosing the open fields of Keyworth can be summarised as follows:

(i)   Setting out of roads and bridle ways
(ii)   Allotment of up to four acres for the excavation of road materials

(iii) Allotment of land to the rector in compensation for his glebe land and other rights (other than tithes)
(iv) Allotments in lieu of tithes
(v)   Allotment to proprietors
(vi) Providing for the poor of the parish

To achieve these ends three matters required immediate attention. The first was for the surveyor to make a map of the parish, the second was to request and examine the claims of the proprietors, and the third to lay out the new road system. Simultaneously the commissioners assumed the responsibility for the farming in the parish. The extent to which they may have exercised this responsibility can be inferred from the Commissioner's minutes for other inclosures. Thus, the farmers in Gedling who occupied 'Tillage Lands' in the fallow fields were ordered to plough them a second time before 1st September. Penalties for not doing so were whatever the Commissioners thought reasonable![27] In East Leake we find proprietors entreating the Commissioner to use their powers: '... it was Represented to us by several of the proprietors that the Lands in the Fields had not been Ploughed and Managed in an Husbandlike manner ... [They] ... ordered that the Lands be Ploughed Stirred and Tilled and that every person occupying Lands in the said Fields, Do Plough, Stir & Till the same in such Manner as shall be thought Proper and Directed by Messrs John Hardy, Daniel Woodruffe & Richard Burrows and that Notice be Given thereof on the Church Door of Great Leake on Sunday next.'[28]

Apart from these supervisory duties there was little that the Commissioners could do until John Bailey had surveyed and mapped the parish. Indeed, the Keyworth Act specifically required that he make such a plan to be 'laid before the said Commissioners as soon after their First Meeting to be held in pursuance of the Act as may be'. This would be the main tool used by the commissioners in reallocating land to the proprietors. It would have to show as accurately as possible the complex distribution of the existing strips and furlongs described in Chapter 3 and illustrated in figure 6. Of necessity it would be drawn at a large scale, probably four chains to the inch (1:3168 or 20 inches to the mile). Few of these maps seem to have survived. Keyworth's, unfortunately, is not among them.[29] It would be necessary to assess the value of all the land in the parish in order to calculate the current value of each man's holding and to compute the area of land to be allotted in a different part of the parish. As the general disposition of these allotments would have to ensure ease of access, the layout of new roads would be an early consideration. Thus a second map would develop which would show the roads and footpaths, the boundaries of each allotment, the position of stiles and the location of sites of pits for roadstone. It would be at this stage that claimants for land would see quite clearly what the commissioners regarded as a fair alternative to the strips they formerly tilled.

By the time of the Bunny and Keyworth inclosures, Bailey was an experienced surveyor highly regarded by the foremost commissioners in this part of the county. Unfortunately, none of his notebooks, even if they still exist, have been located. However, the many records, maps, notebooks and accounts generated in the course of the work of the Fairbank family have survived, and can provide an insight to the work of an inclosure surveyor.[30] Among these are documents relating to the parish of Eckington (near Sheffield) which was inclosed over the period 1795–1800, i.e., about the same time as the inclosure of Keyworth and some of its neighbouring parishes. They include an account book for this survey from which we have a day-by-day record of the progress of the inclosure as experienced by the Fairbank family. This shows that William Fairbank met the commissioners on two occasions in the summer of 1795 and started his survey in October; the fieldwork was completed by the following September, and in November he recorded 'Finished Survey & Working Plans' of the 6800-acre parish.

This survey, albeit of a much larger parish, provides data which can be used to comprehend Bailey's work in Keyworth. The surveyors, two sons of William Fairbank, were in the field for a total of 166 days, so averaged 40 acres per day. This accords well with other estimates of the workrate of eighteenth century surveyors.[31] When applied to the 1400 acres of Keyworth it suggests that Bailey as the sole surveyor could have completed the survey in about three months. Thus Bailey would be surveying the open fields of Keyworth during June, July and August; not a very suitable period in the farming year for such an activity!

Meanwhile the Commissioners would order the proprietors to make their claims in writing, instructing that these should be delivered by a specified date to a local hostelry. At their next meeting, which could last several days, they would evaluate the claims received and set a date for the receipt of those outstanding. When all the claims were in they would be listed alphabetically and posted for all to see. Objections could be made in writing and objectors were invited to attend a meeting at which the evidence by claimants and objectors would be heard. The proprietors were asked to state where they would like their allotment of land to be located.

Roads

We have seen that one of the first tasks of the Commissioners, aided by the surveyor, was to agree the layout of the roads within the parish. The pre-inclosure parish roads would have served two purposes: to provide routes to neighbouring villages and to give access to the open fields. For the latter we could wish for a sight of the map Bailey had made for the commissioners, but this was a working document and if it survived we have no knowledge of its current whereabouts. What we do have is a map of Nottinghamshire which depicts more than just the location of Keyworth relative to its neighbouring settlements, namely, John Chapman's map of 1776 drawn at a scale of 1 inch to 1 mile[32] (Figure 17). Although on too small a scale to show tracks into the open fields, it does show what we now call Main Street, Bunny Lane, Selby Lane, Lings Lane, Thurlby Lane, Debdale Lane, Stanton Lane, Nicker Hill and Normanton Lane which functioned both as routes to nearby villages and as ways to the open fields. Although we can recognise these on Chapman's map there are significant differ-

Figure 17 **A portion of John Chapman's Map of Nottinghamshire, 1776**

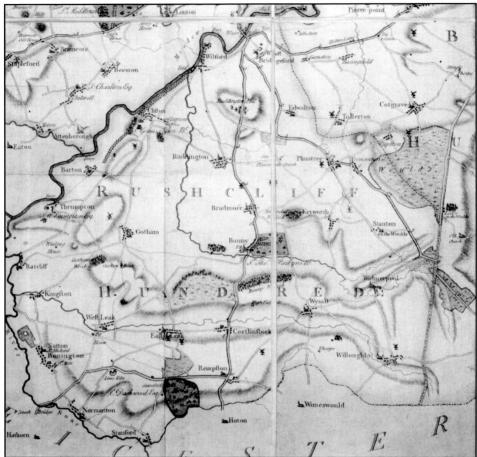

ences from the present day which derive from the decisions made at the time of inclosure. Among the most obvious relates to Lings Lane, then called Pasture Lane, which, in Chapman's time, not only provided access to Woulds Field and the Common Pasture, but was the route from Keyworth to Wysall. Inclosure reduced its status to an access way only and a new road was opened up to Wysall. Another outcome of the commissioners' work was the linking of Price's Corner to Normanton Lane. Prior to inclosure the road from Keyworth to Normanton branched in a north-easterly direction from the old Nottingham road which continued to Price's Corner to turn into Debdale Lane, ultimately leading via Flawforth to Lings Bar and Nottingham. The north-easterly branch of Nottingham Road was reduced to the status of a footpath.

It would be reasonable to suppose that lanes designed primarily to permit ease of access to the proposed inclosures would follow existing paths and tracks leading to different parts of the open fields. It has to be remembered that while the process of inclosure was going on, so was the traditional farming practice. It would not have been a popular move to lay out a new road across a series of cultivated strips. Thus it is probable that Woulds Road (Lane) and Hemsley's Road approximate to older uncultivated areas allowing access to different parts of Woulds Field. Similarly the extension of Debdale Lane beyond the old route to Nottingham may be the successor of an older track into Bunny Gate Field. But what of the new road to Wysall? Here the primary purpose was to create a satisfactory route to that village, but there are questions to be asked about the choice of route. One can readily believe that the short east-west portion of Wysall Lane was a trackway into Bunny Gate Field and that the eastern end of this track marked the departure point for the new road. The road to the parish boundary is nearly straight, but not quite. Why? Why enter Wysall parish at Miller's Gap, and having made the decision to do so, why not go directly to it? We cannot give definitive answers, but we can consider some of the factors which could have been debated by the commissioners.

Although the laying out of the roads was required by the act to precede the allotment of land to the proprietors, common sense suggests that the proprietors, surveyor and commissioners must have had a prior view as to the general disposition of these allotments. However, when Bailey had produced his detailed plan of the parish and the individual claims of the proprietors were being examined it may have become clear that the proposed road system did not quite fit and adjustments would be necessary. In other words the practice of inclosure may well have been one of adjustment by 'trial and error', rather than the simple 'step-by-step' process implied by the Act.

For example: from a road-building point of view, it would have been logical to construct the new Wysall Road in a straight line to the parish boundary. However, from the land-allocation point of view, it was reasonable to allot Sir Thomas Parkyns, in lieu of tithes, land adjacent to his Bunny estate. This roughly triangular allotment was bounded on one side by the Fairham Brook and on another by the Keyworth/Wysall Parish boundary — both permanent features. If the new Wysall road had continued in the same direction as it had departed from the village, then the area enclosed within the Fairham Brook, the parish boundary and the new road would have been about 50 acres — nine acres more than the area due to Sir Thomas. So, it is suggested that the line of the new road was adjusted westward to provide the third boundary to Sir Thomas's correct allocation — hence its present rather unexpected alignment. (See map, Figure 18.)

The relative importance attached to the different roads is revealed by their widths as defined in the Award and are testimony to the need to allow for the shifting of the road proper as a section became impassable by virtue of the deep ruts and tenacious mud. Thus the road from Plumtree to Stanton, and then via today's Willow Brook to Widmerpool was directed to be 50 feet between fences, while Selby Lane, Bunny Lane, Nottingham Road, Normanton Lane and the new Wysall Lane were to be 40 feet wide. Roads serving the new inclosures and the roadstone quarries varied in width from 20 to 30 feet. Similarly, the widths of the road surface would vary. The minimum width required to permit the safe

Figure 18 **Map showing roads described in Keyworth's Inclosure Award**

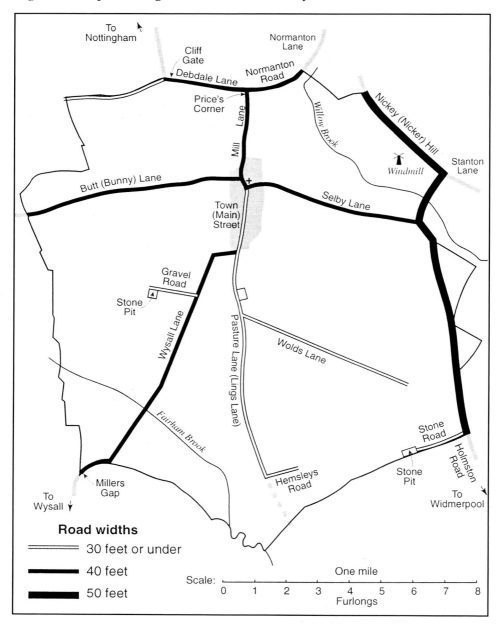

passage of two wagons would be approximately 12 feet, but where traffic was light with few on-coming vehicles, 9 feet would be adequate, especially when supplemented by passing places at the top of 'steeps', a circumstance which we might imagine applied to most of Keyworth's roads outside the village. That the roads were expected to be constructed to some standard, however vague, is suggested by the requirement that they be certified at quarter sessions.[33]

From what is known of road construction in the eighteenth century we may envisage that a central strip of the staked out road would be cleared of all vegetation, excavated, lined with brushwood and filled with broken stone, roughly graded, the larger pieces at the bottom, smaller nearer the top. The commissioners had located two areas in the parish from which road materials were to be extracted. One west of Wysall Lane behind New Holme farm was accessed by the appropriately named 'Gravel Lane'. According to The British Geological Survey the gravel here is from the fluvio-glacial deposits from the outwash of the Anglia Ice Sheet, consisting mainly of pebbles of quartzite, sandstone, Jurassic limestone and flint.[34] The stone pit near Wolds Farm was dug into the Lower Lias clays containing flaggy limestone.[35] Thus it seems probable that the foundations, or bottomings, of the enclosure roads in Keyworth were of this limestone overlaid with sand and gravel.

Land

With the web of roads centred on the village established, the commissioners could turn their attention to the division of the parish land between the various claimants. Their first obligation was to the Rector, not as a tithe holder but as the custodian of the land owned by the rectory — the glebe land. The 89 acres allotted as 'a full Satisfaction and Compensation for his Glebe lands and other Rights and Interests (except Tithes)', extended from the Rectory Close to Normanton Lane and Nicker Hill.

The quantity of land to be allocated to the five tithe holders was crucially dependent upon John Bailey's survey, for it was calculated *in toto* on specified fractions of the already inclosed land ($2/17$ths), the pasture ($2/17$ths) and the remainder ($2/11$ths). The Rector was the recipient of about half (116a 3r 0p) of the 238 acres to be allotted in lieu of tithes, 49 acres of which was to be situated adjacent to his glebe land to create the largest compact holding in the parish. Together with his remaining 68 acres in one lot along the west side of Lings Lane he also became the largest landowner. The other half of the land to be allotted in lieu of tithes was divided between four claimants, the Rectors of Gotham and Clifton, the Vicar of Bunny and Sir Thomas Parkyns. (See Appendix VIII.)

Next in the procedure set out in the Act was the allotment of land to the proprietors. Factors affecting the siting of these would have included (i) the status of the claimant, (ii) the location of an existing farmhouse and (iii) accessibility. Keyworth farmhouses were situated exclusively within the village, the majority on either side of Main Street (see Figure 19) Thus they imposed a strong radial pattern to the post-inclosure landscape. (See map on p.134.) On the east

Figure 19 **Buildings and closes in the vicinity of Main Street, Keyworth, from the Inclosure Award Map of 1799**

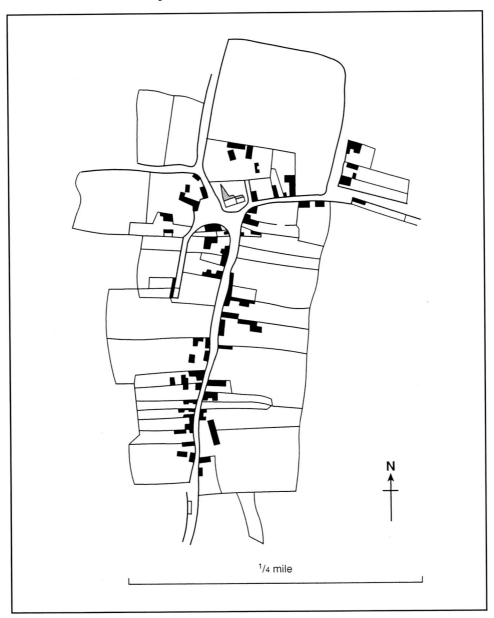

N

¹/₄ mile

side of Main Street and immediately south of Selby Lane, 94 acres were allotted to Rev. Dr. Milnes. This reached across the Widmerpool Road to include the nearly thirteen acres of Old Hedge Nook, one of the two triangular areas between the road and the zigzag eastern boundary of the parish. Adjacent and to the south of the Milnes allotment were the 86 acres granted to Richard Tookey, including the second triangular area known as New Hedge Nook. Between Tookey's land and Wolds Lane was Samuel Greaves allotment of 79 acres. A similar but less prominent pattern can be seen to the west of Main Street, Commercial Road and the Square. Thomas Hemsley was allotted 55 acres to the north of Bunny Lane which were easily accessible from the Manor House Farm which he owned and lived in.[36] Samuel Smith's 74 acres stretched westward from Main Street into Bunny Gate Field and north to Bunny Lane and south to Fairham Brook parallel to Wysall lane, from which it was separated by land allotted to Langford Nevill. Wysall Lane and Lings Lane emphasised the radial pattern and determined the layout of blocks of land owned by Nevill and by Richard Attenborough. Elsewhere in the parish the pattern of ownership was determined by access from Bunny Lane to both north and south, from Lings Lane to the east and Wolds Lane to the south. In general these inclosures ran at near right angles to the roads and lanes so that the radial pattern centred on the village gave way to a patchwork of rectilinear plots near the parish boundary. (See Appendix IX for a complete list of the proprietors and acreage of their allotments.)

The Act provided for old inclosures to be exchanged for land intended to be inclosed. The purpose was to meet the case where such an exchange provided a practical advantage to the proprietor, e.g., by consolidation of his holdings. In contrast to the situation in Tollerton where considerable areas were exchanged, this opportunity was exercised in only three cases, viz. Murdin's Close, The Pingle and Motley Close, a total area of only one acre!

Inspection of John Bailey's map reveals some curious allocations. Why separate Henry Hebb's allotments in Wolds Lane by that of William Cooke? Why did the rector not receive the sixteen acres allotted to William Hemsley? Indeed, why did so much fragmentation of landholding still obtain? Did it reflect pre-inclosure consolidation, or was it the consequence of attempting to achieve equivalence of value of the pre-inclosure ownership? The location of the plots for the extraction of road building materials was determined by the presence of suitable stone or gravel, but what determined that of the plot for the Trustees of the Keyworth poor? What significance, if any, can we attach to the location of the Bell and Loundes plot?[37]

We cannot answer these questions but perhaps the reasons were well understood by the proprietors as they assumed overnight the responsibility for managing their newly defined property.

The commissioners, surveyor and solicitor were left to complete the legal business, drawing up the accounts and preparing the Award, while the proprietors began the creation of a new landscape.

Digging ditches, planting hedges and building fences

The straight roads with wide verges represent an important component of the post-enclosure landscape. However, they take second place to the effect of the pattern of hedgerows imposed upon the open fields. A row of stakes was adequate as a temporary allotment boundary, but something more durable was required to ensure permanence and to keep stock from straying into a neighbour's holding.

The solution was elaborate, labour intensive and costly to create and maintain. It comprised a combination of hedge, ditch, mound and timber fencing.[38] Two variations are to be found in the Keyworth award. The allotments to the tithe holders were to be ring-fenced (i.e., a continuous fence around the perimeter of the holding) at the expense of the proprietors. This fence was to comprise '...good young Hawthorn Quicksets properly planted and guarded on each side with good Oak posts and treble row of Oak or Ash Rails on the outside and a double row of Oak or Ash rails on the inside thereof and Ditch of sufficient dimensions on each side of the said Fence'. The non-tithe holding proprietors did not ring-fence their allotments, simply because they shared a common boundary with a neighbour who would be responsible for one or more of the fences separating one allotment from another. These fences were almost certainly not ditched on both sides as were the ring-fences of the tithe holders' allotments, for the proprietors were only required to construct 'mounds and fences'. The lack of a detailed description suggests that these fences were to be constructed according to a commonly understood pattern, possibly similar to that described by William Marshall in 1790 and reproduced in Appendix XI.[39] A further requirement was for the quicksets to be planted not less than four feet from the staked boundary. According to Lowe the preferred quickset in Nottinghamshire was whitethorn which was planted in one or two rows, on the flat or slope of the bank.[40]

We might have expected that the ditch would have been dug on the proprietor's side of the quicksets, but not so. This is clear from the instructions in an eighteenth century manual for surveyors:

> Observe (in the Boundaries of the Estate you are to measure and map) the Hedges & Ditches, that is to whom do they belong: And note if the Ditch is between the Field you must measure and the Hedge, that ditch belongs to the neighbouring Gentleman's Land and therefore you must allow 4 feet or 6 links from the quick Roots in the Hedge, ... , but if the Hedge is between the Field you are measuring and the Ditch then it must be measured there with.[41]

The village roads — now much improved, but in places still bounded by their eighteenth century hedges — remain for us as reminders of the work of the commissioners appointed to inclose the parish. So too do many of the hedges planted by the proprietors of the time. Not so obvious are the effects of these on the pattern of ownership and development during the two hundred years since the division of the parish between the proprietors. We get occasional glimpses of the longevity of these decisions in the maps accompanying planning applications, property sales, and more rarely, but comprehensively, in wide ranging surveys such as the National Farm Survey 1941–1943.

Notes

1. The inclosure of Sneinton was first proposed in 1787 by John Musters of Colwick Hall, but it was nine years later before a Bill was put before Parliament; a delay due in part by a failure of Musters and Pierrepont to agree on the tithe allotments. NUMD, MaB248/19, MaB 248/7. See also MaB241/16 which suggests that relations between the two men was not good. Pierrepont's accounts for the Cotgrave inclosure (1790) were not closed until 1803, MaB242/32.
2. East Leake Inclosure, Commissioners' Minutes, NA DD SD 1/1.
3. Nearly 80% of the open field Parliamentary Inclosure Acts for Nottinghamshire over the period between 1755 and 1850 had been published by 1798, the date of the Keyworth Act. See chapter 5.
4. Charles Pierrepont made a member of the Board of Agriculture when it was formed in 1793.
5. An attempt to inclose East Leake in 1781 failed because it lacked the support of Sir Thomas Parkyns; NA DD3P 4/1.
6. NUMD, MaB99/18.
7. This was unusual: only two other Nottinghamshire parishes, Elkesley/ Normanton (1777) and Trowell (1787), were inclosed in this way.
8. NUMD, MaB99/20, William Sanday to Charles Pierrepont 6th Sept. 1791: '...the chiefest reason why I recommended ... that the lands should first be divided and allotted and afterwards to apply to Parliament is that Lord Chesterfield & Mr. Smelt [the rector] will have the right for each to appoint a Commissioner and you only one, which would be a majority against you ... and not so likely to pay that attention to your interest as they would to that of their employers ....'.
9. NUMD, MaB99/26.
10. NUMD, MaB99/24.
11. Dec. 19th 1791; NUMD, MaB99/25.
12. An earlier move to inclose East Leake was frustrated by Sir Thomas Parkyns, for the proposed bill did not take account of his rights to a Coney Warren. NA DD3P 4/1.
13. William Pickin to Mr Jamson 30th November 1801; NUMD, MaB243/59.
14. NUMD, MaB 247/3.
15. NUMD, MaB 99/30.
16. William Pickin to Mr. Jamson 30th Nov 1801, NUMD, MaB 243/59.
17. East Leake Inclosure Accounts, 19th Dec. 1797, NA DD SD1/2.
18. The East Leake Accounts include £5 for the expenses of the proprietors.
19. William Sanday to William Picken 19th Dec 1797, NUMD, M3321/44a.
20. NUMD, M3321/44b.
21. 'The power granted by most of these Acts to Commissioners, is an extraordinary circumstance in the History of Enclosure. They are a sort of despotic monarch, into whose hands the property of a parish is invested, to recast and distribute it at their pleasure among the proprietors; and in many cases without appeal.' Arthur Young, *General Report on Enclosure drawn up by Order of the Board of Agriculture* (1808), p.61.

22. East Leake Inclosure, Commissioner's Minutes, 30th July 1798.
23. This requirement accounts for the definition of parts of Keyworth's parish boundaries as shown by the Ordnance Survey, PRO OS 27 4186.
24. East Leake Inclosure, Commissioners' Minutes.
25. Bailey was involved in six inclosures with Awards dated either 1798 or 1799. See Appendix V.
26. William Calvert's Case & Protest with queries thereon, NUMD, MaB 99/7.
27. Inclosure of Gedling, Stoke Bardolph and Carlton 1792–1796, Commissioners' Minutes, NA DDMI 90.
28. East Leake Inclosure, Commissioners' Minutes, NA DD SD 1/2.
29. John Chapman, 'Some Problems in the Interpretation of Enclosure Awards', *Ag. Hist. Rev.*28, 1980, p.109, 'Pre-enclosure maps ... are occasionally attached to the awards, but this does not seem to have been a very common practice.'
30. Eckington Survey Accounts 1795–1801, Sheffield Archives, Fairbank's Collection, MB 192.
31. Bendall, 1992, p.138.
32. Nottinghamshire, surveyed in 1774, published in 1776, by John Chapman.
33. East Leake Inclosure Commissioners' Minutes, 23–25/9/1799. The commissioners urged that the roads be completed in the spring of the following year for certification at the mid-summer sessions.
34. Crofts, 1989, p.31.
35. R.L. Sherlock, of British Geological Survey, in his survey of 1907 described this location as being 17 feet of loamy clay with pebbles overlying shale and blue-grey clay with thin sandy fossiliferous shale, some fragments of flaggy limestone.'
36. For the history of Manor House Farm see Hammond, 1997.
37. This plot is adjacent to the boundary between Keyworth and the township of Normanton-on-the-Wolds. Inspection of the 1798 Land Tax returns revealed that a John Bell owned land in that township so it may be that the 1½ acres allotted to him in Keyworth were adjacent to his holdings in Normanton-on-the-Wolds.
38. See J.V. Beckett, B. Cowell & M.E. Turner, 'Parliamentary enclosure hedges and landscape preservation', *The Local Historian,* February 1999, which appeared just before this publication went to press.
39. Marshall, 1790, Vol.I, pp.87–88; Vol.II, p.295.
40. Lowe, 1796.
41. Burns, 1771, p.88.

Chapter 8

Counting the Cost

We have seen that, from time to time during the process of allotment, the Commissioners levied a rate on the proprietors to cover costs incurred or anticipated. But these did not represent the total cost of inclosure. Here we examine the totality of the costs involved and note that proprietors not only had to pay their share of the expenses of the redistribution of parish land, but pay for the fencing of their own property. Thus we recognise two categories of cost. First, what we might call the Communal cost attributable to the work of the Commissioners and paid by the proprietors in proportion to the value of their holding. Second, the Individual cost incurred by each proprietor in respect of his own property. In the absence of any similar Keyworth material we will use the extant documents — minutes and accounts — relating to the contemporary inclosure of East Leake to provide data to assess both categories of cost and apply the findings to the inclosures of Keyworth.[1]

Communal Costs

From entries in the East Leake Minute Book we see that three rates were levied between October 1798 and December 1800 to raise a total of £4379. Of this sum, £649 8s 6d was allowed for the fencing of the Rector's allotment and £1602 for making the roads. The solicitors' bill amounted to £995 15s 8d. Thus these three items represented three-quarters of the communal cost.

There were certain unavoidable expenses attached to the Parliamentary process and the preparation of the Award. The former we can extract from the detailed accounts of the solicitors, John Harrison and John Blunt (see Table 4). The total, £480, is close to the average cost implied by figures quoted by The President of the Board of Agriculture, Sir John Sinclair, in 1796. In seeking leave to bring in a Bill for the inclosure of waste lands, he remarked, 'There had already passed in all 1900 Private Bills, the expense of which had been at least £800,000.' i.e., an average cost per Bill of £420.[2]

The completion of a parliamentary inclosure was signified by the Award which, with a few exceptions already noted, was an integral part of the process. These costs from John Harrison's accounts are shown in Table 5.

Table 4 Cost of obtaining the Act for the Inclosure of East Leake

	£	s	d
Drawing & Engrossing Petition		13	4
Paid for Parchment		2	6
Making Fair Copy of Bill to send to Messrs White for the Printer	4	0	0
Messrs White's Bill of Fees for passing the Act	284	0	0
Journey to London to solicit & attend passing of the Act of Parliament 28 days at £2:12:6/day & expenses	147	0	0
His Clerk 28 days at £1:11:6	44	2	0
Making a total of	479	17	10

Table 5 Cost of preparation of the Award for the Inclosure of East Leake

	£	s	d
Drawing the Award Fol 650	32	10	0
Fair copy of Award as settled	10	16	0
Ingrossing the Award	21	13	4
Parchment & Duty	45	16	0
Making a total of	110	15	4

Thus the indispensable expenses, or fixed costs, associated with the requirements of the legislators was approximately £590, about 60% of Harrison's bill of £996 (see table 6 on p.130). His other costs were incurred in responding to the decisions of the Commissioners, e.g., variable administrative costs such as arranging the printing and posting of notices and securing the agreement or signatures of proprietors.

To account for the quarter of the total bill for which no detail is available requires a number of assumptions. From the minutes of the commissioners' meetings it appears that their official deliberations occupied some 66 days. Each commissioner would receive a fee of two guineas a day plus expenses of, say, half a guinea. There were five commissioners in this case, hence the total cost would amount to 825 guineas, or £866. The cost of the survey and making of the map to accompany the Award would approximate to £74. A further cost which one might have expected to be included in expenses is shown separately in Harrison's accounts and also those of William Fairbank for his part in the inclosure of

Eckington. It was for horse hire, the eighteenth century equivalent to modern day 'travelling expenses'. Harrison claimed 4s a day.[3] It seems reasonable to assume that the East Leake Commissioners would submit similar claims, which, therefore, could amount in total to £66.

In summary the communal costs incurred in the inclosure of East Leake were as shown in table 6.

Within this data, which we can use to estimate the cost of the Keyworth inclosure, are two kinds of cost: the fixed costs largely independent of the parish to be inclosed, and variable costs which are dependent on both the number of proprietors and the size of the parish. Clearly where there were few proprietors, the expenses would be reduced, but with larger numbers negotiations could become more complicated necessitating more of the solicitor's and commissioners' time. Common sense suggests that the increased costs would be more than proportional to the number of persons involved, but it is by no means clear what the relationship might be. At the risk of overstating these costs for Keyworth (where there were fewer proprietors than at East Leake) we have ignored this complication. To some degree the errors of this approach may be offset by our ignorance of the costs associated with the negotiations surrounding the tithe allotments. The commutation of tithes was always a contentious issue and the existence of five tithe holders in Keyworth must have increased the cost of negotiation. (The curious fractions used to compute the allotments in lieu of tithes in Keyworth may hint at some hard bargaining.[4]) On this basis the solicitor's cost for Keyworth's inclosure are estimated as £590 (fixed cost) plus £255 (variable cost). The same simple approach suggests that the Keyworth commissioners were occupied for 41 days for which each of the three commissioners would receive £2 12s 6d in fees and expenses per day; a total of £323. John Bailey's fees and expenses for attending the commissioners would be £1 11s 6d per day; assuming that he attended every meeting, this would amount to £65.

The costs of ring-fencing the tithe holders' allotments and the construction of roads (to which the tithe holders made no contribution) have been computed from the East Leake costs and the lengths of the fences and roads in the two parishes (derived from the appropriate OS six-inch map). They amounted to £540 and £1100 respectively. Finally, travelling expenses have been assessed on the basis of 4s per day for each commissioner and the surveyor. We thus arrive at the summary shown in Table 6.

The higher cost per acre compared with that of East Leake suggests that the total cost of £2940 may be an overestimate and that the inclosure of Keyworth required less commissioner time than has been assumed.

The average cost for a proprietor of £92 obscures the widely differing amounts to be met by individual landowners, who were charged on the basis of their land tax. Thus the cost to individual landowners could vary from £12 for Job Eggleston's three and a half acres to £385 for the Samuel Smith's 131 acres.[5]

Table 6 **Comparison of Inclosure Costs for East Leake (actual) and Keyworth (estimated)**

	East Leake (actual) £	Keyworth (estimated) £
Solicitor's work, fixed	590	590
variable	406	255
Fencing	650	540
Roads	1602	1100
Survey	74	35
Fees and expenses	932	420
Unaccounted for	125	
Total	4379	2940
Cost per acre	35s	42s

Individual costs

The additional cost to individual proprietors was that of fencing their allotments. While the communal expenses were shared in an equitable manner between proprietors, this was by no means the case when fencing their own land. In broad terms, value was equivalent to area; but fencing costs relate to the boundary of that area and not to the area itself. The effect of this is shown as follows: Let us suppose we have a square field the sides of which are two units long: its area is four square units. Compare this with another field with sides four units long: its area is 16 square units. The length of fencing required is twice as much for the larger field, but the cost per unit area is only half that for the smaller.

Perimeter of field
Area of field

i.e., for the smaller field 8/4=2 and for the larger field 16/16=1

Thus the costs per acre for the smaller proprietor were higher than for his more affluent neighbours. For all proprietors fencing would be relatively more or less expensive depending upon the number and shape of their allotments.

But what exactly did the proprietor have to do, and what were the costs? The surveyor had staked out the property boundaries and in general the owner was required to dig a ditch and plant a quickset hedge four feet from the staked boundary.

Figure 20 **Equivalent 1998 values of the pound 1760–1850**

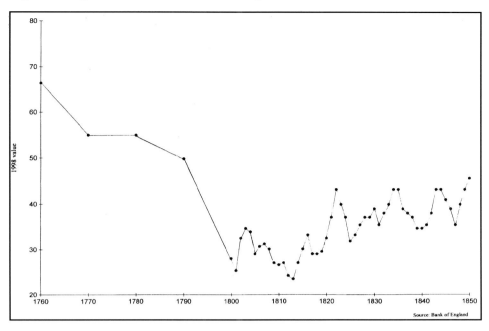

William Sanday produced detailed accounts for the inclosure of Charles Pierrepont's estates in Cotgrave which show the variety of costs which had to be met by proprietors in South Nottinghamshire at this time.[6] Trees had to be felled, the timber cut to size, rails shaped and the posts mortised. The post and rails then had to be transported to the staked-out inclosures, hawthorn plants purchased and labour paid for planting, ditching and fencing. Gates were needed to secure access to the new inclosures. These were constructed from heavier timber; particularly the posts which were often 'rived' out of oaks growing in the hedges of the old inclosures, gunpowder sometimes being a necessary agent in the process.[7] All the gates needed iron hinges and fastenings. Overall the inclosure of a parish required large amounts of timber, considerable labour, a variety of skills and substantial sums of money. It took Pierrepont several years to fence his Cotgrave estate, during which time he bought over half a million hawthorn plants and spent £2900. A substantial proportion of this cost was for the acquisition and preparation of fencing materials, viz. £1300.

The cost of fencing reported by different authors varies from as low as 8d per yard to as high as 19¾d (see Appendix IX). These various figures cannot be directly compared. Not only is it uncertain as to the exact nature of the combination of hedge, fence and ditch the costs refer to, but inflation, which was rampant at the turn of the eighteenth century, cannot be ignored. (See graph, Figure 20.) Fortunately, we have available the cost for fencing the Rector's allotment in East Leake which we can apply to the tithe holders' allotments in Keyworth. By transferring the boundaries of the rector's allotment from the award map to an

Figure 21 **Keyworth Proprietors' Fencing Costs**

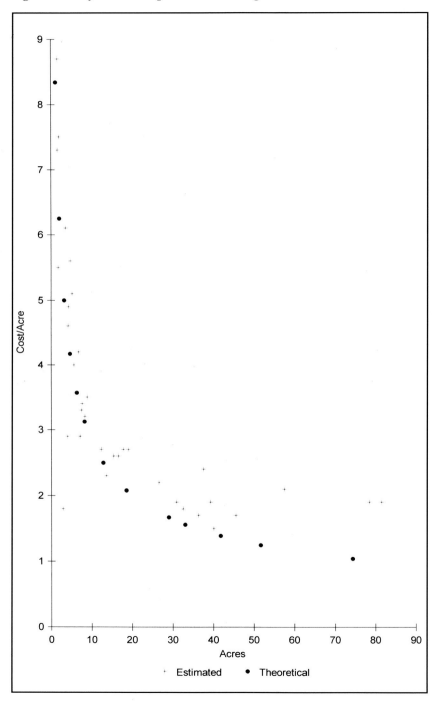

OS six-inch map and measuring their length we can derive a cost per yard (15½d) which can be used by a similar procedure to compute the cost of fencing the Keyworth tithe holders' allotments. The proprietors' fencing costs would be somewhat lower for, as we have shown in Chapter 5, their fencing and ditching requirements were to a different, imprecise, but simpler specification. In the light of these uncertainties we may either, arbitrarily reduce the figure of 15½d by say 2d, or recognise that its use will result in an overstatement of these costs. We have used the latter approach in computing the data shown in Appendix X and illustrated in Figure 21. From these we see how the smaller proprietor had to bear a disproportionate cost in physically inclosing their new holdings. Thus while it cost Job Eggleston £22 to fence his three and half acre holding and Samuel Smith £207 for his 131 acres, these costs represented £6 2s and £1 12s per acre respectively.

Notes

1. Commissioners' Minutes NA DD SD 1/1, Solicitors' accounts NA DD SD 1/2.
2. Quoted from the report of the debate published in *The Nottingham Journal*, 6th February 1796.
3. William Fairbank, working out of Sheffield, charged only 2s 6d!
4. See p.121.
5. These figures have been calculated by applying the appropriate percentage of the Land Tax to the estimated total communal cost. See Appendix XII.
6. NUMD; MaB16/111, and MaB16/66/1.
7. NUMD; MaB 16/101/2. Richard Tugman's Bill for felling 34 rough hedgerow oak trees for gateposts for the Cotgrave inclosure included an item for 6lbs of gunpowder at 1s 6d per pound 'for the use of getting the trees in pieces'. 'Riving' was the term used for this dismemberment.

Figure 22 The major property boundaries created under the Inclosure Act, 1798, superimposed on a 20th century OS 6" map of Keyworth (reduced).

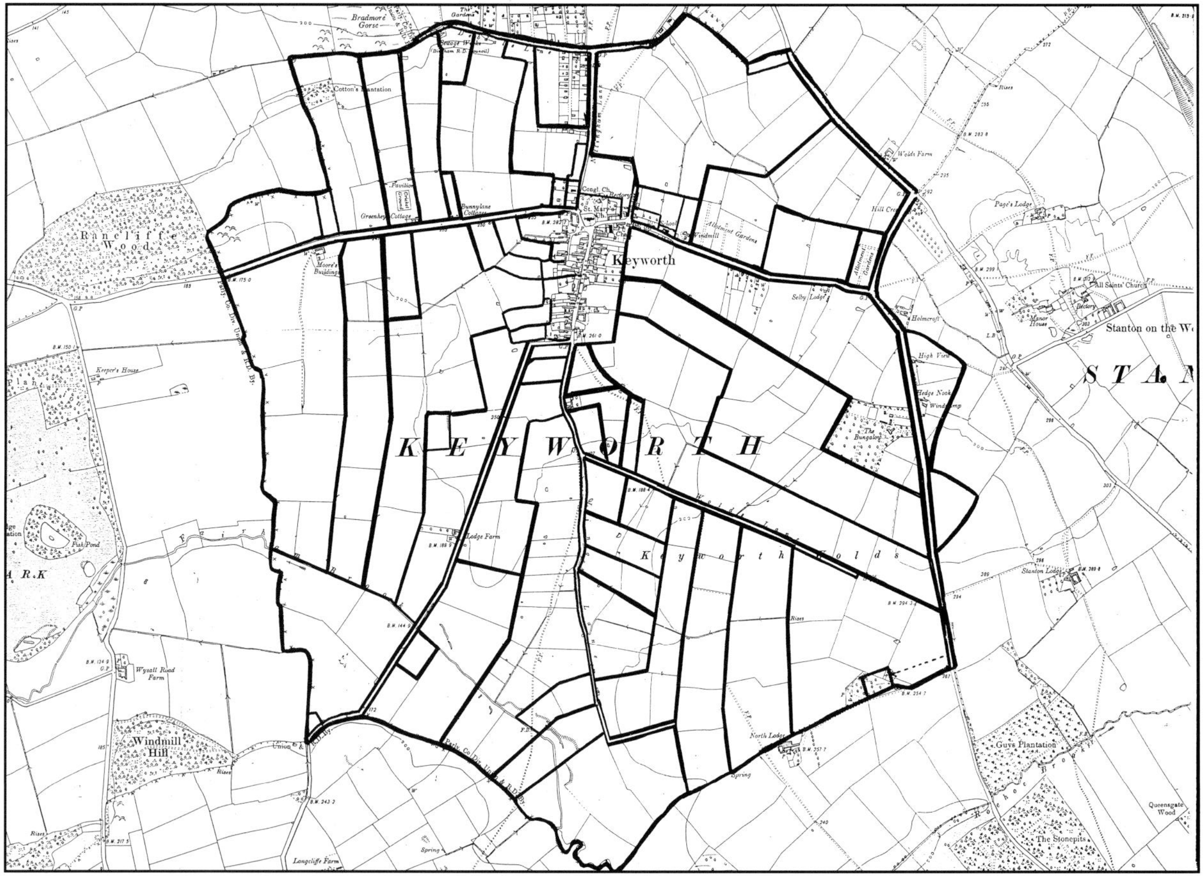

PART III: A VILLAGE TRANSFORMED

Chapter 9

The New Keyworth

It is tempting, from our late twentieth century viewpoint, to assume that the inclosure award in Keyworth signalled a sudden and far-reaching revolution in the life of the parish. That the award drastically altered the pattern of land ownership and eventually of land use is true, but it was the natural consequence of developments that had been taking place both nationally and locally for many decades, even centuries. 1798–9 was the point at which Keyworth came into line with what was going on elsewhere. We also need to remember that there were here, as in every village society at the time, sections of the community whose work was not directly or immediately affected by these changes — such people were those engaged in rural support services, such as blacksmiths, makers of agricultural implements, traders such as bakers, butchers, shoemakers, tailors and so on. Although Parliamentary inclosures were in their way revolutionary for each individual parish, similar events were commonplace and part of an apparently inevitable economic trend moving steadily across the countryside.

Apart from the visible hedges and ditches marking the new boundaries of fields, the evidence for the direct effects of inclosure on the parish of Keyworth is scant, and surmises have had to be made based on the experience of other parishes in the locality and in the East Midlands as a whole. There were other tendencies going on at the same time — the spread of industry to rural villages for example — and it is difficult to say to what extent such developments would have taken place in any case in a given parish. At least it would seem that in many respects 'closed'[1] parishes such as Bunny and Tollerton retained their former rural characteristics longer than many others. Keyworth, being a parish with no resident lord of the manor to preside over village affairs, was relatively more open to outside interests and developments. It is perhaps useful to start by imagining a return to the village after the inclosure award had had time to take effect, and comparing it with the description we have already read.

If we were to return to the viewpoint described in Chapter 2 and survey the village from the church tower again about a generation after the inclosure award, we might see what changes had taken place. The village street and buildings would not have greatly changed. Looking south along Town Street, the same muddy lane would be visible, possibly slightly improved as a result of that part of the inclosure award which allocated sites to the parish for the extraction of stone, sand and gravel for the maintenance of the local roads.

The rebuilding of houses, especially farmhouses, resulting from the increased prosperity of the farming community would have begun, but as we are not sure of the dates of building of many of the houses in Town Street, we cannot picture this in detail. Certainly some framework knitters' workshops would have appeared, sometimes separate from the houses, sometimes attached to them, typified by their long windows.[2] On the other three sides, looking from the church tower, the buildings would be similar to those of our previous picture: the Manor Farm house, the Independent chapel, and the only building to be added in this area, as far as we know, for some years after inclosure, the Primitive Methodist chapel of 1828, now converted to a house (no.12 Elm Avenue). There may have been one or two other cottages, since we know that some on Selby Lane and Old Lane (Elm Avenue) appeared at some time between 1801 and 1840.

But if we looked beyond the village cluster we would find an almost total change in the appearance of the landscape. No longer would there be wide open fields divided into strips, but a patchwork of smaller fields separated by quickset hedges, rails and/or ditches. The hedges would be grown to maturity and neatly laid to ensure that stock could not wander from one field to the next. The present-day pattern of medium-sized hedged fields, typical of a large part of the English countryside, would have come into existence. Some of these fields would still be under crops, and some would have been turned into pasture, which was probably more profitable on heavy clay land such as that of Keyworth parish. In winter, on the pasture lands especially, it would have been possible still to trace the outlines of the old strips, in the form of ridge and furrow, but over years ploughing gradually eliminates most such markings. Even today (1999) however, some such traces still survive in the parish, notably on the Rectory Field and on the hillside north-west of Wysall Lane; these examples may well indicate that here we have areas which have rarely or never been under the plough since 1799.

We have no direct evidence about the actual use of land in the parish in the years following inclosure, but there are indirect indications. The old post-mill was replaced in 1820 by a brick-built tower-mill on Selby Lane, suggesting that the miller's business was in good shape[3]. Enough grain crops must have been grown locally to maintain this development. This was very understandable during the Napoleonic wars, when corn prices were high and corn-growing was profitable, but the date quoted seems to indicate that the miller's business remained good even afterwards, when prices fell. On the other hand, this was the time of improvements in stockbreeding and animal husbandry, thus encouraging the use of land for pasture. (Robert Bakewell, who had been a leader in this field, had farmed in the East Midlands at Dishley, near Loughborough.) The relatively large fields and holdings that were more consolidated than formerly, together with the post-inclosure freedom on the part of farmers to arrange their own systems of crop rotation, may have meant that there was more mixed farming. Farmers could respond more quickly than before to the fluctuations in market demand for crops, not only of the traditional kinds, but those gradually being introduced as a result of the agricultural revolution in the country as a whole.

Partly out of sight from the church tower, the roads leading out of the village would be seen to follow traditional trackways, but to have been fenced and to some extent maintained in accordance with the stipulations of the award (the exceptions being the roads to Wysall and Widmerpool, which had been re-aligned). One characteristic of many East Midland parishes, which is largely absent from Keyworth, is the scattering of isolated farmhouses away from the village centre. The lands allotted to farmers in Keyworth tended to radiate in elongated areas from Town Street, or to include some detached lands away from the main farm. This can be clearly seen from the map outlining the individual holdings (see p.134). There was therefore no advantage in moving the whole farm establishment out into the fields, and much advantage in staying within the central area. The majority of farmhouses thus remained alongside the village street, and many are still there, even though they are no longer used as farmers' residences. Six such houses are shown on Neville Parker's pictorial drawing of Keyworth at the turn of the twentieth century, together with Manor Farm opposite the Parish Church: others exist outside the range of this drawing. (Oldham's Farm, also shown, is of a later date.)[4]

The land holdings after inclosure[5]

This brings us to a discussion of the greatest immediate change resulting from the inclosure award. Chapter 7 explains the reorganisation in ownership and occupation of the individual farms. Of these the most considerable was the increase in allocation to the rector, in lieu of tithes, a total of 116 acres (added to his 89 acres of glebe). A further 122 acres went to four other former tithe holders. It does seem, however, that in general the land was being worked by the same people as before. A comparison of the land tax returns for 1797 (just before inclosure) and 1802 (soon after inclosure) shows very few changes of ownership, apart from the increase allocated to the rector, by now the Rev. Mr. Beetham. 29 of the 37 properties are held by owners who held similar areas or at least paid similar amounts of tax before inclosure: the majority of these are either worked by the owners or tenanted by the same persons in 1802 as in 1797. By 1802 the rector had twelve tenants, as opposed to two in 1797, and nine of these appear as owners or tenants on both the 1797 and 1802 returns. Some of these tenants had evidently taken the opportunity to increase their holdings over those they held formerly. As the land tax returns for 1797 and 1802 show a largely identical list of amounts, apart from the lands held by Sir Thomas Parkyns, the Lord of the Manor, and the rector, it would appear that the increase in lands held by the rector and Sir Thomas is accounted for by the inclosure of hitherto unoccupied land. This is not to say that the Parkyns family simply appropriated to themselves the common lands, but that these lands were put into the 'pool' to be divided up by the commissioners. Two of the 'new' names among the rector's tenants (John Pike and William Murden) appear to belong to Keyworth families still known today in the village: the third 'new' name is Elizabeth Burrows, the widow of John Burrows who already figured in the returns.

Other changes from 1797 to 1802 are few. Henry Hebb increased the land he owned, and was farming it entirely as owner-occupier in 1802: his tenant of 1797 now rented land from the rector. One or two other changes of tenancy also took place in these years.

Although the total land tax levied in the parish in 1802 is less than that of 1797, the difference is exactly accounted for by the three proprietors who by 1802 are recorded as having redeemed their liability.

The overall impression is that through the award the smaller owners received allocations of land comparable to those that they held previously; tenants had broadly similar holdings as well.

The land tax returns for the following years likewise show little change: by 1810 for instance there are a few new names, but the same people or, in some cases, their relatives or descendants are farming the same amounts of land in the parish. By 1810 two more proprietors have redeemed their liability, and once again this accounts exactly for the reduction in total tax for the parish in that year. In this respect then the farming life of Keyworth continued as before for some years after inclosure. The difference would have been that those who owned or worked the land no longer had their land scattered in many parcels throughout the parish, and they had more discretion in the use of the land than previously, now that they were free from the binding decisions of the manorial court or vestry meeting.

Even in 1820, twenty years after the inclosure award, only the same slow change is apparent. The Parkyns family had reached higher rank, as Sir Thomas had been succeeded by his grandson Lord Rancliffe,[6] but the land tax on his property is virtually unchanged. Henry Hebb had again increased his holding, and it appears that he, along with the Belshaw, Eggleston and Shepperson families, were the leading farmers of the parish, the two latter having several members among the owners and tenants of lands. The same person may have owned and farmed his own land, rented some land from others, and let land to others.

The land tax returns end in 1832, so it is possible to follow the fortunes of landowners and tenant farmers for a further decade. But even then change is slow. After 31 years, seven owners or occupiers were still farming the same amounts of land as immediately after the inclosure. In addition, the farm owned by Richard Attenborough in 1802, and let to John Shepperson, had by 1810 passed to John Attenborough (probably the son of Richard), who was farming it himself, unlike Richard, who appears to have been an absentee landlord.[8] John Attenborough was still in occupation in 1820, but by 1830 the same land was being farmed by Mary Attenborough (probably John's widow). William Belshaw, though apparently never a landowner, had the largest holding in the parish, that owned by Samuel Smith, as well as two others. These latter two had passed to other tenants by 1802, but Belshaw retained the largest. This holding remained in the family — by 1830 it had passed to George Belshaw. There are other cases of family continuity of this kind. The Shepperson family was much reduced by 1830: the parish register shows three deaths in that family between 1815 and

1821. The Egglestons continued, with some changes of name. The rector's holdings show some variation, and there does seem to be some flexibility here, either for other landholders to increase their holdings or for new tenants to come in. Richard Tookey, an owner-occupier at inclosure, had evidently retired from active farming by 1830, but still owned his land, and his tax rating was the same: he now let it out to a tenant. There is even some slight suggestion of 'social' betterment — one smaller owner (Thomas Metham) seems to progress in the period under discussion from plain 'Mr.' to insisting on being listed as 'Esq.'

Keyworth as an 'open' village[7]

Documentation on Keyworth, other than the land tax returns, for the period from inclosure in 1799 to the 1841 census is scanty. Perhaps the lack of sources is some indication that village life here was relatively undisturbed. Keyworth in the eighteenth century had been an 'open' village, where a fairly large number of farmers shared the land, either as owner-occupiers or as tenants. In 1780 there were 37 occupiers of farmland in the parish, among whom were 15 owners and 23 tenants. There was some overlap: some owners of small holdings also rented land from other larger owners: a few let all their property to others. In 1832 there were 38 holdings, of which 18 were owner-occupied and the rest let to 26 tenants. These figures would suggest that apart from the redistribution and consolidation of the original strips of the medieval fields, and the increase in land available for farming due to the inclosure of commons etc., the social pattern of the village had been relatively little affected by the change. E.P. Thompson's description of the inclosures as 'a plain enough case of class robbery' is hardly an apt comment on the situation here. When one adds the fact that the same names appear to a large extent in the land tax returns before inclosure and as late as 1830, with scarcely more changes than might reasonably be due to changes in the generations in families, this picture is reinforced. A small number of names are reduced in importance or disappear: a few new ones appear. The rector in particular seems to have distributed his new enlarged holdings among a dozen or more tenants: Keyworth seems to show, at least in the early post-inclosure years, a social picture of an 'open' village community not unlike the previous one.

Some of the holdings, both before and after inclosure, appear from the land tax returns to be very small, suggesting that occupiers of these holdings must have had some other means of support, or been in a position to expand their land. For example, Thomas Disney rented a holding worth 1s 8d per annum in 1797: after inclosure he added almost three times this to his farm by renting from the rector. Joseph Disney (brother of Thomas) rented twice as much as Thomas from the rector after inclosure: he was still doing so in 1820, but had disappeared by 1830. On the other hand, Mary Green held an allotment worth 1s 0d annually in 1797, as owner-occupier, and still held it as owner occupier in 1830, while Samuel Holmes, owner-occupier of a holding taxed at 9s 8d per annum in 1797 found his tax liability, for whatever reason (it could have been illness, age or disaster), reduced to 1s 8d per annum in both 1820 and 1830 There seem to have been some gainers as well as losers in the reallocation of land. There may well have been no sharp division in Keyworth between land owners or holders and the waged labourers, rather a gradation from one end of the scale to the other.

A summary of the proportions of land ownership and occupation in Keyworth over the period 1787–1897 is given in Table 7 (p.149), and illustrates the continuity of land holdings over a long time. The columns indicate the number of properties of differing sizes, from those large enough to amount to more than 10% of the total land area of the parish under occupation, to those covering less than 2%. A distinction is made between lands owned and lands occupied, but there would be some overlap between these categories, as some farmers owned land, yet rented further land from other owners, while some occupied more than one holding. The interesting point, however, is the small extent of change in patterns of land ownership and occupation over the whole century.

The agricultural labourers

What this apparent continuity disguises, however, is the fate of the labourers who had no allocation of land in the inclosure award, were not even small farmers in their own right, and depended on work available from those who cultivated the land. About half the householders in the 1801 census had no landholdings, either as owners or tenants. Hard evidence of what became of such persons in Keyworth in the early years after inclosure seems to be nonexistent: we can only surmise from the general picture of conditions in the East Midlands and indirectly from what we know of developments in village life through the early nineteenth century. There are census figures for 1831, 32 years after the inclosure was implemented, which show that 37 males over the age of 20 were then employed as agricultural labourers in Keyworth, presumably by the 10 out of 28 occupiers of land who employed others than their own families on their farms. Some of these could possibly have been employed in other neighbouring parishes.

The biggest change for these people was the extinguishing of customary common rights. Under the old manorial system, there was a considerable area in each parish of land for grazing, where each parishioner had the right to graze one or more cows, allow his pigs to run, and collect food and firewood. Inclosure resulted in elimination of all such common lands, and the disappearance of the accompanying rights. In many parishes this led to considerable impoverishment of the lowest social classes. In Keyworth the Inclosure Award did include 4 acres for the poor of the parish, which were later rented out in the form of allotments, and the resulting income used for charitable relief in the parish. (A part of these 4 acres still remains as the Charity Allotments at the corner of Selby Lane and Willowbrook.) But this can only have been a minimal exchange for the open pasture and rough grazing land which had existed previously. No land, in the form of copses or coverts, was designated as woodland in Keyworth parish, as happened elsewhere.[8]

The employed farm labourer had to move from an economy in which the family was to a considerable extent self-sufficient — a family with a small holding and the right to keep a cow or two, a few sheep and a pig on common land could survive, if not reach a very high standard of living. Some of the smaller farmers also relied on such rights to supplement their living. In many cases such an existence was no longer possible. It is true that many families still had a vegetable garden with fruit trees and space to keep a pig right through the nineteenth century. Inevitably, however, the labourer was drawn further than previously into a money economy, where many things formerly supplied from his own and his family's work had to be bought from the wages he could earn by working for those who now farmed the land. There were considerable fluctuations in wage rates and in prices. The years immediately after inclosure were years when prices, and therefore farmers' incomes, were relatively high due to the Napoleonic Wars. After 1815, however, agricultural prosperity slumped, farmers fell on harder times, the value of labourers' wages often dropped, since rising population, troops returning from the war, and in many places the completion of post-inclosure work brought a surplus of labour. This may not have applied to Keyworth, as framework knitting and employment opportunities in nearby industrial towns could have absorbed the surplus. But over much of rural England there was a deterioration in the standard of living of workers of all kinds. The resulting elimination of smallholders and concentration of land in the hands of a few larger farmers seems not, however, to have been immediately the case in Keyworth.

In many places there were difficulties for labourers due to the working of the Poor Law. Farmers tended to employ men from other parishes, so as to avoid using persons who might become a liability for their own parish. Such men would have to walk perhaps a few miles to their work each day, and return home at night: but they would not be encouraged to settle near their work, since in the event of unemployment they might then be the responsibility of the parish in which they worked. This could lead to difficulty in obtaining work in one's own parish.

Where a man was working in a parish not his own, a statement had to be drawn up declaring that in the event of his becoming unemployed, any poor law relief for him and his family was the responsibility of the parish from which he came originally. A fair number of such statements involving Keyworth parish survive from the eighteenth century, a number tending to rise as the century progressed.[9] This shows that prior to inclosure some migration from parish to parish did take place, in spite of the reluctance of parishes who feared having to support 'incomers' on the poor rate. A change in the law in 1795, however, meant that such statements were henceforth to be made only in cases where the need arose, and not in every case: after this the number of statements dwindled to a very low figure. Migratory labour no doubt continued, even increased, but became a hidden statistic.

Employment was also affected by the new freedom of landowners to change agricultural practices. With freedom from the restraints of the manorial courts (see p.52), farmers could respond much more quickly than previously to changes in the market, and to new procedures in farming practice. In many East Midland parishes there was an increase in pasture and stock-raising as opposed to arable farming. These were the times of the improvements in animal husbandry introduced by such men as Robert Bakewell. There is evidence in many areas of the Midlands of the conversion of arable land to pasture: where there is clearly marked ridge and furrow in the fields, this often means that the land has rarely or never been cultivated since inclosure. Livestock raising was less labour-intensive than crop growing, thus contributing to unemployment. The clay lands of Keyworth, making heavy work for arable farming, could well have encouraged a move to the raising of animals. Temporarily there would have been an increase in employment for labourers in the planting of the new quickset hedge-rows, ditch digging and road construction, but the long-term outlook for employment may have been poor.

Framework Knitting

The above remarks are, however, based largely on what we know of conditions across the East Midlands: it is difficult to form any clear idea of the situation locally. We can be clearer about another development in the lot of waged families, the introduction of the framework knitting industry. This form of cottage industry, whereby an individual could hire or own a framework knitting machine, and receive yarn from a bag hosier travelling the countryside in order to make it up into cloth for resale when the bag hosier reappeared, was already widespread in the district in 1800 — indeed the machine had been an East Midlands invention. It probably made its first appearance in Keyworth during the eighteenth century, possibly as early as the 1730s (see p.45 footnote), but after 1800 there was very considerable growth. The 1831 census records 36 males over the age of 20 as being employed in the knitting industry — the largest total of the villages immediately surrounding Keyworth apart from Ruddington, where this form of industrialisation had taken very deep root. By 1841 there were 49 persons listed in the census returns as framework knitters, together with four apprentices and one journeyman. There is a contrast here with other villages in the neighbourhood, which remained much closer to the old style of farming community. Only one man was so recorded in the parishes of Plumtree, Normanton, Stanton, Widmerpool and Wysall combined. The industry never reached factory proportions in Keyworth as it did in some other villages and towns in the area (though there was later one such enterprise — Messrs. Pike and Gunn). Figure 23 shows clearly the contrast in this respect between Ruddington, Keyworth and Plumtree/Normanton.

The life of a framework knitter was by no means easy. The bag hosiers who provided the goods for working and who bought back the completed material were often hard taskmasters, keeping payments to knitters low. Many knitters were too poor to obtain and own their frames: these were rented, thus making

Figure 23 **Occupations of males aged 20 and over in 1831 for three parishes**

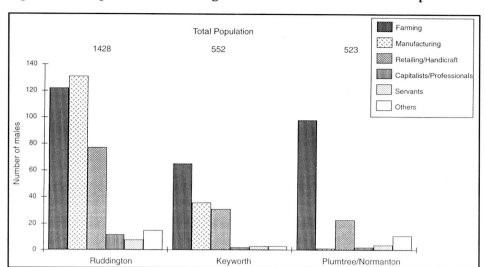

the workers even more obligated to the hosiers or to others. Long hours of work at the frames were necessary to make any kind of profit: often whole families had to be involved, with the husband working the machines and the wives and maybe children employed as well in winding thread or 'sewing up'. According to the House of Commons Journals of the late eighteenth century, quoted by J. D. Chambers, the wealthy Nottingham hosier called Need declared that a man, his wife and two or three children, working twelve hours a day, could earn up to 20s a week, but evidence from the operatives themselves denied this reckoning vehemently[10]. A much lower income than this seems to have been the norm. We can assume, however, that framework knitting provided an alternative to starvation, migration or dependence on the parish: Keyworth's population grew at the rate of the national average, whereas in many rural communities it remained static or fell. This is exemplified in Figure 24.

Some rather circumstantial evidence concerning the labouring class and/or the framework knitters in Keyworth is to be found in the baptismal register of the Primitive Methodist Chapel, which runs from 1834 onwards.[11] Unfortunately this is the only consistent record of this chapel which survives from the early days, and is admittedly for a period sometime after inclosure. The original Methodist movement under John Wesley does not seem to have touched Keyworth, although a chapel was opened at Normanton-on-the-Wolds in 1797 and there are isolated records of the movement's preaching in Keyworth about 1804 and again in 1809. Perhaps this is because non-conformity was already well established in Keyworth, in the shape of the Independent congregation which appears in records as early as 1704 and had had a place of worship in the village since at least 1768. This congregation seems also to have had quite strong connections with the community of farmers, who were probably the class to whom

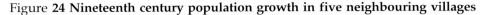

Figure **24 Nineteenth century population growth in five neighbouring villages**

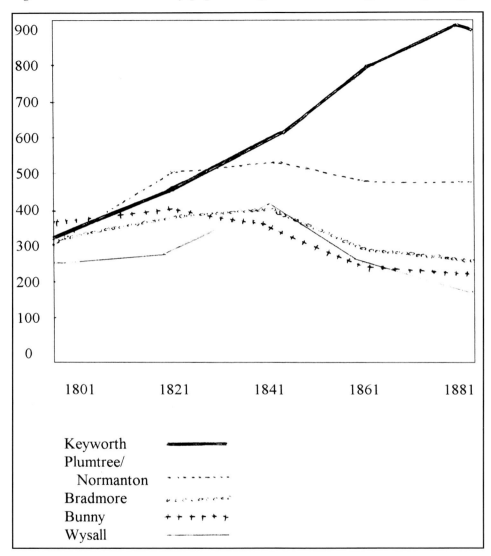

Keyworth	━━━━━━
Plumtree/	
Normanton	▪ ▪ ▪ ▪ ▪ ▪ ▪ ▪
Bradmore	╌ ╌ ╌ ╌ ╌
Bunny	✦ ✦ ✦ ✦ ✦ ✦
Wysall	───────

'Wesleyan' Methodism would have appealed (its strength lay in the artisans and owners of small businesses in the towns). On the other hand it may simply be that the Methodists failed to reach Keyworth earlier because the village lies off the main roads. What is certain, however, is that the Primitive Methodist mission in Keyworth, dating from 1818–21, flourished, leading to the opening of a chapel in 1828. The baptismal register, beginning from 1834, shows that this denomination was composed almost exclusively of labourers and framework knitters — that is, those who by now were more or less exclusively dependent on wage earning for their living. William Eggleston, a tenant farmer with a moderately sized holding of land, and one of the Parish Overseers of the Poor in the 1820s, was one of the few exceptions[12].

It might also be relevant that the Primitive Methodist movement was a recent revival of Methodist-style evangelical religion, which had only begun in 1807. By 1800 Methodism was becoming more associated with manufacturing leaders in its strongholds such as Yorkshire and Lancashire, and retained much of Wesley's autocratic style of organisation. Primitive Methodism, however, instigated by some dissatisfied breakaways in the Potteries, was more democratic in outlook, and indeed appealed nationally to such impoverished groups as the miners of Durham and the agricultural labourers of the Midlands, many of whom had remained outside the earlier evangelical movements. The inclosure settlement in Keyworth may have indirectly contributed to the threefold division of religious loyalties (Church, Independents and 'Prims') which seems to have had a basis in social strata in the village, and which seems to have lasted as long as Keyworth remained a relatively isolated rural community.

Apprenticeships formed another possible means of finding an occupation. Indentures exist for Richard Pyke to be apprenticed to a knitter in Bradmore in 1795, and Samuel Chadwick to one in Ruddington in 1801, though we do not know whether they were paupers. Richard Pyke was only a child (7 years of age).[13] Whether these are isolated cases or just two among many we do not know. It may be that support for Keyworth's unemployed was already working well, perhaps even generously for the period.

The parish baptismal registers[14] and churchwardens' account book[15] for this period also provide some insight into conditions among such people. Between 1813 and 1822 fifteen fathers are recorded as framework knitters. Only one of these — a John Pike (there were three framework knitters of that name in the list) appears in the land tax return (for 1820) as a tenant of the rector. There are also a William Pike and a Robert Pike in that register, who do not appear in the land tax return, and two others who share a surname with holders of land and are therefore probably closely related to them. More interestingly, the churchwardens record the names of seven bricklayers engaged in building the churchyard wall between 1820 and 1825. Three of these names do not occur elsewhere in the records we have. Robert Pike (already mentioned as a framework knitter) is included. The other three, Thomas Disney, Henry Price, and John White were all small landowners at this time, and also rented extra land from the rector (assuming that these are the same people as those listed in the land tax returns). The distinction between labourers and small farmers would seem not to have been absolute: some members of the community could and did turn their hands to a variety of means of livelihood. Perhaps there was pressure from the rector on his tenants to help with maintenance work on the church.

Though new industry provided a living for some of the labouring poor, there would have been others whose support fell upon the parish and its poor rate. Unfortunately the Parish Overseer's accounts for Keyworth have not survived, so no details are available: evidence from elsewhere suggests that often the overseer's job was a thankless one. An obituary survives for William Eggleston (mentioned above) in which he is recorded as having often spoken of his problems in this office.[16] In many cases the parish hired out paupers to farmers and, if necessary, subsidised their wages. This developed into a nationwide system, the Speenhamland system, worked out first in Berkshire in 1795. Here in Nottinghamshire it seems that something similar was operating in Sutton Bonington as early as 1783[17], although we have no evidence about any such scheme in Keyworth. In due course, however, abuse crept into such schemes to the extent that farmers tended to set wages deliberately low in order that public funding should pay the subsidies, and the system was abandoned.

Other Sections of Keyworth Society

There was of course another section of the Keyworth community, many of whom may not have been directly concerned with the inclosure settlement, though they must have been affected indirectly. These are the various tradespeople and professional men. Once again, there is very little indication of the occupations of these people in Keyworth before the 1831 census: they probably constituted about one third of the workforce in the village. In 1831 31 males over the age of 20 were listed as being employed in retailing trades or in various kinds of rural craft. In the 1841 census seven persons were registered as shoemakers/cordwainers, five as tailors or dressmakers, five as bricklayers, seven as joiners, and three as innkeepers. In each of these categories there was one apprentice. In addition the census records the crafts of miller, bracehand, blacksmith, wheelwright and the trades of coal igler, butcher, grocer, baker, hawker and carrier. White's *Directory of Nottinghamshire* of 1832 adds surgeon and vet. The total number of apprenticeships available in Keyworth is not known; it may not have exceeded the four recorded. The cases mentioned in the preceding section show that some apprenticeships were available to Keyworth people in neighbouring villages.

Some trades had more than one representative among the village population. There may have been an element of social mixing in that some probably combined their trade with a small agricultural holding. This section of the community is likely to have been only indirectly affected by inclosure itself, though any resultant fluctuations in trade and in prosperity among the farmers would mean variation in their living standards. The period of the Napoleonic Wars was in general a period of high prices, but financial recession and even collapse could and sometimes did follow after 1815.

The relatively large number of persons in some of these occupations suggests that they served a wider area than Keyworth parish. The miller would no doubt have been a person of importance and of substance, who had been able to rebuild his mill as a brick tower — the one which survived until the 1950s.

The picture that emerges is of a village that in the early nineteenth century was still largely self-contained and self-sufficient in many ways, though with a growing industrial element dependent on outside connections. The professional people of the village were very few, and most in any case would scarcely be affected by inclosure. The rector, of course, had become a very considerable landowner. Rev. W. Beetham may have visited the village periodically in his official capacity, but after Beetham's death in 1833 until 1859 successive rectors left practically everything to curates. There was always an Independent minister in the village, but he was not a landowner or occupier of agricultural land. The Independent Chapel's allocation of land under the inclosure award was not sufficient for a farm: earlier it had probably been let to Isaac Bowley.[18] The 1841 census also mentions a nurse, a schoolmaster and a policeman.

At the other end of the scale there were a few male and female servants, both as farm and domestic workers. These would presumably live on the premises of their employers, and would change perhaps annually as a result of the hiring fairs in local towns. Thus they may not have been native Keyworth residents. This is a small group of whom we know little before the 1851 census: thereafter their place of birth and marital status is recorded. Obviously their employment situation must have often been precarious.

The overall impact on Keyworth

In Keyworth, therefore, in three respects inclosure was a sudden revolution — the radical alteration in land boundaries, giving rise to hedged fields which in future would characterise the landscape; the replacement of communal activity by individually worked farms; and the disappearance of common lands. Serious as this last was, particularly for smallholders and those without land (who were also those with the least voice in the changes), its effect was cushioned in the short term by labouring opportunities generated by inclosure itself — making hedges, fences, and ditches — and in the longer term by new forms of work, especially in the framework knitting trade.

As far as land use is concerned, some such reorganisation as inclosure was inevitable in order that new forms of agriculture and stock breeding could come in. The larger and more compact units made such improvements possible, and the greater freedom to change use of the land at short notice, which farmers received as a result of the demise of the old manorial court, meant a greater responsiveness to supply and demand. In 1809 Arthur Young said, 'The old open field system must die before new ideas become generally rooted.' The inclosure of Keyworth was a local step in a process which was rapidly covering all those regions of England where the open field system had hitherto held sway. In some places there was a tendency for small landowners to become pauperised: this does not seem to have happened to any extent here. As Table 7 on p.149 shows, the most remarkable aspect may be the general continuity of land distribution for a century after inclosure.

It has been said that inclosure was a device on the part of the landowning classes to strengthen their hold on their estates and that their motive was purely economic gain. It was said that this resulted in widespread pauperisation of the labouring underclass, and a drift to towns which contributed to the slums and deprivation of Victorian urban areas. We cannot ascertain how much impoverishment inclosure brought to Keyworth, but we do know of at least one family — that of William Pike — which was pauperised and emigrated to South Africa in 1820[19].

Parishes under the control of one owner were not always turned into efficient economic units; many landowners were not themselves farmers, but may have been content with a 'home farm', which would supply the estate's needs, but little more. In such cases the old subsistence agriculture would continue much as before, with new ideas and techniques only filtering through slowly. But there were also the 'open' villages, where the actual farming community carried much more weight. Keyworth seems to have been one of these — and was not the only one in the East Midlands.[20]

There was a loss of community spirit and a sharper differentiation of social classes. The extent of this varied from place to place. In parishes where inclosure meant the concentration of land and power in the hands of the squirearchy — Tollerton for example — there tended to be a sharp division between the landowning family on the one hand and the cottagers and labourers on the other. Locally these are often parishes where the population remained static and perhaps eventually declined. This effect may have been less evident where, as in Keyworth, an element of industrialisation came in. Keyworth seems to have become a balanced community, with some industry, but still with a strong agricultural basis. Life was still hard — the phrase 'as poor as a stockinger' seems to go back to the mid-eighteenth century. But on the whole Keyworth survived and the population grew.

It is tempting to try to understand the motives behind inclosure in Keyworth. No doubt economic considerations came first — the landowners of Keyworth could well see that greater production and therefore greater profit and prosperity were being obtained in parish after parish where inclosure had taken place. This was not a time when inclosure was still at an experimental stage: it was a tried and tested form of organisation. The Parkyns family were lords of the manor, but their lands and perhaps therefore their influence were not as great as it was in other neighbouring villages such as Bunny. Did the motivation here come as much from the members of the manorial court or vestry meeting themselves as from above, and was this therefore more of a community effort than in other places? There seems to have been no attempt to buy out owners and/or tenants to make them conform. Inclosure may have given greater security of tenure to some occupiers than previously, and certainly gave them more control over the use of their lands. Perhaps the whole enterprise was more community-centred than might be expected. The relatively great rise in population in Keyworth over the following half-century, in contrast to other neighbouring villages, suggests that Keyworth absorbed its problems of labour without much drifting away to seek work elsewhere.

The agricultural revolution, across the country, was a long drawn-out process; in Keyworth as in many other places inclosure was an important step in the evolution of modern society from its medieval past. In some respects it was a sudden break with the past; in others, change came more gradually.

Table 7 **Summary of Keyworth land ownership and occupation** based on Land Tax returns, 1787, 1797 & 1801 and Bingham Union Property Evaluations, 1897

Ownership

Percentage of total values in Keyworth	No. of properties				
	>10%	5 to 10%	2 to 5%	<2%	Total
1787	2	7	4	25	38
1797	2	7	4	21	34
1801	2	7	6	20	35
1897	4	3	5	17	29

Occupation

Percentage of total values in Keyworth	No of Farms				
	>10%	5 to 10%	2 to 5%	<2%	Total
1787	3 (0)	5 (1)	2 (2)	22 (13)	32 (14)
1797	2 (0)	7 (2)	4 (1)	19 (11)	32 (14)
1801	3 (0)	6 (2)	4 (3)	24 (8)	37 (13)
1897	2 (0)	5 (0)	7 (3)	24 (5)	40 (8)

Numbers in brackets are farms wholly or largely owner-occupied.

Before Inclosure, total acreage of privately owned or farmed land was between 900 and 1000 acres. After inclosure, after privatisation of Common Pasture, the acreage of privately owned and farmed land was about 1350 acres.

Notes

1   Historians of English agricultural practice have roughly divided parishes at this period into two categories: 'closed' parishes, dominated by a single landowner or his family, often resident and in a position to dictate on parish and agricultural matters to his tenantry, and 'open' parishes, where power rested with a larger number of landholders, and where the manorial court was not dominated by a single interest.

2   R. A. Hammond, *Keyworth: The First Millennium*, KDLHS, 1998, gives details of buildings in Main Street.

3   R. A. Hammond, 1998, p.32. The post mill was itself a replacement of an earlier one situated near what is now High View Avenue.

4   R. A. Hammond, 1998.

5   This section is based on a detailed comparison of the Land Tax returns for 1797, 1802, 1810, 1820 and 1830.

6   Beryl Cobbins, leaflet on the Parkyns family, 1987.

7   Chapter 9, endnote 1 above.

8   Chapter 7.

9   NA, Settlement Certificates and Removal Orders, PR 1926–7, 1929, 1932–4.

10 J. D. Chambers, *Nottinghamshire in the Eighteenth Century*, p.295.

11 Copy in Keyworth Public Library.

12 Keyworth Methodist Church Centenary booklet, 1981.

13 NA, Parish Apprentices 1731–1801, PR 1928.

14 Copies in Keyworth Public Library.

15 NA PR 1141.

16 Primitive Methodist Magazine, 1830, p.280.

17 J. D. Chambers, *Nottinghamshire in the Eighteenth Century*, p.243.

18 See chapter 2.

19 NA QACP 5/1/6/29.

20 G. E. Mingay, *English Landed Society in the Eighteenth Century*, chapter 6, p.169: 'A few landlords....used their home farms to try out new ideas, but probably most home farms were cultivated quite conventionally, and they were generally of less importance in the spread of improved farming than is sometimes supposed.'

Chapter 10

The Legacy

Inclosure and what preceded it have left their marks on present-day Keyworth in a number of ways. In this final chapter we briefly review, first, the legacy of the open field system, and then that of the inclosure award.

Legacy of the open fields

Perhaps the most significant legacy of the ancient open field system is the village itself. As explained in Chapter 3 (p.56), the fragmented farm holdings of pre-inclosure parishes like Keyworth gave rise to nucleated settlements — villages; while a system of more compact, inclosed farms was usually associated with dispersed settlements — hamlets and isolated farmsteads. Despite the changes that have occurred in the parish over the past two hundred years, the substantial pre-inclosure village layout, together with a few of its buildings and the stone footings of many more still survive as reminders of its open field past. The parish contains no trace of pre-inclosure buildings outside the old village.

The old streets and many of the crofts — small inclosures in which farmhouses and cottages were situated — have probably endured from at least medieval times. Parliamentary inclosure did not directly affect them. The streets are still there: The Square, Main Street and its continuation some way along Lings Lane, the village end of Selby Lane, Elm Avenue and Commercial Road; so are many of the croft boundaries, which have determined the layout of later buildings, the most obvious of which are several long rows of houses and workshops (e.g., Attenborough's Yard and Factory Yard), set at right angles to Main Street within the narrow crofts on which they were built.

Because of the scarcity of nearby quality building stone and because there were few wealthy residents to have stone brought in from a distance, most buildings in pre-inclosure Keyworth were made of mud or low-grade brick, or of cheap, unseasoned timber frames filled with wattle and daub. They therefore had a shorter life than either streets or property boundaries. The oldest building still standing is the parish church (mostly fourteenth century), made of stone. The next oldest, the timber-framed barn, is dated 1651; part of that collapsed in the nineteenth century, and the rest was only saved from a similar fate in the 1970s by £30,000 worth of repair. Other surviving pre-inclosure buildings are few: The Salutation, the brick barn and numbers 2, 3, 4, 39 and 47 Main Street, The Hall on Nottingham Road (1768) and perhaps two houses on Commercial Road. All the rest have gone, most recently Inglenook Farm, behind the timber-framed barn, in 1968; Manor Farm on The Square (demolished in 1970) and the old No. 46 Main Street, now replaced by a modern house with the same number.[1]

Outside the village, the parish was transformed by inclosure, so little of the open field landscape remains. Patches of ridge-and-furrow bear witness to former strip ploughing in fields which have not been disturbed since inclosure. Some post-inclosure fields may correspond to old furlongs — clusters of parallel strips in the open fields — and have been given the same names. Examples are Watersqualls (suggesting springs), Isabell's Arse (perhaps named after a fifteenth century rector of Keyworth, William Isabell) and the Bratlands (see Appendix III).

Unlike some parishes, Keyworth had very few closes before parliamentary inclosure. The two most easily recognised, shown as closes on the inclosure award map, are the rectory field (formerly glebe land, now the recreation ground) at the northern end of the old village, and Motley Close at its southern end. The rectory field has somewhat subdued ridges and furrows, indicating former ploughing and therefore implying that it was taken out of the open fields by being inclosed at some time before the end of the eighteenth century. Motley Close, at the end of the spur carrying Main Street and its continuation along Lings Lane, is thought to be where the medieval 'moot' or village council used to meet.[2] It may also mark the end of the village street before 1349, when the Black Death decimated populations all over Britain, leading to the abandonment of many of the houses.

Country roads before inclosure were not defined by hedges and ditches, but their general course was sufficiently distinct to be mapped by Chapman in 1776[3]; they were forerunners of the present network. Most of the roads traversing Keyworth parish today follow courses shown by Chapman: Bunny Lane, Nottingham Road, Debdale Lane (then the most direct road to Nottingham), Nicker Hill and Selby Lane. He does not, however, show the present roads to Widmerpool and Wysall; those villages were reached by tracks taking off from Lings Lane.

The last surviving pre-inclosure feature worth noting is the parish boundary, which was totally unaffected by inclosure. Until 1894, the parish was essentially an ecclesiastical unit, though also used for secular administration. In that year civil parishes, administered by elected parish councils, took over the secular roles of the old ecclesiastical parishes, but the latter continued as before in all other respects. In most cases, including Keyworth, the boundaries of the post-1894 civil parishes and the ancient ecclesiastical parishes coincided. But in 1984, the civil parish boundary was altered: a large part of Normanton-on-the-Wolds, containing nearly 2,000 people and extending as far as the railway, was added to Keyworth, while small areas along Bunny Lane and Widmerpool Lane were ceded to Bradmore and Stanton respectively. The boundaries of the ecclesiastical parish, on the other hand, remain unaltered. It is perhaps worth adding that Normanton was inclosed without a parliamentary act, probably in the seventeenth century, so that part of the present parish of Keyworth includes a field pattern dating back to that time, with older hedges containing a greater variety of woody species than most Keyworth hedges.[4]

Oddly, the ancient ecclesiastical parish also had an internal boundary: an enclave of Bunny in the heart of Keyworth village. The enclave, which occupied the northern ends of Main Street and Commercial Road, seems to be of medieval origin or earlier; in the seventeenth century, people from the enclave travelled to Bunny for baptisms, weddings and funerals, and in the nineteenth, the more conscientious clergy noted them in the parish registers as living in 'Keyworth in the parish of Bunny', right up to 1878. It seems that the anomaly was extinguished soon after that — there are no further references to it in parish records.

The Legacy of Inclosure

As we saw in Chapter 9, inclosure had little direct effect on the village but transformed the surrounding fields. Because land was allocated in the award so that many of the new holdings radiated from the village (see p.123), it was possible for farmers to manage their new land from the same farmhouses. When the time came to replace them, new buildings were erected on the same site, so that the village streets continued to be lined with farmhouses, their surfaces spattered with droppings of cows traipsing to and from milking. Right up to the 1950s, Main Street was affectionately called Cow-muck Alley. This was unusual: in most parishes inclosed in the eighteenth and nineteenth centuries, farmhouses were built, perhaps a few decades later when the cost could be afforded, on the now consolidated holdings outside the village. In Keyworth during the nineteenth century, only three such farmhouses appeared: Robin Hood Farm on Wysall Lane (now Wembley Lodge), The Owl's Nest (now demolished, off Bunny Lane) and, right at the end of the century, Greenhayes Farm on Bunny Lane. In addition, two buildings on Lings Lane, which could be regarded as an extension of Main Street, were erected to house cottagers and have recently been completely renovated. Meanwhile, there were still more than a dozen farms in the village in the mid-twentieth century, the larger three-storey ones, built either just before or soon after inclosure, reflecting the prosperity which high wartime corn prices, and then inclosure helped to secure.

The most visible legacy of inclosure on today's landscape is the patchwork of rectangular fields bounded by hawthorn hedges and ditches, and devoted to a mixture of grassland and crops. Some of the original hedges have been grubbed up in response to a recent emphasis on arable and its use of clumsy machinery like combine harvesters. But hedgerow destruction has not been on the scale found on the huge estates of East Anglia for instance — probably because Keyworth's farms remain modest in size. Of the hedges planted in the years immediately following inclosure, about a third have been lost to make way for building; while in the remaining farmland 75% still survive. The mixture of crops and grass, and the particular crops grown and animals pastured have varied with demand and market prices. Maps in The Keyworth Hedgerow Survey 1998, coordinated by Margaret Wright, show a striking contrast in proportions of arable to grass before and after World War II: in 1937, less than 20% of Keyworth's

Figure 25 **Map to show coincidence of inclosure boundaries and present-day farm boundaries**

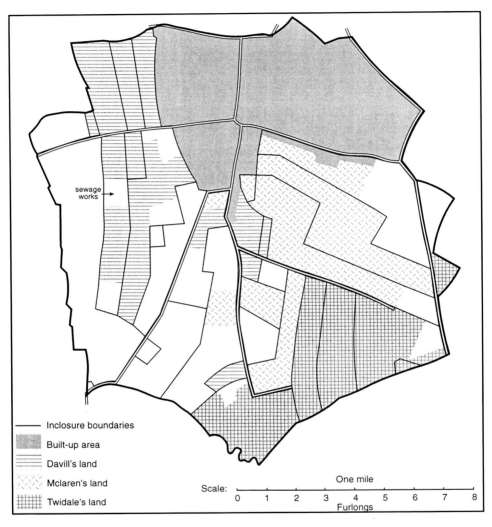

Legend:
- —— Inclosure boundaries
- Built-up area
- Davill's land
- Mclaren's land
- Twidale's land

Scale:
One mile
0 1 2 3 4 5 6 7 8
Furlongs

farmland was arable and the rest grass; in 1998, the percentages were reversed.[5] And among the crops grown there have been important newcomers in recent years: rape — rarely seen thirty years ago — has been widely grown in response to high EU support prices; more recently still, flax has made an appearance. Also fallow — almost eliminated by inclosure — has come back thanks to EU setaside grants.

Property boundaries established at inclosure have persisted almost as much as hedges, as Figure 25 illustrates. Some properties remained in the same family for generations — for instance, the descendants of Samuel Smith, named in the award, were still among Keyworth's principal landowners, at least up to the

Figure 26 **Map to show coincidence of inclosure boundaries and present-day street lay-out**

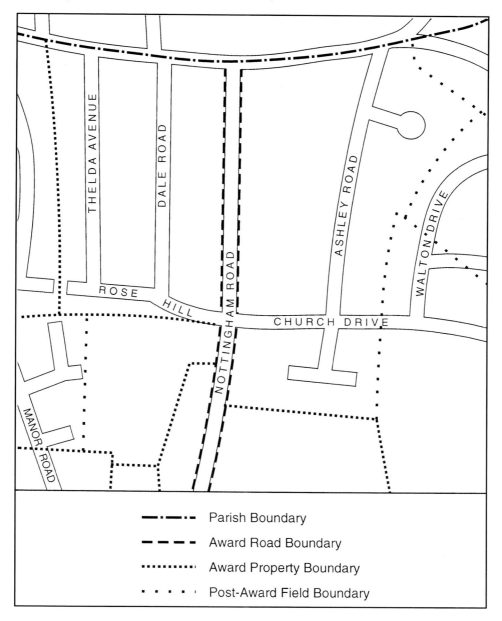

Parish Boundary

Award Road Boundary

Award Property Boundary

Post-Award Field Boundary

1920s: they owned Shaw's Farm, one of the largest in the parish. And while the rector of Keyworth sold most of his glebeland inherited from inclosure during the agricultural depression between 1880 and 1940, successive rectors of Clifton have held on to their Keyworth inheritance, which is now administered by Southwell diocese.

Property boundaries are not in themselves a landscape feature, but may be an important factor underlying patterns of land use. Although farms are not synonymous with properties (a farmer may rent land from several property owners) many of their boundaries correspond. Each farm is a system of interrelated activities: a mixture of crops and their rotation, of grass and livestock, inputs of capital and labour, and of end-products for market, the whole managed by an individual farmer. Farm boundaries therefore represent breaks between systems, perhaps between a predominantly cash crop farm on one side of the line and a dairy farm on the other. Figure 25 illustrates the way in which most present-day farm boundaries follow property demarcations made by the inclosure commissioners and surveyor. It also shows that the western edge of the built-up area of Keyworth corresponds with inclosure boundaries.

It is not only in the open country that inclosure has left its mark. When developers bought land to build long after inclosure, particularly when they did so on a small scale, they bought individual plots which had generally been allocated by the award, and the subsequent layout of streets and houses reflects the shape and size of those plots. This is illustrated in figure 26, showing how the land allotted to Joseph Barnett was used, first in the mid-nineteenth century to build the cottages on Nottingham Road; then in the early twentieth century to develop Dale Road and Thelda Avenue. All are aligned parallel to the long boundaries of Barnett's plot. Again, the land on the other side of Nottingham Road, all allocated to the rector at inclosure, was subdivided into fields soon afterwards. The present alignment of Ashley Road, Ashley Crescent and Wynbreck Drive, reflect these post-inclosure field boundaries. On the other hand, when the wholesale development of the 1960s occurred, involving the purchase by builders Wimpey and Goulding of numerous contiguous fields, the new street layout took little account of former field boundaries.

The inclosure award also determined the present pattern of country roads in the parish. It stipulated quite precisely the route and the width of each road outside the village itself. As we have seen, most followed the course of pre-inclosure tracks, defining them between hedges and ditches. Completely new roads were laid down for the routes to Wysall and Widmerpool. All the inclosure roads are still in use, between the same hedges and ditches that were planted and dug 200 years ago. No other country roads have been constructed in the parish since.

One of the characteristics of inclosure roads throughout Britain is their straightness and width. They were planned instead of evolving piecemeal, as did the narrow, winding and often sunken country lanes of the Sussex Weald, or of Cornwall for instance. They generally make a bee-line for their destination,[6] with bends only to negotiate steep slopes, as when crossing the valley of Fairham Brook. Their width was stipulated in awards, to take account of the rutted condition into which they degenerated in winter, especially on clay, before surfaces were underlaid by stones to provide hard, well-drained carriageways. In Keyworth, the main roads had to be 40 or 50 feet between ditches (see p.119) — a far greater width than is needed on modern by-roads surfaced with tarmac. So today, the roads, generally between fifteen and twenty feet in width, are flanked by broad grass verges and well set-back hedges and ditches. In some neighbouring parishes, the awards required most roads to be 60, or even 80 feet wide; hence the extraordinarily wide verges in, for instance, Willoughby and Wymeswold. The grass on these verges was originally a source of revenue to the surveyor of highways: the hay could be sold to farmers and the proceeds used to pay for the roads' upkeep. Today, it is usually collected by any farmer who can take the trouble to do so, without any payment.

In addition to public roads, the award also stipulated the course and width of bridle roads and footpaths, which are, with few exceptions, still the only public rights of way outside the built-up area for walkers and horse-riders where cars are excluded. The bridleways, like Lings and Wolds Lane, were to be of specified width and defined by hedges and ditches, ensuring that they remain clear landscape features today. Footways on the other hand were not; they were of no specified width and were not identified on the ground by any markers, so that today signposts are used to help walkers and minimise trespass as the paths cut across fields, vulnerable to the farmer's plough.

Finally, in outlining the inclosure legacy, mention must be made of the allotments on the corner of Selby Lane and Willow Brook; and of the Stonepits and Gravel pit to the west of Widmerpool and Wysall Lanes respectively, set aside for road maintenance by the parish highways surveyor. The allotments were to alleviate the problems of the poor: they could rent a small area to grow their own vegetables, and the money so obtained would be distributed amongst the most needy. Allotments are less popular today and half the original four acres was sold to a developer for houses flanking The Fairway. Income from the rent of the remaining allotments is still received by the Parish Council and distributed locally — for instance, to Community Concern, a voluntary group which works among the elderly and disabled in the parish. The Community bus often seen ferrying people to shops, the Village Hall and Centenary Lounge, is in small part financed out of a provision made in the Inclosure Award — though most of the funds to keep it going have to be raised in other ways.

Road maintenance is no longer a parish responsibility and the Stonepits and Gravelpit have ceased to be used for the purpose designated by the inclosure commissioners. The Stonepits had, in any case, yielded most of its usable stone and was exchanged by the parish council for the land on which it developed the Conservation Area at the end of Lings Lane in the 1980s, while the Gravelpit, never so much in use, was bought by a neighbouring landowner.

Conclusion

The main motivation for the inclosure of Keyworth, as elsewhere, was economic: greater productivity and profitability from the land by bringing under individual cultivation nearly a third of the parish until then under common management (the pasture); and making possible a more rational farming system on compact holdings instead of on thousands of scattered strips. In this it probably succeeded in the short run and certainly in the long term: modern farming techniques, involving underground drainage, the deployment of combine harvesters and other machinery as well as intensive use of artificial fertilisers and pesticides, and the selective breeding of livestock, would have been impossible under the open field system. But the economic legacy of inclosure has become intermingled with subsequent developments so that it is no longer possible to identify it with any particular elements of the local economy. Likewise the social consequences: in the immediate aftermath, large landowners and large tenant farmers were probably made more prosperous, while the landless were impoverished by loss of common rights; while social cohesion must have been undermined by the elimination of communal routines in the common fields. But 200 years later it would be difficult to attribute disparities of wealth and poverty, or any lack of social cohesion, to inclosure — too much else has intervened, including a thirty-fold increase in population.

Two undiminished legacies of inclosure remain, however. The first is conspicuous by its absence: the almost complete lack of common land and the concomitant right to roam anywhere in Keyworth's countryside other than along the few footpaths prescribed in the award. More positively, it is the hedges and rectangular fields they surround, and above all the open, straight roads with their wide verges — an almost incidental by-product of inclosure — that are its clearest visible legacy two hundred years after they were laid out.

Meanwhile, Keyworth has changed almost beyond recognition, obscuring much of its past with estates and the paraphernalia of twentieth century life. The bucolic, self-contained farming community of pre-inclosure times turned, first, into a predominantly industrial village in the nineteenth century, and then into a residential satellite of Nottingham in the twentieth, with many residents spending the greater part of their waking hours elsewhere, either at work, shopping, or in leisure activities. Its population grew from little more than 300 at inclosure, to 800 a century later, and to over 8,000 today. Much of this change came about gradually and incrementally, so that people barely noticed while it occurred — the steady growth and later decline in framework knitting, or the increasing amount of commuting following that decline, for instance. Occasionally the pace hotted up, as in the 1950s and 1960s, during which population quadrupled and Keyworth exchanged much of its character from rural to suburban — a process that only the blind could have failed to notice.

As we saw in Chapter 9, inclosure in Keyworth was long anticipated, and some of its subsequent effects emerged only slowly. Nevertheless, inclosure arrived virtually overnight: one day, common land occupied over a quarter of the parish, the rest divided into thousands of narrow strips, worked under communal management; the day following, all common land and communal management were gone, the whole parish divided into compact, individually run farms waiting to be defined on the ground by the ditches and hedges we see today. There are few sharp turning points in history, and fewer still that coincide with the turn of a century, but inclosure in Keyworth was one such. We shall no sooner finish marking its bi-centenary than the millennium will be upon us.

Notes

1. See R. A. Hammond, 1998, pp.20–21.
2. S.P.Potter, 1935, p.7.
3. Map of Nottinghamshire on a scale of one inch to one mile, by Chapman, 1776.
4. Wright, 1998, pp.14–16: local hedges have been dated on the proposition (Hooper's Rule) that the age of a hedge can be **roughly** estimated in centuries by the average number of woody species contained in a sample of 30 yard (27 metre) lengths. Most ex-Normanton hedges contain 3 or 4 species, indicating ages of about 300 or 400 years; in the rest of Keyworth they mostly contain one or two species, indicating ages of about 100 or 200 years.
5. ibid. pp.11–12.
6. See p.119 offering a possible explanation of a minor deviation of Wysall Lane to take account of land allocations.

Appendix I

Tithes

The reason for this note is two-fold: (i) tithes, a form of 'church tax', were paid by most Keyworth households before inclosure and were then extinguished, the former recipients being granted land in lieu; (ii) Keyworth was unusual in having five tithe-holders before inclosure, a fact that calls for some explanation.

Origin of tithes

The word 'tithe' (often spelled *tythe* in the eighteenth century) derives from an Old English word meaning simply 'a tenth', and originally tithes comprised a tenth of every layman's income, to be set aside for God. In practice, this meant they were set aside for the clergy, enabling them to discharge their role, that of looking after the spiritual needs of their flock. They were also meant to cover expenses incurred in relieving poverty, and provided, together with the output or rent from glebe (land belonging to the local church) and charges for conducting marriages and funerals (sometimes called 'surplice fees'), the source of a priest's income. They were intimately bound up with the demarcation of parish boundaries, because these determined the priest to whom people paid tithes.

This may explain a curious annual payment of six shillings and eightpence made by the rector of Keyworth to the rector of Plumtree over several centuries and recorded in a series of Plumtree terriers between 1664 (the earliest extant) and 1786.[1] A possible explanation is that Keyworth parish was carved out of Plumtree, depriving the rector of Plumtree of some of his tithe-payers, for which the annual payment was compensation. The payment seems small, but if it originated in the early middle ages or before, the value of six-and-eightpence was then much greater (it was not inflation indexed!), while populations and therefore tithepayers lost to the new parish would have been relatively few, requiring only modest compensation.[2]

How tithes were paid

Originally, most tithes were paid in kind. They consisted of two types: great tithes, being a tenth of all corn, hay and wood produced in the parish; and small tithes, chiefly fruit, wool and young livestock (e.g., one of a litter of ten piglets). This created difficulties in making fair estimates (a cow never had ten calves; crop yields varied wildly, depending on weather and pests) and in storage and handling (priests needed tithe barns and had to know, or employ someone who knew how to deal with farm produce). The payment of tithes came to be bitterly resented, particularly where the priest was an absentee who neglected his parish, the more so among dissenters, who even had to pay tithes on their Normanton Meeting House.[3] Resentment became particularly strong towards the end of the eighteenth century, which was no doubt why so many inclosure acts of the period included clauses to end them. There were disputes over whether tithes should be levied on new crops like potatoes and turnips, many of the latter grown in labourers' garths and only visible to a prying priest.[4]

Eventually but at varying speeds throughout the country, the value of tithes was translated (alternative terms used were 'composed' or 'commuted') into their estimated cash value. In Keyworth, they were still mostly being paid in kind in 1770,[5] though Lowe, writing about Nottinghamshire as a whole less than thirty years later, stated that 'more tythes are paid by composition (i.e., in cash) than in kind.'[6] He goes on to say that 'these compositions are much lower than the real value of the tythe', so there was resistance from many clergy to 'composition'.

On the other hand, clergy must have been aware of the unpopularity of tithes, and of how it could undermine their ministry. Where tithes were paid in cash, some would relieve the tension of 'Tithe Audit Day' — the day when tithes were due — by throwing a party. Parson Woodforde, rector of Weston Longville, near Norwich, who made this an annual event, wrote in his diary[7] on 2nd December 1783:

'This being my Tithe Audit Day, [twenty]... people attended and paid me everything that was due... They all dined, spent the afternoon and evening till 10 o'clock... I gave them for dinner a leg of Mutton boiled, and Capers, some Salt Fish, plenty of Plumb Pudding, and a Couple of boiled Rabbits with a fine large Surloin of Beef roasted. Plenty of Wine, Punch and Strong Beer after Dinner till 10 o'clock. We had this Year a very agreeable meeting here, and were very agreeable — no grumbling whatever. Total recd. this Day for Tithe £286. 15. 0.' The fact that he noted 'no grumbling' on this occasion suggests that there had been tension in the past. Certainly Parson Woodforde had little to complain about: he had just received from his parishioners what might be the equivalent of between fifteen and twenty thousand pounds in today's money!

It was not until the Tithe Commutation Act of 1836 that all tithes had to be converted into cash payments, based on the average value of wheat, barley and oats over the previous seven years, and not upon crop yields. This not only reduced their variability, but also meant improvements introduced by farmers did not have to be shared with clergy who made no contribution to those improvements. By this time, tithes had been abolished in Keyworth, but people in neighbouring Normanton were still paying them, so a Tithe Award with accompanying map was produced in 1840 for that parish — a valuable document for the local historian. Horn comments: 'Although the Tithe Commutation Act of 1836 could not make payments palatable, at least it removed some of the main grievances which had clouded relations between clerics and their parishioners over the years.'[8] The grievance was reduced further from the tenant farmer's point of view when the onus to pay tithes was shifted from the farmer to the land owner in 1891, though the latter may sometimes have countered by raising the rent.[9] These charges were finally disposed of in 1936 when landowners began to pay an annuity over sixty years in order to redeem all tithes by 1996.[10]

From what has been said, it may be thought that tithe payments were confined to farm produce, but this was not so. For instance, in a Keyworth Terrier of 1781,[11] after outlining the main sources of tithes, the following is recorded: 'Also every commonable house [i.e., house carrying rights of its occupier to graze stock on common land] pays two shillings tythe of wool and lamb.' Again, a Bunny terrier of 1786 listing tithe amounts due, includes 'the tenth swarm of bees, sixpence a swarm' — presumably the vicar did not relish having them in kind! — and 'every servant pays a farthing for every shilling of wages'. As we shall see two paragraphs further on, this Bunny terrier also applied to part of Keyworth. Tithing arrangements were complex, arising out of piecemeal bargaining between priest and parish over many centuries.

Why Keyworth had five tithe holders

Apart from the rector of Keyworth, the other tithe holders fall into two groups: the lay rector (see below) and the vicar of Bunny; and the rectors of Gotham and Clifton. Different explanations may apply to each group.

There had for many centuries been an enclave of Bunny in the heart of Keyworth village, whose origin is obscure, but which can be traced from the sixteenth century to 1878 by reference to court rolls and parish registers. It may be assumed therefore that people living in that enclave, which took in about one sixth of the whole population of Keyworth[12] paid their tithes to Bunny.

'Lay rector' is harder to explain. In medieval times, a landowner who had originally founded a church, or his heirs, often gave land and/or the right to tithes to a nearby monastery. If the monastery had tithe rights it became the rector of the church. However, as it would not be located in the village itself (and may have belonged to a contemplative order, whose monks were withdrawn from secular society), it could not minister to the needs of the parishioners directly, so a vicarious rector — a vicar — was appointed to act on its behalf. The monastery then received the great tithes and the vicar the small tithes. The priest of a parish with no such arrangement with a monastery was rector and received both great and small tithes; a vicar received only small tithes and, unless he had a large amount of glebe land, was generally worse off than a rector.

After the dissolution of the monasteries and later of chantries in the 1530s and 1540s, all their lands and tithes became crown property. However, over the next few decades most were sold off to finance wars and other kinds of royal and government expenditure. In this way land and the right to tithes came into the hands of wealthy men or institutions, who thereby acquired the status of lay rector, with the right to receive tithes and appoint vicars in the same way as the monasteries had done before the dissolution.

It appears that the whole of Bunny, including the enclave in Keyworth, went through this process of having its tithes transferred first to a monastery (Ulverscroft, near Loughborough), then to the Crown and then to a wealthy local family — the Parkyns — who appointed a vicar to minister to the people of Bunny. Something similar may have happened to parts of Keyworth parish, which were given, along with the church, to Thurgarton Priory in the twelfth century. Although they were returned in the thirteenth,[13] it is possible that the priory retained the tithes which, after royal confiscation and sale in the sixteenth century finished up as tithable to the rectors of Gotham and Clifton. Unlike the lay rector of Bunny, however, they did not need to appoint a vicar because that role was already being performed by the rector of Keyworth. In fact, some deal seems to have been struck in the case of the rector of Gotham who, though he had more tithe-holders in Keyworth than the rector of Clifton, was only entitled to the great tithes on his Keyworth lands, the small tithes going to the rector of Keyworth. The rector of Clifton took both from his tithe-lands.

Commutation of Keyworth's tithes

The Inclosure Act for Keyworth provided for the extinguishing of tithes and the granting to former tithe holders of land in lieu, indicating what the size of grants should be. These provisions are outlined in the main text (p.121). They more than doubled the land owned by the rector (glebe), making him the largest landowner in the parish. Altogether, the five former tithe holders were awarded 238 acres out of a total of 1336 acres of farmland in the parish. But in one respect Keyworth was fortunate: it had, prior to inclosure, a high proportion of its land under common pasture — much more than 238 acres — so the tithe-holders' compensation could be given without reducing the amount held by other landowners. And a severe bone of contention was removed, at a stroke.

Notes

1.   NA DR/1/3/2/26/1-13.
2.   The hypothesis fits what is known of the origin of nearby parishes: Plumtree, Keyworth, Edwalton and Ruddington were originally served by a minster church and group of priests based at Flawforth. They became separate parishes, probably in that order - Plumtree certainly has the oldest church.
3.   NA PR1140.
4.   Horn, 1980, p.153.
5.   Church terrier NA PR1140.
6.   Lowe, 1798, p.141.
7.   Woodforde, 1978, pp.217–7.
8.   Horn, 1980, p.155.
9.   Trevelyan, p.514.
10. Hey, loc cit.
11. NA DR/1/3/2/17/1-13.
12. About a sixth of the entries in the parish registers which record place of residence of the people involved give it as 'Keyworth in the parish of Bunny'.
13. See Hammond, 1997, pp.1–2.

Appendix II

Summary of Keyworth Terrier, 1752[1]

In 1752, a terrier or inventory of the rector's glebe and tithe land was produced. It identified 2101 items — separate, individually worked units in the three open arable fields, mostly lands — of which 288 were glebe and the other 1813 tithable to the rector. The latter figure represents 49% of all tithable land in the parish (the other 51% were tithable to four other tithe holders); so the total number of items of tithable land was probably about 3700 (1813 x 100/49), to which must be added the 288 items of glebe, giving a total of 3988 — say 4000 in the whole parish.

The area of arable land in the three open fields at the time was about 1000 acres, so each item averaged a quarter of an acre — perhaps 220 x 5.5 yards, or one furlong by one rod (pole or perch), the rough equivalent of a single ridge one furlong in length.

The majority of these items were individual 'lands' bordered by 'lands' belonging to other people, though some were amalgamated with adjoining items to form wider units. These units, whether composed of single or multiple items are here called strips. The terrier identifies 1484 individual strips of which 140 are glebe, leaving 1344 in land tithable to the rector. So the total number of strips in the parish would be approximately 1344 x 100/49 + 140 = 2883 — i.e., nearly 3000 strips.

These 3000 strips were distributed among three open arable fields and belonged to an unknown number of proprietors. The rector received tithes from 19 landowners, but there were probably as many again paying tithes to the other four tithe holders. (Other eighteenth century terriers shows that the rector of Gotham had 11 tithe holders in Keyworth.)[2] Land tax returns and the Inclosure Award indicate there were between 36 and 42 landowners towards the end of the century, six of whom were absentee landlords owning half the total parish area. The land was, therefore, highly fragmented — the rector's glebe, for instance, comprised about 90 acres which were scattered among the three fields in 140 strips.

Of the 2101 items identified in the 1752 terrier, 655 in two of the three fields are said to be 'in the pasture', implying that a large proportion of these two fields had recently been taken out of arable use and put down to grass. It amounted to nearly a third of the parish land in which the rector had a financial interest and it is likely that the rest of Keyworth's arable — i.e., that which was tithable to the four other tithe holders — was treated similarly. (One of the two fields affected, Brook Field, was renamed Bunny Gate Field 'by reason of the pasture being taken out of it' so that it no longer reached down to the brook.)

The landowners whose strips were put down to (common) pasture were compensated by being allotted 'New land being the equivalent to that which is in the Pasture'. But the new land only comprised 141 items to compensate for the 655 lost to pasture. However, 46 of these new items were called flats, a term which usually denoted a group of 'lands', while most of the remaining 95 were single 'lands'. If we assume the new land (not to be confused with 'lands') to be equal in area to land lost to pasture, with L standing for one 'land' and F for one flat, we have the equation:

$$95L + 46F = 655L$$
$$\text{hence, } 46F = 560L$$

and one 'flat' = twelve 'lands' (as a rough average; measures were not standardised in the mid-eighteenth century).

The new land must have been taken out of what was formerly pasture or waste — perhaps significantly, a large part was taken from land alongside Long*moor* Field, which subsequently changed its name to Mill Field. Among the freshly created furlongs (in the sense of clusters of parallel strips) were Debdale and Nickey Hill *(sic)*, indicating where the new arable was.

Notes

1. NA PR/1139.
2. NA DR/1/3/2/77/1–14.

Appendix III

Keyworth Field Names

Of the 211 fields numbered on the accompanying map, the names of some 70 have been identified and are given below. Those asterisked are found in the 1752 terrier (See Appendix II) and relate to post-inclosure fields presumably occupying roughly the same locations as furlongs (clusters of parallel strips) with those names in the pre-inclosure fields. Many of the others are of more recent provenance — e.g., Cricket Field (No.27) where cricket was played in the early part of the twentieth century.

5/6 The Penns*	10 Cliff Nook	21 Long Mere	22 Thunderpits*
27 Cricket Field	32 Greenaids	39 Parson's Close End*	40 Water Willows*
44 Parson's Close*	54 Stanton Gate*	56 Allotments	60 Church Rein*
61 Wine Ho*	66 Long Bunnygate	67 Short Bunnygate	68 Rampart Close
73 Barrowslade*	75 Homefield (Shaw's Farm)	78 Nether Wine Ho*	79 Owl's Nest
82 Bunker's Hill	89 Sandpits (or Sandholes)	98 Brookfield	105 Town End*
110 Co-op	111 Pickard's Field	112 Fox Hill*	124 Brook Close
126/132 Beyond the Brook	127/9 Joey Dodds	136 Church Meer	137 Church Land
140 Meerside	142 House Close	143 Tom Croft*	144 Kennel Hill*
145 Short Bratlands*	146 Long Bratlands*	147 Top Bratlands	148 Town Close
150 Hillfield	153 Bottom Bratlands	154 Flank Bratlands*	155 Old Hedge Nook*
157 Home Field	158 Kennel Bottoms*	160 Well Field*	161 Wold Side
162 Top Wolds	164 Well Field (No.2)	166 Motley Close*	170 Little Kennel Bottoms
171/2 Red Hill	175 Springfield (or Wells)	177 Bottom Wolds	179 New Hedge Nook
181 Burrowgate Lees	182 Duckpool Close	183 Chekles	184 Marl Hill
186 Watersqualls*	187 Isabelle's Arse	188 Duck (or Dock) Foot	189 The Sun
191 Bakergate	198 Lady Sick*	205 Against ye Sun*	210 Upper Meer Side

Figure 27 **Map of known Keyworth field names**

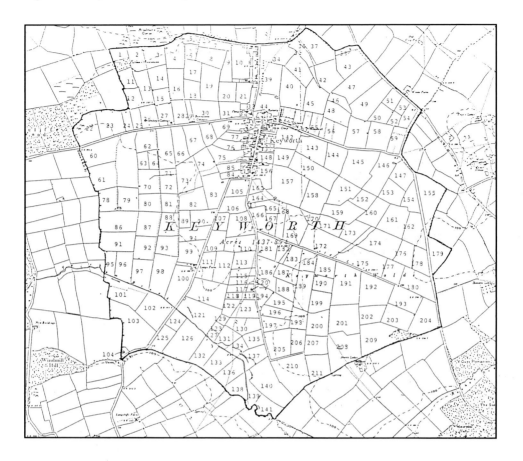

Appendix IV

Inclosures for which Jonas Bettison was a Commissioner

ACT/AWARD	PARISH	FELLOW COMMISSIONERS	SURVEYOR
1789/91	Arnold	John Beighton John Renshaw	James Dowland
1792/92	Lambley	Wm. Fillingham John Renshaw	John Bailey
1792/97	Basford	Thos. Fletcher John Renshaw	James Dowland
1795/98	Upton	Wm. Fillingham* John Ince John Kirk	Wm. Attenburrow
1795/98	Woodborough	John Ince John Bailey	John Bailey
1795/1801	East Stoke & Elston	Wm. Fillingham* Samuel Turner John Renshaw	Richard Gee
1796/98	Sneinton	Wm. Calvert Samuel Wyatt	John Bailey Wm. Calvert
1796/1803	Weston	Wm. Calvert Benj. Chambers	?
1796/1801	East Bridgford	John Renshaw	Richard Gee
1797	Bunny	Jos. Boultbee	John Bailey
1798/99	Keyworth	Jos. Boultbee John Renshaw	John Bailey
1800/01	Normanton- on-Trent	John Kirk** John Saunders John Brown	John Brown
1800/01	Wysall	John Renshaw	John Bailey

1802/04	Cropwell Bishop	John Kirk	John Bailey & John Brown
1802/06	Walkeringham	Jonathon Teal Wm. Whitelock Wm. Kelk	John Brown
1802/04	Widmerpool	James Dowland	John Bailey & Wm. Chatterton
1803/15	Dunham & Ragnall	Wm. Bilby Wm. Kelk*** Wm. Bailey John Brown	?
1804/06	Gotham	Robert Padley John Bailey	John Bailey & John Brown
1804/10	Alverton	Wm. Ashton	John Brown
1805/07	Plumtree & Clipston	John Bailey	John Bailey & John Brown
1806/09	Beeston	John Bailey	John Brown
1809/09	Annesley & Annesley Woodhouse	Bettison sole commissioner	John Brown
1808/09	Gamston	James Dowland	James Dowland ?
1809/14	Eaton	Bettison sole commissioner	James Dowland

*Died 18 October 1795
**Died January 1806
***Died 8 October 1808

Table compiled using information from the following sources:
Tate and Turner, 1978.
Unpublished data collected by Professor Roger J.P.Kain and Dr Richard Oliver of the University of Exeter in their study of 'Government-sponsored, large scale mapping of England and Wales before the Ordnance Survey'.

Appendix V

Nottinghamshire Inclosures for which John Bailey was the Surveyor

ACT/AWARD	PARISH	AREA ACRES	COMMISSIONERS
1769/70	Blidworth	1508	Barnas Lucas John Harvey Thomas Clark
1771/72	Stapleford and Bramcote	1325	Rev. Tristram Exley William Fox Thomas Olknow John Stone
1774/75	Sutton Bonington (St. Annes)	1435	Thomas Oldknow John Darys (?) William Fox William Fillingham John Watkinson
1775/76	Hickling	2866	Thomas Oldknow John Renshaw William Fillingham
1779/80	Calverton		Thomas Oldknow Hugh Platt John Ince George Padley George Kelk
1787/88	Cropwell Butler and Bishop	2090	William Fillingham Joseph Outram William Sanday
1789/90	Whatton	1760	John Kent John Renshaw William Fillingham
1792/96	Lambley	560	William Fillingham Jonas Bettison John Renshaw
1792/96	Gedling, Stoke Bardolph and Carlton	4540	William Pearce William Calvert John Renshaw Samuel Wyatt Samuel Deverill

1795/98	Woodborough	1945	Jonas Bettison John Ince John Bailey
1796/98	Sneinton	911	Jonas Bettison William Calvert Samuel Wyatt
1796/99	Lenton and Radford	261	John Renshaw Robert Padley William King
1797/98	Bunny	2137	Joseph Boultbee Jonas Bettison
1798/99	East Leake	2530	Edward Dawson Joseph Boultbee John Seagrave John Bailey John Chamberlain
1798/99	Keyworth	1438	Joseph Boultbee Jonas Bettison John Renshaw
1799/1801	Grassthorpe	3514	John Renshaw William Ashton Paul Pearson
1800/01	Wysall	1554	Jonas Bettison John Renshaw
1802/4	Cropwell Bishop	1375	Jonas Bettison John Kirk
1802/04	Widmerpool	2106	Jonas Bettison James Dowland
1803/06	Tollerton	436	James Green John Farmer John Bailey John Brown
1804/06	Gotham	2563	Jonas Bettison Robert Padley John Bailey
1805/7	Plumtree and Clipston	2798	Jonas Bettison John Bailey

Appendix VI

Work undertaken by John Bailey for the Borough of Nottingham, 1783–1801

Source: *Records of the Borough of Nottingham*, Vols VII & VIII

1783, Dec. 'To measuring the Streets in Nottingham to calculate the expence of Flagging the Footpaths, and paid a man for assisting me'   £0-10s-6d

1785, Aug. 'To Surveying and making a Terrier of an Estate in the Liberties of Nottingham 58 acres'   £1- 9s-0d

1795, Mar. 'To measuring and valuing Land belonging to the Corporation and taken for the Grantham Canal'   £0-10s-6d

1796, Feb. 'To measuring Lands of the Corporation taken for the Nottingham Canal and making out Particulars of the Lands'   £1- 1s-0d

1796, Mar. 'To measuring and Planning the Coppice 104 acres at 6d   £2-12s-0d
'To Vellum for Map'   £0- 3s-6d

1802, Feb. *Corporation Estates*
'Ordered that Mr Bailey be applied to in the name of the Corporation to furnish for their use a Plan & Survey of all the Land in the Lordship of Nottingham belonging to them either as Chamber, Bridge or School Land.'
NOTE: The outcome of this decision is unknown.

John Bailey's Maps of the Keyworth Inclosure Award

John Bailey drew two maps, one which accompanied the Award and is now in the Nottinghamshire Archives, EA 59/1, the other for the enrolled copy lodged with the Public Record Office, KB 122/723 rot 1081. The only essential difference between them is in the decorative cartouche embracing the title. The map in Nottingham has a simple garden scene with the title displayed on an ornamental feature, the other a rural scene, trees, shrubs, a fence and, in the distance, a church. The following describes the PRO map.

Title: PLAN / of the TOWNSHIP of / KEYWORTH / in the County of Nottingham / _____/ Inclosed by an Act of / Parliament passed / 38th Geo. III 1798 / Bailey/ Surveyor

Scale: approx. 1:5740, no scale given on map.

Size: Sheet: 65 x 57 cms (height, width)
                 Within borders 62 x 55 cms.

Orientation: Top is north north west.

Material: Parchment

Features: Pre-inclosure closes coloured green, property boundaries black, proprietors' names in black.
Inclosure Award allotment boundaries, red, ownership of boundaries indicated.
Allotment numbers in red (Arabic).
Proprietors' names in black, lower case except for Rectorial property which is in upper case lettering.
Area of allotments, Acres, Roods and Perches, in black.
Parish boundary in black with outer edge coloured red, purple, blue, or yellow to distinguish the boundaries of adjacent parishes.
Buildings, other than church, shown in plan in a red-brown colour partly outlined in black. Church shown in elevation from the south.
Roads: pre-inclosure: black.
inclosure: defined by the red boundary lines of adjacent property.
Footpaths: blue single pecked line labelled with origin and destination.
Waterway: Fairham brook, un-named, uncoloured between black borders.
Woodland: tree symbol.
Outside parish boundary: Names of adjacent parishes in upper case black lettering
Routes in and out of the parish shown; in general, 'From' the south 'To' the north.

Decoration: Eight compass points, four identified; north by *fleur-de-lis*, east by a cross, south by S and west by W. Located top right-hand corner.
Title Cartouche: Title within a wreath supported on circular plinth. To left: a tree. In background, a double railed fence, trees and shrubs. to the right a distant southern view of the church. The colours are faded grey, brown and green. Located in bottom left hand corner.
Border: one broad line and one narrow line on inside.

Keyworth Inclosure Allotments
in lieu of Tithes

	Allot. No.	a	r	p	a	r	p
Sir Thomas Parkyns	1	18	0	21			
	33	41	1	4			
Total					59	1	25
Rector of Keyworth	14	48	3	0			
	37	68	0	0			
Total					116	3	0
Rector of Clifton	47	16	3	39			
Total					16	3	39
Rector of Gotham	51	43	0	9			
Total					43	0	9
Vicar of Bunny	2	2	0	33			
Total					2	0	33
Total for Tithes					238	1	26

Appendix IX

Calculation of fencing costs

In his study of the development during 1774–6 of Radley Farm, Southwell, Nottinghamshire, Hardstaff computed the cost of fencing to be 8d per yard.[1] This figure contrasts with that found by Russell for the inclosure of Hibaldstow, Lincs, 1796, viz. 18·9d per yard and the 19·8d per yard quoted by Williams for inclosures in the Mendips.[2] The difference between the lower and higher figures is greater than can be accounted for by the rate of inflation during the last quarter of the eighteenth century.

Using data from William Sanday's accounts for the inclosure of the Pierrepont property in Cotgrave[3] and John Harrison's accounts for the Inclosure of East Leake[4] estimates of fencing costs have been made which yield intermediate figures.

(i) From Sanday's accounts have been extracted those items directly related to fence construction. Knowing the number of quicksets purchased an estimate can be made of the total length of fencing. This estimate depends crucially on two assumptions: the proportion of the purchased quicksets which was fit to plant and the distance apart at which they were planted. We can be reasonably certain that not all the young quicksets supplied were fit to use — what the proportion was we cannot say, but here we have arbitrarily assumed 90%. For the spacing of the plants we have available contemporary recommendations, albeit from another part of the country. J. Billingsley farmed in the Mendips, was a commissioner for at least seven inclosures in the area, and was a great advocate of the hawthorn quickset. He was said to have inclosed 3-4000 acres of his own land creating in the process 100 miles of hedging. He advocated planting the quicksets four inches apart.[5]

Extracting from the accounts those items directly related to fencing, the total cost amounted to £2911 13s 11d or 698,807d

Number of quicksets purchased: 587,000

Number planted: 528,300

Spacing: 4", 9 per yard

Number of Yards planted = 528,300/9 = 58,700

Cost per yard = 698,807/58,700 = 11·9d

(ii) A more direct approach involved measuring the length of fencing as shown on a contemporary map. Some years after the inclosure of Cotgrave when Lord Newark had completed the inclosure of his land he commissioned William Calvert to make a map of the parish showing his holdings.[6] On this map field boundaries on recently inclosed land are shown in red. The assumption was made that all red boundary lines represented hedges which Lord Newark caused to be planted. These were measured and the total length computed from the map scale.

Measured length = 69,929 yds

Total cost of fencing = 698,807d

Cost per yard = 698,807/69,929 = 10d

(iii)   The East Leake Inclosure accounts show that £649 8s 6d was allowed for the fencing of the Rector's allotment. By transfering the boundaries of these allotments to an OS 6 inch map, measuring the length of boundaries which, according to the Award, were to be fenced at the expense of the proprietors the cost per yard was calculated as 15·5d per yard. This figure has been used in the calculation of the fencing costs of the Keyworth Inclosure as fewer assumptions have been made in its derivation, there is greater certainty of the boundaries measured and the original data is most appropriate in terms of its time and origin. Furthermore it is in close accord with the 15d per yard suggested by William Marshall in 1790, see Appendix XI.

Notes

1   'Radley Farm, Southwell', Bob Hardstaff in *Farms and Fields of Southwell: A Study of Enclosures*, Ed. Philip Lythe; University of Nottingham Centre for Local History, 1984.
2   'The Enclosures of Barton-on-Humber and Hibaldstow', Rex C. Russell; 'The Enclosure and Reclamation of the Mendip Hills, 1770–1870', Michael Williams, *Ag. Hist. Rev.* (19) 1971, 73.
3   loc.cit.
4   loc.cit.
5   Williams, loc.cit.
6   *Manor of Cotgrave in the County of Nottingham, the Estate of The Rt. Hon. Charles Ld. Viscount Newark subsequent to an Inclosure of the Open Lands which was confirmed by an Act of Parliament in the Year 1790.* Undated but later than 1796 and prior to 1806.

Appendix X

Keyworth Inclosure
Allotments and Fencing Costs

Allot. No.	Name	Area			Fencing		
		a	r	p	yards	cost £	cost/ acre
1	Sir Thos. Parkyns for Tithes	18	0	21	572	37	
2	Vicar of Bunny for Tithes	2	0	33	220	14	
3	Thos. Mettam	32	0	12	895	58	1.8
4	Ann Bennett	19	0	25	792	51	2.7
5	John Shepperson	17	3	18	763	49	2.7
6	F. Eggleston Jr.	4	3	10	410	27	5.6
7	Wm. Shepperson	1	2	17	220	14	8.7
8	Thos. Hemsley	39	1	19	1195	75	1.9
9	Thos. Hemsley	15	1	36	630	41	2.6
10	Joseph Barnett	13	2	30	499	32	2.3
11	Dissenters' Meeting Hse.	1	0	18			
12	Rector for Glebe	89	1	19	1159	75	0.84
13	Bell & Loundes	1	1	30			
14	Rector for Tithes	48	3	0			
15	Keyworth Poor Trustees	4	1	2	323	21	4.9
16	Wm. Hemsley	16	2	24	660	43	2.6
17	Rebecca Holmes	2	0	0	235	15	7.5
18	F. Eggleston Jr.	4	0	10	191	12	2.9
19	John Eggleston	0	1	33			
20	Thos. Disney	0	1	26			
21							
22	Thos. Hemsley	0	2	17			
23	Rebecca Holmes	0	1	33			
24	Thomas Mettam	4	1	1	308	20	4.6
25	Wm. Shepperson Jr.	6	0	23	440	28	4.6
26	Langford Nevill	2	3	16	73	5	1.8
27	F.Eggleston Sr.	1	2	23	191	12	7.3
28	Samuel Smith	74	1	35	1672	108	1.5
29	E.Walker	8	1	23	410	27	3.2
30	Wm. Shepperson Jr.	45	2	17	1203	78	1.7
31	Sir Thos.Parkyns as Lord of the Manor						
32	Sir Thos. Parkyns	78	1	10	1613	104	1.3
33	Sir Thos. Parkyns for Tithes	41	1	4	1267	82	

34	Wysall Church	0	3	2			
35	Wm. Griffin	3	1	22	117	8	2.4
36	Langford Nevill	42	1	5	1071	69	1.6
37	Rector of Keyworth for Tithes	68	0	0	2420	156	
38	Richard Attenborrow	26	2	25	909	59	2.2
39	F. Eggleston Sr.	2	3	23			
40	F. Eggleston Sr.	1	3	10	161	10	5.5
41	Langford Nevill	37	2	16	1423	92	2.4
42	Surveyor of Highways	2	2	0	220	14	5.6
43	Henry Hebb	5	2	30	358	23	4
44	Wm. Cooke	7	2	14	387	25	3.3
45	F. Eggleston Jr.	8	3	26	484	31	2.5
46	F. Eggleston Jr.	7	3	0	425	27	3.4
47	Rector of Clifton for Tithes	16	3	39	821	53	
48	Henry Hebb	30	3	34	906	59	1.9
49	Keyworth Ch. Wardens	6	3	12	455	29	4.2
50	Henry Hebb	11	3	24			
51	Rector of Gotham for Tithes	43	0	9	836	54	
52	Thos. Hemsley	36	1	21	968	63	1.7
53	Wm. Shepperson Jr.	40	0	20	909	59	1.5
54	Surveyor of Highways	1	2	0			
55	Samuel Smith	57	0	0	1540	99	1.7
56	Samuel Greaves	78	2	15	2525	165	2.1
57	Job Eggleston	3	2	14	337	22	6.1
58	Wm. Hallam	6	0	32	411	27	4.4
59	Wm. Hallam	0	1	32			
60	Samuel Wells	5	1	7	411	27	5.1
61	Samuel Greaves	0	1	7			
62	Samuel Greaves	0	0	38			
63	Richard Tookey	78	2	6	2273	147	1.9
64	Richard Tookey	7	0	30	323	21	2.9
65	Rev. Dr. Milnes	12	2	28	528	34	2.7
66	Rev. Dr. Milnes	81	2	3	2391	154	1.9
67	Wm. Hallam	0	0	16			
68	Wm. Hallam	4	0	32			

Appendix XI

William Marshall, *The Rural Economy of Midland Counties*, 1790, 2 vols.

Vol.I Chapter 5 FENCES

p. 84 RAISING NEW HEDGES
'Garden quick' the universal hedge wood, formerly (within living memory) gathered from natural woodland.
'A gentleman from Tamworth was the first who ventured to plant garden quick on a large scale.'
'The quantity now raised at Tamworth and its neighbourhood, for the Birmingham and other markets, is extraordinary. Its price even at Tamworth, seven shillings a thousand, at Birmingham eight or ten shillings: yet at those prices one gardener sells, even when no public inclosures are going forward, three or four hundred thousand annually.'

p. 86 *The time of planting* autumn preferred

p. 87 *Method of Planting* said to be that of putting the plants into a broad flat mound: generally planting *two* rows ten or twelve inches apart, and a similar distance from the brink of the trench, by the side of which they are planted, ...

p. 87–88 Two rows of posts and rails are the common guard; incurring an expense equal to twice that of a deep ditch and banklet on one side, and a high bank on the other. If the hedge be planted behind a shelf of sufficient width, and part of of the mould of the ditch be applied in forming a banklet on its outer brink, the load incurred by the remainder is little, if any, impediment to the progress of the young hedge.

Vol.II

MINUTES/ ON/ WOODLANDS, LIVE HEDGES,/ AND/ PLANTING/ IN THE MIDLAND COUNTIES
Minute Number 123.

STATFOLD, May 1784. Finished the NEW FENCE between No2 and 3

The *ditch* an equilateral triangle each side or slope, as well as the width, being exactly a quarter of a rod, namely four feet inch and half [*sic*].
The *bank* on the fence side, formed of three spits of mold: a *banklet*, as a guard to the outer brink of the ditch, of the fourth spit, and the pointing: the last being raised with a narrow pointed tool.
The *hedgerow,* hawthorn transplanted, with an oakling at every rod, laid in with the hawthorn plants.

The *method of planting*. The first spit — the cultivated corn mold — a good loam forms the bottom or foundation of the bank; over which the second spit, a brick earth, being spread evenly, the face was adjusted and the top levelled; and a line stretched a foot from the angle of the mound,* a narrow trench was opened down to the first spit, and drawing back the loose mold. In this trench the plants were set, from four to six inches apart, nearly upright, and their roots bedded in the finest of the mold, in the nursery manner, planting them *in* the best of the subsoil, upon the cultivated corn mold; and casting the third spit behind the line of plants.

The *guard* in *front*, a sharp ridge or banklet, formed on the opposite brink of the ditch with the fourth spit and the pointing: behind a low stiff stake-and-edder hedge; set on the bank formed by the third spit. The edders being well beaten down with a beetle, and the stakes re-driven to within a hand's breadth of the edders, the face of the hedge was trimmed so as to prevent the spray from dripping upon the plants. The hedge strong enough to bear a man's weight: a stile [sic] from end to end.

Lastly the bank was made up , with sufficient slope to stand firmly, and sown with ray [sic] grass and white clover.

The whole expense of the sixty seven statute rods, including labour, plants and materials, £7 9s 8d. Not quite two shillings and threepence a rod; not five pence a yard.

*It is observable, however, that this width though favourable to the infant plants, is too great when sheep are pastured on the ditch side, first or second year after planting. Even long wooled sheep, after they were shorn, leaped across the ditch: and, getting foothold on the platform injured some of the plants.

Estimated communal cost of inclosure to named proprietors

Name	*Rate%	Allot. Nos	Area acres	**Rate £	Rate/Area
Richard Attenburrow	2.9	38	27	85	3.1
Wm. Cooke	0.8	44	8	24	3
F. Eggleston Sr.	3.7	27, 39, 40	6	109	1.7
Job Eggleston	0.4	57	4	12	3
F. Eggleston Jr.	1	6, 18, 45, 46	26	29	1.1
Samuel Greaves	8.2	56, 61, 62	79	241	2.9
Thos. Hemsley	7.7	8, 9, 22, 52	92	227	2.5
Wm. Hemsley	2.3	16	16	69	4.3
Henry Hebb	1.3	43, 48, 50	49	39	
Rev. Dr. Milnes	7.3	65, 66	94	213	2.3
Thos. Mettam	4.2	3, 24	37	123	3.3
Langford Nevill	6.7	26, 36, 41	83	196	2.4
Samuel Smith	13.1	28, 55	132	385	2.9
Richard Tookey	7.5	63, 64	86	221	2.6
E. Walker	1.1	29	8	33	4

*Percentage of the total land tax paid by the proprietors in 1798 and applied to the estimated communal inclosure cost of £2940 to arrive at the individual contribution of the proprietor and shown as the **Rate £.

Bibliography

CUP: Cambridge University Press
OUP: Oxford University Press

Albert, W.	*The Turnpike Road System in England, 1663 to 1840*	CUP, 1972
Allen. R.C.	*Enclosure and the Yeoman*	Clarendon Press, 1992
Atkins, J.	*Keyworth Methodist Church Centenary Booklet*	Keyworth Methodist Church, 1981
Bailey, T.	*Annals of Nottinghamshire*	W.F.Gibson, 1852
Baker, A.R. & Butlin, R.A.	*Studies of Field Systems in the British Isles*	CUP, 1873
Beckett, J.V.	*The Agricultural Revolution*	Blackwell, 1990
Beckett, J.V.	*A Centenary History of Nottingham*	Manchester Univ.Press, 1997
Bendal, S.	*Maps, Land and Society*	CUP, 1992
Bendal, S.	*Dictionary of Land Surveyors & Local Map Makers of Great Britain and Ireland, 1530 to 1850*	British Library, 1997
Brewer, J.	*Pleasures of the Imagination*	Harper Collins, 1997
Burns, A.	*Geodaesia Improved or a New and Correct Method of Surveying Made Easy*	1771
Cantor, L.	*The Changing English Countryside, 1400 to 1700*	Routledge & Kegan Paul, 1987
Chambers, J.D.	*The Vale of Trent, 1670 to 1800*	CUP, 1957
Chambers, J.D.	*Nottinghamshire in the Eighteenth Century*	Cass, 1966
Chambers, J.D. & Mingay, G.E.	*The Agricultural Revolution, 1750 to 1880*	Batsford, 1966
Chapman, J.& Seeliger, S.A.	*A Guide to Enclosures in Hampshire, 1700 to 1900*	Hants.County Council, 1997
Charnock, J.	*Biographia Navalis*	R.Faulder, 1794
Clowes, L.W.	*A History of the Royal Navy*	1900
Collins, H.	*Variation in Farm Lay-out in South Notts. at the Time of Parliamentary Enclosure*	M.A.Thesis,Univ.of Nottingham
Coope, R. & Corbett, J.Y.	*Bromley House, 1752 to 1991*	Notts.Subscription Library, 1991
Cossons, A.	*The Turnpike Roads of Nottinghamshire*	Nottingham Historical & Geographical Associations, 1934
Crofts, R.G.	*Geology of Keyworth District*	British Geological Survey, 1989
Deane, P.	*The First Industrial Revolution*	CUP, 1979
Deering, C.	*The History of Nottingham*	Ayscough & Willington, 1751

Derry, T.K.&
  Blakeway, M.G. *The Making of Britain to the*
                  Close of the Middle Ages   Murray, 1968
Dahlman, C.   *The Open Field System and Beyond*   CUP, 1980
Dexter, A.&   *The Egglestons of Derbyshire &*
  Eggleston, B. *Nottinghamshire*   The authors, undated
Dickinson, W.   *The History of Antiquities of Newark*   M.Hage, 1816
Fellows &
  Freeman   *Historical Records of the South Notts.Yeomanry* Gale & Polden, 1928
Fussell, G.E.   *Village Life in the Eighteenth Century*   Littlebury, 1947
George, D.   *England in Transition*   Penguin, 1953
Godfrey, J.T.   *Notes on the Churches of Notts;*
                  Rushcliffe Hundred   Bemrose, 1887
Hadfield, C.   *The Canals of the East Midlands*   David & Charles, 1968
Hall, D.   *The Open Fields of Northamptonshire*   Northants.Record
                                                                Society, 1995
Hammond, J.   *The Practical Surveyor*   T.Heath, 1750
Hammond, J.L.&
  Hammond, B.   *The Village Labourer*   Longmans Green, 1948
Hammond, R.A.   *Keyworth Manor & Manor House Farm*   Keyworth & District
                                                                LHS, 1997
Hammond, R.A.   *Keyworth: The First Millennium*   Keyworth & District
                                                                LHS, 1998
Harris, R.W.   *England in the Eighteenth Century*   Blandford Press, 1963
Hey, D.   *The Oxford Companion to Local &*
                  Family History   OUP, 1996
Hollowell, S.   *Maidford 1718–1788: The Effects of*   UNMD, PZ LH 89
                  Parliamentary Enclosure on Life in a   (unpublished)
                  Northants. Village
Horn, P.   *The Rural World, 1780 to 1850*   Hutchinson, 1980
Hutton, C.   *A Treatise on Mensuration both in Theory &*
                  Practice   1802
Kerridge, E.   *The Agricultural Revolution*   Allen & Unwin, 1967
Langford, P.   *A Polite and Commercial People,*
                  England 1720 to 1783   OUP, 1989
Lowe, R.   *General View of the Agriculture of the*
                  County of Nottingham   Board of Agriculture,
                                                                1796
Lythe, P.   *A History of Nottinghamshire Farming*   Cromwell Press, 1989
Malthus, T.R.   *An Essay on the Principle of Population*
                  (1798 & 1830)   Penguin, 1970
Mantoux, P.   *The Industrial Revolution in the*
                  Eighteenth Century   Harper & Row, 1961
Marshall, D.   *English People in the Eighteenth Century*   Longman Green, 1956
Marshall, W.   *The Rural Economy of the Eastern Counties*   1790
Mason, A.S.   *Essex on the Map: The Eighteenth Century*
                  Land Surveyors of Essex   Essex Record Office,
                                                                1990
Matthias, P.   *The First Industrial Nation*   Methuen, 1969

May, T.	*An Economic & Social History of Britain, 1760 to 1970*	Longman, 1987
Mingay, G.E.	*English Landed Society in the Eighteenth Century*	Routledge & Kegan Paul, 1963
Mingay, G.E.	*Enclosure & the Small Farmer in the Age of the Industrial Revolution*	Macmillan, 1968
Mingay, G.E.	*Arthur Young and his Times*	Macmillan, 1975
Mingay, G.E.	*A Social History of the English Countryside*	Routledge, 1990
Namier, L.& Brooke, J.	*The History of Parliament: The House of Commons, 1754 to 1790*	HMSO, 1964
Neeson, J.M.	*Commoners: Common Rights, Enclosures and Social Change in England, 1700 to 1820*	CUP, 1993
Orwin, C.S.	*The Open Fields*	Clarendon, 1967
Pawson, E.	*Transport & Economy: the Turnpike Roads in Eighteenth Century Britain*	Academie Press, 1977
Platt, C.	*The Parish Churches of Medieval England*	Secker & Warburg, 1981
Plumb, J.H.	*England in the Eighteenth Century*	Penguin, 1950
Potter, S.P.	*Keyworth and its Story*	Keyworth & District LHS, 1995
Priestland, P.	*Radcliffe-on-Trent, 1710 to 1837*	Ashbracken, 1990
Robson, E.	*The American Revolution in its Political & Military Aspects*	Batchworth, 1955
Russell, R.	*The Enclosure of Barton-on-Humber, 1793–6,*	WEA, Barton-on-Humber, 1968
Russell, R.	*The Enclosures of Scauby, 1770–71, Kirton-in -Lindsey, 1793–1801 & Hibaldstow, 1796–1803*	WEA, Barton-on-Humber, 1970
Scarfe, N.	*A Frenchman's Year in Suffolk: Innocent Espionage*	Boydell Press, 1988
Scarfe, N.	*Innocent Espionage: La Rochefoulcauld Brothers' Tour of England, 1785*	Boydell Press, 1995
Schofield, R.E.	*The Lunar Society of Birmingham: A Social History of Provincial Science & Industry in 18th.Century England*	Clarendon Press, 1963
Slicher van Bath	*The Agrarian History of Western Europe, AD 500 to 1850*	Arnold, 1963
Smith, A.	*The Wealth of Nations (1776)*	Penguin, 1970
Tawney, R.H.	*The Agrarian Problem of the Sixteenth Century*	Longmans Green, 1912
Tate, W.E.	*The Village Community and the Enclosure Movements*	Victor Gollancz, 1967
Tate, W.E.	*The Parish Chest*	Phillimore, 1983
Tate, W.E. & Turner, M.E.	*A Domesday of Enclosure Acts and Awards*	Reading Univ.Press, 1978
Taylor, C.	*Fields in the English Landscape*	Dent, 1975
Taylor, E.G.R.	*The Mathematical Practitioners of Hanoverian England*	CUP, 1966
Thirsk, J.& Mingay, G.E.	*The Agrarian History of Britain, Vol.VI, 1750 to 1850*	CUP
Thompson, E.P.	*The Making of the English Working Class*	Penguin, 1968

Thompson, F.L.	*Chartered Surveyors: The Growth of a Profession*	Routledge & Kegan Paul, 1968
Thorne, R.G.	*The House of Commons, 1790 to 1820*	Secker & Warburg, 1986
Thoroton, R.	*The Antiquities of Nottinghamshire (1677), edited & enlarged by John Throsby*	E.P.Publishing, 1797
Trevelyan, G.M.	*English Social History*	Longman Green, 1946
Turner, M.E.	*English Parliamentary Enclosure: Its Historical Geography & Economic History*	William Dawson, 1980
Turner, M.E.	*Enclosures in Britain, 1750 to 1830*	Macmillan, 1986
Webb, S.&B.	*English Local Government*	Longmans Green, 1924
Webster, W.F.	*Nottinghamshire Hearth Tax, 1664 & 1674*	Thoroton Society, 1988
Woodforde, J.	*The Diary of a Country Parson, 1758 to 1802*	OUP, 1978
Wordie, J.R.	*Estate Management in the Eighteenth Century*	Royal Historical Society, 1982
Yelling, J.A.	*Common Fields & Enclosure in England, 1450 to 1850*	Macmillan, 1977
Young, A.	*A Six Weeks' Tour Through the Southern Counties of England & Wales*	1768
Young, A.	*A Six Months' Tour Through the North of England*	W.Strahan, 1770
Young, A.	*A General Report on Enclosures*	Board of Agriculture, 1808

Index

terrier 49, 61, 69, 161, 162, 165–7
Thoroton, Robert, Historian 64
Thorpe-in-the-Glebe, Notts 64, 98
tithes 56, 69, 81, 111, 114, 121, 129, 137,
    161–3
Tollerton, Notts 65, 90, 123, 135, 148
Tookey, Richard 67, 123, 139
transport, *see* canals, roads
turnpike roads, *see* roads

urbanisation 11–12, 44, 147

vestry meeting, role of 31, 37

Walkeringham, Notts 88
Watt, James 15
Wedgewood, Josiah 15
White, John, of Keyworth 145
Widmerpool, Notts 25, 58, 65, 67, 90, 119,
    137, 142, 152, 156
Willoughby, Notts 25, 36, 41, 65, 67, 98,
    157
Woodborough, Notts 91
Wright, Ichabod, Nottingham banker 105
Wyatt, Samuel, commissioner/surveyor
    103, 104, 115
Wymeswold, Leics 25, 65, 157
Wysall, Notts 58, 67, 90, 98, 118–9, 137,
    142, 152, 156

Young, Arthur 15, 19n, 28, 125n, 147